RAVES FOR *WHAT FALLS AWAY*

"Farrow's book possesses an elegance of prose and sensibility that elevates it way beyond the typical gorefest of sex, gossip, and betrayal."
—*USA Today*

"A stellar new memoir . . . it's all there, every wondrous, scandalous, inhumanely difficult thing."
—*Mirabella*

"Mia Farrow tells the story of her fascinating life with uncommon grace and insight."
—William Styron

"Word by word, page by page, we're convinced. We believe her."
—*Newsday*

"One of the best writers to ever come out of Hollywood. She writes with extraordinary wit and polish. This is good news for Frank Sinatra, André Previn, and the hundreds of other celebrities who make cameo appearances in her fabulous life, but it is very bad news for Woody Allen."
—Pat Conroy

WHAT FALLS AWAY

A Memoir

MIA FARROW

BANTAM BOOKS
New York   Toronto   London   Sydney   Auckland

This edition contains the complete text
of the original hardcover edition.
NOT ONE WORD HAS BEEN OMITTED.

WHAT FALLS AWAY

A Bantam Book / Published by arrangement with Doubleday

PUBLISHING HISTORY
Doubleday hardcover edition published March 1997
Bantam paperback edition / January 1998

Published simultaneously in the United States and Canada

Bantam Books are published by Bantam Books, a division of Bantam Doubleday Dell Publishing Group, Inc. Its trademark, consisting of the words "Bantam Books" and the portrayal of a rooster, is Registered in U.S. Patent and Trademark Office and in other countries. Marca Registrada. Bantam Books, New York, New York.

Printed in the United States of America

For my mother
and my children
who have stood by me,
and to those grandchildren and
great-grandchildren whom I may never meet

For their encouragement, company and faith along the way, I am grateful to my children, Mike Nichols, William Goldman, Maria Roach-Carpenter, Casey Pascal, Leonard Gershe, Barbara Daitch, Tom Stoppard, Stephen Sondheim, Rose and Bill Styron, Peter Wooster, Garson Kanin, Prudence Farrow, Maureen O'Sullivan, James Cushing, Patrick Farrow, Johnny Farrow, John Tavener, Tisa Farrow, Felice Farrow, Sheila Mooney, Liza Minnelli, Carly Simon, William Beslow, Mavis Smith, Judy Hollister, Judy Hofflund, Nancy Sinatra, Quincy Jones, S. and J. Herman, Tracey Seaward, Nan Talese, Lynn Nesbit, Susan Kinsolving, Maureen Orth, and Rock Brynner.

I would also like to express my gratitude to Eileen Taylor, Yul Brynner, Marcel Hunter, Ruth Gordon, George Cukor, Salvador Dalí, Mary O'Sullivan, John Farrow, and Michael Farrow.

I wake to sleep, and take my waking slow,
I feel my fate in what I cannot fear,
I learn by going where I have to go.

We think by feeling. What is there to know?
I hear my being dance from ear to ear.
I wake to sleep, and take my waking slow.

Of those so close beside me, which are you?
God bless the Ground! I shall walk softly there,
And learn by going where I have to go.

Light takes the Tree, but who can tell us how?
The lowly worm climbs up a winding stair;
I wake to sleep, and take my waking slow.

Great Nature has another thing to do
To you and me; so take the lively air,
And, lovely, learn by going where to go.

This shaking keeps me steady. I should know.
What falls away is always. And is near.
I wake to sleep, and take my waking slow.
I learn by going where I have to go.

—THEODORE ROETHKE, *THE WAKING*

Chapter One

I was nine when my childhood ended. We had celebrated my birthday the day before, which was a Saturday, and it hadn't gone well. Healthy, noisy kids were all over my backyard, and I had a feeling that had become familiar to me during those last weeks: that I was watching everything from a great distance. My mother had taken me to a number of doctors, but they could find no reason for the fatigue or the insomnia that now plagued me.

So on this day of my ninth birthday party I was used to being tired. That it hurt to move wasn't unusual either, and I was sitting on a low wall watching my friends playing ball down the driveway. When the ball smacked the bricks under my feet, everybody yelled, Come on kick it back, hurry up, and even though I clearly remember thinking, Don't, I pushed myself off the wall and a surprise pain, a bad one, shot through my legs, back, and neck as I dropped straight down onto the pavement. As my friends crowded around, I tried to laugh. I was mortified. It was my birthday and I couldn't even get up. Then Eileen, our Irish cook, and Barbara or Lucille, I forget which nanny, carried me to bed, where I lay flat and quiet, listening to the party outside my window.

The next morning was Sunday, and missing Mass was a mortal sin in the fifties, but again I fell to the floor. Everything hurt. It was a bad sign when Dr. Shirley, our pediatrician, came into the nursery and didn't even smile. His daughter Becky went to school with me every day on the bus, but now he was showing me a big long needle, saying he was going to put it into my spine so he could get fluid and find out what's wrong with me, it's called a spinal tap. I never knew there was fluid in my spine. I felt like throwing up.

I had to curl into a ball so he could get inside my actual spine. My mother said she had to do something like this too, every time she went to have a baby—that's seven times. But I was nine, and I didn't want babies. I didn't want any of this. I considered Dr. Shirley among the most handsome of my parents' friends, so it was embarrassing being curled up in front of him with a needle in my spine. I didn't even like him seeing me in my undershirt, and I certainly didn't like to hear him breathing so loud and close. I shut my eyes tight; he was taking forever and it really hurt. I went through the Ten Commandments, the Seven Deadly Sins, all my times tables, and the planets, starting with Mercury. But the main thing I kept thinking was, *I just hope I don't die.*

Then Dr. Shirley took my fluid away and we had to wait. In the next room I could hear the drone of the Rosary. Beside my bed was a pretty miniature wooden chest with flowers and birds painted all over it. I kept my best stuff in the drawers: my First Communion prayer book with the pearl cover, some dolls' eyes, a piece of blue eggshell, almost all the parts from my first watch including the changeable colored bands that you could wear as bracelets, a parrot feather from Mexico, a real silver bullet, my dead turtle's dried-up shell, a pen-and-pencil set that was too good to use, the thumbtack my brother Johnny had stuck in my foot when I was asleep, three Irish coins, a painted fan, a desiccated beetle, our collie Billy's tooth. I can't remember everything, but I picked out what I thought each of my brothers and sisters would want, dividing everything fair and square into six neat piles, eldest at the left . . . Then an ambulance's siren drowned out the prayers of my family.

Dr. Shirley walked in, not looking me in the eye, picked me up, and carried me out of the bedroom past my mother, who was cheerfully saying how she got to ride in ambulances whenever she had to go to the hospital to have babies. I heard him tell her, "Better burn all that," referring to the six piles, each with a note. There were no good-byes. Perhaps my brothers and sisters waved from the window, but I didn't look back.

My father, my mother, and I were headed to the public wards for contagious diseases at Los Angeles General Hospital. Inside the ambulance I squeezed my mother's hand while, through a rear window, tall, drab buildings skimmed past. I had never seen downtown Los Angeles before. It was nothing at all like Beverly Hills.

After entering the hospital, I was abruptly taken away from my parents, without explanation, and wheeled into an elevator. That was when I came apart. I screamed all the way upstairs to a big room where there were curtained cubicles and lots of children, all on gurneys, all screaming, just like me. A nurse wearing a mask over her nose and mouth hissed, Be *quiet*, you're only making things worse for everybody, but I was beyond terror. I threw up. Everything hurt —my back, neck, legs, arms, and chest; it even hurt to breathe.

Somewhere downstairs my parents were eventually informed that the second spinal tap confirmed the diagnosis of polio. I didn't see them for two days, until visiting time, which was twenty minutes, three times a week, behind the glass window at the end of my room. By then, I was a different person.

The nurses and doctors dressed protectively and kept contact to a minimum. They always seemed busy, which of course they were, and some of them seemed frightened of their patients. Who could blame them? It was 1954, and polio was sweeping the country. Nobody knew how it was spread, so you didn't go to movies or swim in public pools because of germs. But we lived in Beverly Hills, and we had our own screening rooms, our own swimming pools. I used to worry about leprosy. I never thought I'd get polio.

It was supposed to be a children's ward, but the iron lungs that lined the halls must have contained some adults too. I could hear men's voices wheezing and shouting in the night. When my turn came to be in the iron lung, I kept calling out, I'm okay, I feel fine now, please. But nobody came, and you can't even scratch your own nose.

There were four beds in my ward, and a crib in which lay a little girl about two years old with brown curls, a quiet little thing who never made a sound, except for an occasional soft whimper, but I don't remember seeing her move. One night the lights went on and the curtains were pulled around her crib, and doctors and nurses all crowded into that corner in a hurry, talking loudly. I pulled the covers over my head and tried to pretend I was somewhere else, but that's not so easy when terrible voices fill the room. The next morning the crib was empty, and then I had to put that quiet little girl right out of my mind.

The nights were hardest. I started sleeping with my head under the covers all the time. Cathy's bed was across the room from mine. She was ten, and unlike me she never cried, even if it hurt, except for once when nobody came at visiting time. Cathy was lionhearted brave, and I tried my best to be like her.

Life in the hospital settled into a routine. As I improved, there were daily hot-pack treatments—loathsome—and later water therapy, which was almost fun. When I was accidentally given a pair of boy's pajamas with fire engines on them, instead of those humiliating gowns that open at the back, I wore them for a week, and hid each day's clean nightgown under my mattress. This small thing gave me some sense of control and was a boost to my morale.

The days passed without much variance until one afternoon, with cold mashed potatoes still on my dinner tray, I hung on to the doctor's hands and, staring hard into his bored face, I stood trembling on my own two feet.

But that didn't mean I could go home. Every day they made me try to do two more things. You stand and put your palms flat on top of the doctor's, and then you try to get up on your tiptoes without putting any weight on the doctor's hands. Well, one day I could do that—I did it, even though it still hurt. And I could touch my chin to my chest too, which was the other thing you had to do before you could go home, and which I couldn't even come close to doing at first. The doctor's expression never changed—but two days later my father came to take me home.

He carried me out to the car and there were a couple of photographers outside the hospital, who asked me to wave. I still have the clipping. It shows a thin, happy little girl in a bathrobe being carried by her relieved-looking father. My mother is not in the photograph. She didn't visit the hospital that last week, nor was she there when I came home. I was told she was in another hospital resting, and I didn't know what that meant. Why couldn't she rest at home? What special kind of rest did she need? My deepest, unutterable fear was that I had given her polio and contaminated my entire family and all my friends too.

When I returned home the house was being repainted, with workmen on ladders everywhere. Carpets had been torn up, the swimming pool drained, the lawn reseeded, furniture re-covered. Our dog, Billy (grandson of the real

Lassie but bringer of flies and germs), had been given away, and my brothers and sisters had moved to our beach house in Malibu. I wasn't allowed to see them or any other children for months, but against the orders of both sets of parents, Maria Roach, my fearless little friend and next-door neighbor, appeared at the window to chat and cheer me up. Maria and I have been close friends since earliest childhood; the bonus for me was that she lived next door.

While I was in bed I read *Jane Eyre, The Adventures of Tom Sawyer, The Hunchback of Notre Dame, Kidnapped, Treasure Island, Black Beauty, Great Expectations, The Little Lame Prince*, three volumes of *Six O'Clock Saints* (biographies of the saints), and all the comic books my parents would buy.

In September I returned to school, but only for half days until after Christmas because I tired so quickly. Because of me, every guest at my ninth birthday party had to endure the first, experimental Salk vaccine, a series of three painful injections. There had probably been frightened talk in homes throughout the fifth grade, because many of my classmates steered clear of me at first.

I cannot with any accuracy describe myself then. I was much as I am now: a pair of eyes on a stalk, a soul no different from most souls, forever trying to understand, needing to give and to love, not daring to hope for much (and hoping far too much), full of uncertainties, and unable to protect myself from pain. If polio marked the end of my childhood, it also left me with embryonic survival skills. I discovered that whatever your losses, you can still for the most part choose your attitude. If you have your health, a little courage, and imagination, then you have the internal resources to build a new life, and maybe even a better one. I saw how fragile our life structure is and how easily you can be plucked from it, and thrown into the land of uncertainty, fear, pain, and death. I learned that you can't truly own anything, that true ownership comes only in the moment of giving. And I learned a little about friendship and how it can light the darkest abyss.

From a distant fragment somewhere in the mind of God I was shown a different earth, a giant orb howling out its long symphony of pain—all the sounds of mortal anguish, in the silence and indifference of the stars. So my childhood was extinguished, innocence and oblivion were replaced by a powerful and unforgettable knowing. And with knowledge comes responsibility . . .

These awarenesses have governed my life.

The gray mansion of my mother's childhood overlooks undulating land where the rivers meet. This was my earliest extended memory. I was three. It was summer in the west of Ireland.

But this is the remembrance of a storm. A storm that stopped my heart and split the night skies over Roscommon, spewing a fury of rain that pounded the old house where I sat upright in a strange bed.

Looking out the window beyond the walled gardens, jagged glimpses of the black peat bogs and churning rivers trembled in coruscating light. Trees bent low under wild winds that rushed down the chimneys and through the dark hallways. The old house groaned and sighed.

Through these sounds a man's voice startled me.

"What are you crying for—great big girl like you?" He stood in the doorway holding a candle. Warm light leaped crazily all over the white walls of the little room. He had a mustache—it was my first.

The hand not holding the candle was tucked into a black sling. And his face, beautiful in candlelight, was the saddest I had ever looked into.

"I want Mummy. I'm scared."

"Let her sleep," he said sorrowfully. "She's tired."

"Are you Jesus?" I wondered.

"Not at all," said he, "I'm your grandfather."

As my mother did, Eileen Taylor, our cook, told me stories of Ireland that were thrilling, powerful, and beautiful; they summoned things ancient and yet to come. Eileen was a quick-witted, warmhearted woman with high cheekbones and a handsome face, and my invaluable ally in the adult world. Most afternoons we had tea in the "grown-ups' kitchen," and my teacup was a little replica of her larger one. When we finished, she'd tell my fortune with the tea leaves on the bottom of the cup. In the mornings, while I waited for the Marymount school bus with Eileen in the bay window seat of our living room, I listened in awe to her accounts of banshees, the warrior Cuchulain, fairies in the woods and at the bottom of the garden; of rocks with magical powers, and children who disappeared from sodden fields or their nursery beds, and of lamp-lit houses with more rooms than anyone could count, where ghosts did mischief. These stories were seamlessly woven with those of Jesus and His miracles, the cross, the nails, the crown of thorns, an agony beyond comprehension, and out of everything the rising in an exultation of angels, and oh the glory and mystery of all these things.

When the school bus came, I said tearfully, "I'm already homesick." But the big girls on the bus were jolly, singing "Put Another Nickel In," and "Good Night, Irene," and eventually I sang too.

I was frightened of the nuns waiting at school, frightened then and, in varying degrees, throughout the thirteen years of my Catholic schooling. I wonder what my life would have been like had I not been afraid of so many things. Sitting on that school bus, I was afraid (in no particular order) of amputations, nuns, God, the devil (especially the devil), certain diseases but mainly leprosy, and my nannies—all of them, even Mary Red Socks, who only came on weekends. I worried about saying or doing something that would make my mother or father love me less, or that my parents or my siblings would die, vacuum cleaners, killing someone, getting lost, and grown-ups in general— not including Eileen of course, or Jess the gardener, or our neighbor Mr. Boyer.

My first nine years were spent in Beverly Hills, California, in a ranch-style house, U-shaped around a brick patio with a tile fishpond at the center. I liked watching the goldfish doze in the sun and dart beneath the slimy lily pads. At half an acre, our garden was large by Beverly Hills standards, an explosion of orange, lemon, magnolia, banana, and olive trees, a profusion of flower beds. We had to watch out for the sprinklers when we ran barefoot on the large, manicured green lawns.

Our right border marked the beginning of the even bigger property of Hal Roach, a producer responsible for *Our Gang*, and the Laurel and Hardy movies that he screened for us on special occasions in the oak-paneled basement of his Tara-like mansion. In his late fifties he had fathered three little girls, the eldest of which was my closest friend, Maria. The two gardens were separated by an easy fence for climbing, and a strip of woodland that was for us comparable to Sherwood Forest. Their swimming pool was far grander than ours or anybody else's: Olympic-sized, it was tiled all around with lifelike pictures of sea creatures. You could swim down to the deepest bottom and stab the octopus in the eyeball with a rubber knife. Our playhouse, however, had it way over theirs, with its two full rooms, a slanted shingled roof, shuttered windows, and a tiny white picket fence defining its front yard.

But the Roaches lived in an honest-to-goodness mansion, containing whole corridors we children were not permitted to explore, and this lent an air of mystery and foreboding to their house. I wondered too at the tiny figure of Mrs. Roach, endlessly at work around the grounds, weeding and sweeping and weeping into her broom.

My own mother, moving gracefully through the house and garden, arranging flowers, breakfasting on a white wicker tray in her bedroom, was easily the most beautiful creature imaginable. She was Maureen O'Sullivan, a famous movie star, and her voice was soft with a light Irish accent. She seemed possessed of magical qualities, an unending supply of stories, and the ability to make me feel safe and happy. She was, of course, unaware of her own perfection or the unsettling, elusive quality that could flood me with yearning and loneliness. At night I lay in bed listening for the rustle of silk or taffeta, waiting for her perfume to overpower the scent of jasmine.

That time shines now like a beautiful, far-off, golden dream: gentle sunshine, dappled shade, butterflies in February, and barefoot summers, the nurseries of Beverly Hills, where children were tended by British nannies in crisp, white uniforms, and fêted with clowns, ponies, magicians, castles for cakes, and personal soda fountains.

There were seven children in my family. Our father had fought in World War II, which might explain the gaps of several years between and after the births of my older brothers. Michael was the oldest, then Patrick, and I followed as the senior of the ensuing cluster of five.

Mike was so smart that even when they skipped him a grade, he got straight A's. And he was handsome too, an Adonis, people use to say. The girls were nuts about him. I could tell from the way they got all mushy around him and they called so often that my parents had to get him his own phone number. There was always a bunch of his friends around, tinkering with cars on the driveway, in and out of the swimming pool, with music going, chasing here and there, cutting up—Mike had it all. He was the bright and shining hope of my family. He's gonna be the President, I used to think, and the topper was that he loved me. I never doubted it.

"How's it going, Mouse?" he'd say, because I was a runt, and I'd feel my face go all hot and I could scarcely look at him for happiness. The presence of my brother's friends around the house almost chased away lingering tendrils of the dark nights and made the world seem well and happy and safe.

During the summer after polio, Mike got his first steady girlfriend, Joan Bailey. She was Mike's age, fifteen, and I tried unsuccessfully not to like her. I discovered that Joan and Mike had a magical gift: they could transform any mundane, done-it-a-thousand-times-before dumb thing into a mysterious, thrilling, never-done-it-before adventure, and their delight in it and in each other was a revelation. I was mesmerized and trailed around after them, hoping they would take me into their enchanted circle.

"When I first met you," Joan Bailey remembers, "you were going around pinching your cheeks, and I asked Mike why. He told me you'd had polio, and said, 'She thinks if she looks healthy, Mom will let her ride her bike to the store with the others.' You wanted to go with everyone else but you were so pale and thin, your parents were always worried about you, and kept you quiet. You were reading all the time. I remember that summer you read *David Copperfield* to your brothers and sisters."

Johnny, a year younger, was closest to me in age and interests. For years, we could credibly pass for twins. If wishing was all it took, I would have been a boy too, entranced as I was by explorers, knights, pirates, soldiers, cowboys, jockeys, deep-sea divers, Robin Hood, and Superman. What exactly it meant to be a woman wasn't at all clear to me. I teetered on my mother's pointy high-heeled shoes, and studied her strange undergarments—the girdles, stockings, garter belts, corsets, brassieres—and I worried.

My sister Prudence, next in line to Johnny, was tall, willowy, and a fast swimmer. (All my brothers are tall. I'm the shortest one in the family, perhaps because of polio.) Prudy's dimples were much admired, and her glasses with pale blue plastic frames were forever sliding off her small, freckled nose. She was wildly emotional, totally honest, adventurous, and quick to laugh.

Like our father, Mike, and me, Stephanie, the next to the youngest child, was blond and, in those days, on the chubby side. Her eyes, huge and round, gave her a startled look, as if she had just witnessed a train crash. The rest of her face was pinkish and tranquil; it made no statements. When she grew up, she was so pretty that for as long as she wanted she earned a living as a model. Steffi never said much, but she observed the goings-on within the family, and occasionally revealed a position of sorts with her amused, surreal comments. In our brawling family, her neutrality and detached, off-center humor earned respect.

If the Farrow kids pooled freckles, we'd have sunk a dinghy. It was a toss-up whether Patrick or Tisa, the youngest, had more. The nanny liked her best—she was a good kid, smart and funny. When she was six or seven she'd memorize the whole *TV Guide* and go around announcing what was going to be on—stuff nobody'd even heard of, because we were only allowed to watch *The Mickey Mouse Club* and *The Lone Ranger.*

Next door the Roach girls, Maria, Jeannie, and Kathy, fitted perfectly into the gaps between our ages. Other kids came and went, but this was our essential gang. Being so much older, Michael and Patrick had no interest in our activities, which for the most part were pretty standard stuff. We climbed trees, built forts and clubhouses, argued, raced, explored, spied, played on rooftops, rode bikes, roller-skated, and swam. After our toddler years, the nannies didn't even try to keep up with us: we ran wild and unchecked between the two properties and in the alleyways of Beverly Hills.

In front of our house, the ivy lay thick and tangled in the soft shade of eight gnarled olive trees that, though beautiful, were not much good for climbing. But at the tip of the narrow strip of woods that divided the Farrow-Roach terrain there grew a giant pine of rare perfection to which we gave a no-frills name, the Big Tree. Its branches reached far out over the sidewalk to meet the tall palms that lined Beverly Drive, and they were so powerfully seductive that even my parents were discovered, one magical evening none of us will ever forget, trying to climb up into them.

At the highest attainable level of the tree, the massive trunk parted and branched up toward the sky, forming a nest. It was to this place, above the rooftops of Beverly Hills, that I brought the small pets that had passed through my life——the dead hamsters, lizards, guinea pigs, birds, and turtles of my affection, each in an open box covered tightly with Saran Wrap. I placed them there, among the branches, and over time, with deepest respect, I watched them rot.

So often in my dreams I am there still, where the ivy tangles. I see my parents standing in front of my house. They are young, and the sun is in their hair. They are calling me to dinner. I run toward them with all my child feelings, hot from play, out of breath, muddy hands, a wiggly tooth——but I do not cross the threshold of my home. I never enter, although I have dreamed this dream thousands of times. For I know that if I go inside, if I take my place at the table, I will have to live my life from that moment all over again, and invariably the weight of this thought awakens me.

As children of show business, we came naturally to the business of shows. Rarely was the Roach/Farrow clan without a play in production. They were meandering, melodramatic scenarios constructed around any characters that caught our fancy. Consistently and shamelessly, I took all the best roles, female and male.

Our audience was likely to include an occasional valiantly patient and tactful parent (usually Mrs. Roach or my mother), and any member of the household staff or stray friend we could beg or bully into attendance. When my grandmother was over from Ireland she would be there, cigarette between her lips, oblivious to the long ash that I found so absorbing and that dropped just anywhere at all. Granny was a "character," the grown-ups used to say, and for that I loved her all the more. We had a club, the two of us, down in the cellar, with the suitcases pushed around to make a little, secret place. There she talked about Ireland and the strangeness of growing old, and she would show me her hands, and pinch the veins to make them stand up all by themselves. It was hard to believe that my mother was really Granny's daughter, and it was troubling to hear them speak to each other in distant, chill voices.

Tour buses crept up and down the streets of Beverly Hills, pausing in front of each celebrity's house while a guide chirped starry anecdotes into a microphone—you could hear them coming a half block away. We accepted their presence as inevitable and unremarkable as the sunshine, or the grand houses, crystalline swimming pools, nannies, cooks, gardeners, and the gaze of strangers. It was obvious that for the quizzical faces peering out of the bus windows, movie stars' houses, their kids, and even their dogs were of interest—along the lines, we speculated, of a visit to the zoo, or even a Disneyland ride. That was a lot to live up to. So for the folks on the buses, our shows were frantic, in the broadest, operatic style. We spattered ourselves with ketchup-blood that was stored, along with the rubber dagger, under the rhododendron bush. We strangled, stabbed, staggered, crawled, rolled, and writhed. And we howled and screamed at the top of our lungs.

Drawn by dreams, and some mysterious brew of talent, determination, looks, and luck, our parents came from towns and cities across the United States and Europe too, to their positions in the Hollywood constellation. Once there, in that rarefied setting, it was easy to lose touch with origins, roots, people, perspective.

They couldn't know how their gifts had come to them, or how long they would endure. They worked and played, and fashioned their lives in dazzling light, while insecurity and apprehension curled into tight little balls, and burrowed deep into unacknowledged silence. But over the years, a creeping awareness of the precariousness of their place fed the dark, hidden things that grew, malignant, demanding light, pushing through the cracks in the smooth, polished surface . . .

I loved my parents with a fierceness and an incomprehension that was terrifying.

My mother was born in 1911, above a draper's shop in the little town of Boyle, Roscommon, in the west of Ireland. Whatever magic is in her soul, she tells me, comes from there. Her own mother, Mary Frazer, was a beautiful and amusing woman, but not a happy one. She found marriage difficult, and never learned to cook or keep house. When her husband said he liked lamb, she bought a whole sheep and hung it over the bathtub, where it dripped blood for days.

My grandfather went off to fight in World War I, but returned in a few months, his right arm shattered. Doctors recommended amputation, but he refused, and fought all his life to keep it. My grandmother couldn't face suffering, and nervous breakdown followed nervous breakdown.

My mother, her father's favorite, went to the Convent of the Sacred Heart in Roehampton. She hated it. They had to wear vests in the bath, and were told that "whistling on the stairs makes Our Lady cry." Vivien Leigh was in the same class, the only girl in the school, according to my mother, who had any sense of direction: from the age of eleven she knew she would be an actress. The others just wanted to be socially successful and travel the world. Vivien Leigh was voted "prettiest girl in the school," and when my mother came in second, she cried all day, unable to believe that anyone thought she was pretty.

Mom was indeed pretty and was "discovered," Hollywood-style, by the director Frank Borzage, who was in Ireland looking for an Irish colleen and a little boy to play in the movie *Song o' My Heart,* starring the famous tenor John McCormack.

My mother describes it this way: "It was the last night of Horse Show week and I wanted to celebrate. I was invited out by a very attractive young bachelor from Trinity College. My mother thought I looked tired and told me not to go out, but I went anyway. There was a dance band. Frank Borzage was sitting at the next table with a group of people and they were watching me. I knew exactly who they were. Everybody knew. They were looking for a young girl for a part in the film. The most beautiful girl in Dublin, Grace McLaughlin, went for an interview. A lot of my friends had tried out, and been turned down or were working as extras. But I didn't. I didn't think I was good-looking enough. Actually, they had given up looking for an Irish girl and were going back the next week, having decided to use a Hollywood actress. Eventually my escort wanted to go home, but I had a feeling something was going to happen, and I said, 'No, let's stay and have one more dance.' That dance sealed my fate. When I came back to my table and sat down, the headwaiter brought over Frank Borzage's card, on the back of which was written, 'If you are interested in films, will you come to my office tomorrow at eleven?' Frank signed me for three pounds a week." In October 1929, eighteen-year-old Maureen O'Sullivan, with a six-month contract, set sail for Hollywood, accompanied by her mother.

Three years later, my mother was signed by MGM and began work on *Tarzan, the Ape Man*, the first of six Tarzan movies she made with Johnny Weissmuller. She says she got bored of being rescued from mad elephants, alligators, and hippopotamuses. She found the monkeys particularly loathsome, and said they were "all homosexuals" who adored Johnny and were jealous of her, biting her at every opportunity. To this day she refers to Cheetah the Chimp as "that bastard."

She says she was "extremely fond of Johnny, but he would drive me crazy with his practical jokes. I remember once on my birthday he brought me a huge cake, and when I put the knife in, the whole thing exploded in my face. While all America thought we were having an affair, there was never a glimmer of a romance between us."

To date, my mother has played leading roles in sixty-two movies, including *The Thin Man* (1934), *Anna Karenina* (1935), *A Day at the Races* (1937), and *The Big Clock* (1948), one of several films she starred in that was directed by my father.

John Villiers Farrow was a conflicted, incongruous figure in Hollywood. He was a movie director, but failed to see film as art, and so could not respect his own endeavors. He read serious books and he wrote serious books, which he *did* respect, and he fraternized with Jesuits. He was a devout Catholic, and a womanizer of legendary proportions.

He was born in Sydney, Australia, in 1904. According to

Farrow family lore, he was the product of a relationship between Lucy Savage and King Edward VII. Whatever the truth, it went to the grave when beautiful, nineteen-year-old Lucy died during my father's birth. All he ever possessed or knew of his mother was the oval portrait he kept with him throughout his life. He never knew his father, Joseph Farrow, so "Jack," as my father was then known, was raised by an aunt, and at fifteen sent to Winchester College in England to complete his education. But a restless spirit and some measure of unhappiness led him to lie about his age and run away to sea. He spent his youth in the merchant marine and the Royal Canadian Navy.

Of all the distant ports, my father loved Tahiti best. During one of his numerous extended visits, he assembled the first French-English-Tahitian dictionary, and wrote a novel, *Laughter Ends*. He kept a scrapbook with black pages and careful white handwriting. The tiny photographs show a very fit, handsome young man, flaxen-haired, with a dazzling smile and a flowered cloth sarong around his waist, in various poses with native women of Bora Bora, Tahiti, and Mooréa, and a beautiful, bobbed brunette named Lila.

It was in Tahiti that he learned of the life of Father Damien, and came to admire him deeply. Among my mother's notes I found the following account of how that came about, in my father's words:

"After a wretched passage on a small trading cutter we reached one of the more remote islands. The sudden peace of the lagoon so enchanted me that I determined to stay there a few days. A consultation with the amiable half-Chinese, half-Tahitian captain soon settled the matter. He would proceed to the next island, pick up a cargo of copra, then after three days' time, return for me. But given the ways of mariners in those pleasant waters, it was not surprising when he did not return for nearly three months.

"Excepting for a gendarme who lived in a different village, I was the only white man on the island and as such was treated as a personage. One hospitable family came forward, insisting I should stay with them since they actually had a bed, an unusual and prestigious article of furniture in those regions, which defined the owner as being a person of wealth, culture, and initiative. My hosts were rightly proud of their bed. It was a huge and grand affair, made of glittering brass and shining mother-of-pearl, ornamented with colored shells and swathed in clouds of mosquito netting. Each evening when it was time to retire, my solemn-eyed friends would gather to wave farewell as I disappeared through the tall curtains. For about two weeks I had been sleeping there in great comfort when, one morning as I was going to the lagoon to fish, I met the gendarme. 'If you are interested to know,' he told me in the most casual of tones, 'the bed you are sleeping in is the bed of a leper.'

"A frantic check revealed this to be true. The son of my hosts was a leper, who had been relegated to a hut of his own behind the main house. I further learned that we had been sharing the same dishes. I got hold of the stongest disinfectants available and scrubbed till the blood ran. After a week had passed, drawn by boredom and the pessimistic certainty of my own fate, I began to visit the leper and we became friends. He was only twenty-five and resigned to his affliction. He strummed the guitar and in a patois of French, Tahitian, and English, he told me stories about the leper colony and the exploits of a character so heroic as to seem highly fictitious—called Kamiano. Tale after tale, punctuated by bobbings of reverent salutes, filled me with curiosity. When at last I sailed back to Papeete I learned that Kamiano was the native name for the priest who had worked and lived among the lepers until he too contracted the disease, and died a leper's death. His name was Father Damien."

My father's biography of Father Damien, *Damien the Leper*, was published in 1937. In the foreword, Hugh Walpole wrote: "I scarcely know how Mr. Farrow has been able to leave so vivid a picture of Father Damien in the reader's mind with so few words . . . I feel that I have Damien as a companion for the rest of my days. This is an addition to one's spiritual experience." Pope Pius XI responded to the book by naming my father a Knight of the Grand Cross of the Order of the Holy Sepulchre.

In one port, San Francisco, my father lingered to pursue a seventeen-year-old beauty from a prominent local family. Always a voracious reader, he took the opportunity to formalize his education and earned a degree in literature from Loyola Marymount University, staying afloat by painting portraits of socialites. A brief, stormy marriage to that same young woman produced his mirror-image daughter, my half sister Felice.

In 1927, while writing for a local theater, my father became friends with the producer David Selznick, who tried to convince him to become an actor. But while Dad had no interest in acting, David's stories about Hollywood were intriguing enough to bring him to Los Angeles, to try his hand at screenwriting.

His first credit for a screenplay came that same year, for *The Wreck of the Hesperus*, based upon Longfellow's poem. Before long he had a contract with Paramount, where he wrote scripts for, among others, William Wellman, Gary Cooper, William Powell, Victor Fleming, and Clara Bow. His short stories were by then appearing in *The Atlantic Monthly*.

My parents first met in 1931 at the Cotton Club in Culver City. My mother's escort that night was Oscar Levant; she says my father was "flirtatious" that evening, and his date, Dolores Del Rio, was furious. "He was, without any doubt, the most colorful, fascinating character on the Hollywood scene," she told me, "and at twenty-six, he had the worst reputation in town. When he asked me for a date, he told me that the first evening he had free was in two weeks' time. Here I was with every night of the week free! But I was very excited about going out with him. He wasn't like other people in the industry: he was a complete mystery to me, which was all part of the attraction."

When my mother returned to Hollywood from a trip to Ireland they started seeing each other again, but before long he ran off to London and almost married one Mary Churchill. That fell through, and one night he rang up my mother to ask if she'd go to Tahiti with him. "You must be crazy!" Mom replied. "I've read in the papers what you've been up to. You're too unreliable for me!" And she hung up. A few days later she found out he'd flown to Tahiti with another girl, where he stayed for most of that year.

"He was my first real beau," my mother explained. "I didn't know anything. I was very angry and broke it off. But somehow he'd always get around me, and eventually we got back together, but I never got over it."

They had been living together for two years, which was unheard-of at the time, when, one day at a gas station in Culver City, he said to my mother, "I guess I'd better marry you."

"Why?" she asked.

"Because you make me happier than anyone else," he answered.

Shortly after Michael was born, the war broke out, and my father rejoined the navy. He received decorations from Spain, France, and Romania, and was honored as a commander of the British Empire. But after contracting a severe case of typhus, which left his heart permanently weakened, he was sent home to Beverly Hills, where my mother cared for him. While recuperating, he wrote two books, *The History and Development of the Royal Canadian Navy* and *Pageant of the Popes*, a history of the papacy.

In 1943 at Paramount he filmed *Wake Island*, for which he won the New York Film Critics Award for direction, and received an Academy Award nomination. Of the seventeen films he made in the forties, the best known was *The Big Clock*, in 1948, with Ray Milland, Charles Laughton, and my mother, which has been praised over the years as bravura filmmaking. *Alias Nick Beal*, in 1949, is one of my favorites. Ray Milland, its star, recalls, "I loved that picture. Farrow was a strange man . . . We got along very well together. He was the most disliked man on the lot, but a good director." In 1950 he directed one of his finest films, *Where Danger Lives*, the first with Robert Mitchum; later that year they teamed up again to make *His Kind of Woman*. For *Around the World in Eighty Days*, made in the mid-fifties, we went to Mexico. I remember it well. I sat on a beehive, and had my first puff of a cigarette with the Mexican star Cantinflas. But Dad feuded with producer Mike Todd, and after a month or so of shooting, walked off the movie. Still, he received an Academy Award for his screenplay. In all, he made forty-three films.

I was too young to be aware of what my father went through during the McCarthy years, so I asked Joe Mankiewicz, who, as the head of the Directors Guild at that time, had been in the eye of the storm. Joe wrote me in 1993, as he was dying, which was extraordinarily generous of him. It seems that Cecil B. De Mille and his cohorts had proposed a guild amendment calling upon every screen director in the United States to sign a public oath of loyalty —otherwise, their director's credentials would be nullified. A petition to have Mankiewicz removed as guild chairman was also being circulated. It was my father who warned Joe of these shenanigans.

In his autobiograpy, Elia Kazan filled in some details. "George Marshall, one of the old-timers, had shown up at Farrow's house in the sidecar of a motorcycle. He walked into John's house and said, 'Here, sign this.' John said, 'I will not sign it.' "

John immediately tried to reach Joe at the home of his brother Herman, to warn him. Joe wrote: "He came over

and gave me a whole bunch of totems and amulets, all
blessed by various popes . . . and said, 'You must carry
these tomorrow at the meeting.' I did carry them in my
pocket . . . and I couldn't prove they didn't help." Sure
enough, Joe won the vote, and the morning papers read,
MANKIEWICZ IN OVERWHELMING VICTORY.

As Kazan summed it up, "The men who beat De Mille,
an extremist of the right, were not from the left. Many were
reactionaries, like John Farrow or Jack Ford . . . What
they were defending was classic Americanism, our basic way
of living . . . And they'd succeeded."

I can only imagine the Kafkaesque climate of the Mc-
Carthy era. The stakes were high—my father had seven
kids. As it happened, his career was not damaged by his
righteous stand, but at the time he had no idea what would
unfold. He did what he always told me to do: stand strong
for what you believe in.

My father taught me how to sail by the winds and navigate
by the stars. He talked about tall ships and distant lands so
that I, like him, longed to see the world. He loved the sea
and poetry, he could cook and he could tell a story. My
father filled a room. He was not simple, but he was direct.
He was an insomniac who read two books a night. He
spoke about "honor" and "responsibility." He told me
about war and showed me his beautiful glory medals for a
hero's work; awed, I touched them in their boxes lined with
black and purple satin, and wondered whether I too would
be brave.

I say all this as if there is one coherent picture, as if I
knew him, as if I understood, but in truth I didn't—I was a
child, I saw only fragments. With a crayon I could draw his
eyes exactly the right shade of blue. I remember him worrying, and laughing. He had a beautiful smile. Everybody
looked at him; it wasn't just me. His monogrammed silk

shirts were made by Turnbull & Asser in London. Suits and
tweed jackets were from London too, and his shoes were
custom-made by Lobb. He was proud of his memberships
in London's Naval and Military Club, and the Athenaeum;
still, he satirized their stuffiness in *Around the World in Eighty
Days*.

I remember my father leaning over a steamy pot, sipping
spaghetti sauce from a wooden spoon. I remember sitting
beside him listening to Gregorian chants, and I remember
struggling to understand when he read aloud the poems of
John Donne.

I didn't know about all the women then. Except for Ava
Gardner. When I came into his office at the studio I caught
a glimpse, a flash, a tear in the fabric, just a little slit, quick,
close it back up. He was very handsome—everybody said
so. After he died, women used to come up to me and they'd
look at me a certain way and I knew what they were going
to say: *I knew your father*. I never knew what to reply, or what
expression to wear.

When I was about ten, I got hopping mad and called the
nanny a fat bastard and ran away to the Wonder bread
factory, across the Santa Monica tracks. I hid out there for
a while, and when it got dark, I came home. My father was
waiting, and he whacked me clear across the room. He had
an almighty temper. When I was six or seven, my brothers
and I put together the filthiest poem we could think of—
we even got it to rhyme. Only somehow my mother got
hold of it. She said, "You just wait till your father gets
home," which was the scariest thing imaginable. After a
long, hellish wait, he sent for me. I had to hang on to the
big beige chair, and I thought he'd break my back with his
walking stick. Jesus. He was something.

He slept in a different bedroom from my mother, which
had its own private entrance. Mom says she had that put in
during his affair with Ava Gardner in 1953, while they were

filming *Ride, Vaquero!* "I thought I'd be so annoyed if I heard him coming in in the middle of the night," she explains.

The door leading from the nursery into the grown-ups' part of the house was memorable for its knob: a larger-than-usual, perfectly round crystal sphere, a universe of tiny bubbles. Permission from an adult and then two small hands were all it took to turn it and step into our mother's dressing room, where every surface was mirrored, reflecting light and countless images of our wide-eyed selves. It was a dazzling, magical passageway into our parents' domain.

There was always the sense of important things going on in the grown-up world of our home. When my parents gave parties, there was great excitement in the house. Eileen would have three extra girls to help cook and serve. The two nannies brought the children out at sevenish, to be kissed and complimented. The four girls were dressed in matching floor-length silk bathrobes, and the three boys were smart in their flannel ones. The main attraction was a man named Tony who played the accordion and kept on his shoulder a tiny monkey wearing a hat. Then we were put to bed and tried to fall asleep to the sound of the accordion and the civilized chatter and laughter.

I thought of my mother and father who were good to me, and Eileen, in her black uniform with the white starched apron, and my siblings, so vulnerable in their sleep, and the tiny monkey in his hat, and the beautiful guests moving and laughing so confidently under the California stars. Overwhelmed by the mystery of my home, I finally fell asleep.

Chapter Two

My first visit to a movie set came sometime in my early childhood. I remember my terror that a sound would escape my tightly clamped lips. I could almost feel it building inside me: some frightful, uncontainable explosion of sound, a devil's noise that would leap out and smash to smithereens the amazing pretend-buildings that were only facades, the cowboys with hats and holsters who smoked and swaggered through saloon doors with Kleenex fluttering around their necks, the bored horses at the hitching posts, the women at their mirrors with their lovely dolls' faces, and countless blazing lights on stilts and hanging from the catwalks. One eruption from my lips would blast the whole illusion right up to the painted canvas sky.

I was about three years old when John Wayne, the tallest person I had ever seen, scooped me up and placed me on the tallest chair in the world. I arranged my pretty dress so that my underpants wouldn't show (there was always that concern when anyone picked me up), and I sat quietly, just as I was instructed. After a while John Wayne forgot about me and strode off down the dusty street. I couldn't see my mother or the nanny or any familiar face, and the chair was so high I couldn't get down—I couldn't even *try* without my underpants showing, and I couldn't make a sound, no matter how badly I needed to go to the bathroom; so there I waited, on that lofty perch, in mute desperation.

When I was about ten, I was taken to visit my mother at a studio where she was working. It was after school, so I was still wearing my uniform when I walked onto the dark soundstage. In a tiny, brightly lit room, my mother was being kissed on her mouth, a strange man was squeezing her arms, pulling her toward him. I had never seen kissing like that, not anywhere, and I couldn't make a thought. Then someone yelled, Cut!, and Mother was moving toward me with the man she introduced as Mr. Joseph Cotten, who said, How do you do?

For the most part, my visits to the soundstage were less alarming. I loved studying the specialized tasks of the grips, the prop-men, the makeup and wardrobe crews: highly skilled men and women working under immense pressure. Growing up, we watched them on our parents' movie sets. We Hollywood children had no social contact with people from other professions—except, in my family, for priests—unless they were hired by our parents in some capacity. Doctors, lawyers, teachers, tradesmen: everyone seemed to function as a sort of satellite. It was a catastrophic distortion, unintended by our parents, but it damaged healthy role models for so many children in my hometown. If kids grow up in some other one-business town, where it is logical to dream the local dream, and they are educated and work hard, and they have family connections helping a little, it is reasonable to suppose they have a shot at making the dream come true. But if you are a movie star's child, and you grow up in Beverly Hills or Brentwood or Bel Air, and you dream that dream because it is all you know, then you go to acting school, and take advantage of your connections, and you give it everything you've got. But even with all this going for you, it's unlikely you'll be able to earn a living in your parents' profession, let alone become a star.

We didn't know that then. We dreamed, and outgrowing our charmed childhoods, we scrambled to find our own footholds. And when the doors closed, it was a shock. Even the toughest kids were ill-equipped to make their way in the real world, because most of them honestly didn't know what that was. If there had been more explaining at the beginning . . . I wonder whether that would have helped push some of the peculiar aspects of our existence into a more comprehensible shape, and lent perspective to life structures that were, with hindsight, conspicuously out of whack.

But our parents were busy improvising their own complex existences on an uncharted, high-pressured frontier. My parents were pioneers: talkies were brand-new when my mother came from Ireland to make her first film, and I was among the first generation of movie stars' children. The future was presumed to be golden for them, and for us. There were no explanations—not about fans or stars, the preferential treatment, or the way people stared. There was no talk about what being famous meant, as perceived and projected by the community in which we lived, or how far from typical our small American town was, and why. Of a simpler world, Ralph Waldo Emerson observed: "I trust a good deal to common fame . . . If a man can make better chairs or knives or crucibles or church organs than anybody else, you will find a broad hard-beaten road to his house." A child could understand this sensible description of "common fame," but I wonder what Mr. Emerson would have thought about motion pictures, and the immense industry that took root and flourished around them. For those who made their lives within that colony, traditional values were not easily maintained, and for the children growing up there, it was nearly impossible to envision the broader landscape, or ponder its possibilities. Like our community, we were not focused on the world outside.

On Saturday mornings, with seventy-five cents' allowance in my jeans pocket, I would ride my bike down Beverly Drive, poke around the fish pond in the park, and climb the wonderful tree that still dominates the corner of Santa Monica and Beverly. You had to cross the railroad tracks to get to the stores, and it may be just as well that the train never stopped there, because if it had, I might have climbed aboard and gone wherever it took me. As it was, if a train was coming, I'd lay a penny on the track. Flattened pennies could always be traded at school.

At the five-and-dime, I'd order a chocolate milk shake at the soda counter, and stock up on M&M's and jujubes. Then I might try out the new Yo-Yo's, or look at the comic books, or buy caps for my gun. Last stop was the Beverly Pet Store. George, the owner, had an accent and could be grouchy, but I was extra polite. Want me to clean the mouse cage for you, George? Can I hold this puppy, please? How much are the lizards? George got used to me hanging around and after a while he'd let me play with all the animals except the puppies, and I'd bring home anything my parents would allow me to keep. They were pretty good about that. At one point or another, apart from the dog and cat, which were everybody's, I had a duck, five guinea pigs, a garter snake, two turtles, a horney toad, a shoebox full of roll-up bugs, and eighty-seven hamsters. I took excellent care of them all.

My three brothers teased me into shape. "Sissies play with dolls," they would taunt me, so I didn't flinch when they took out the eyes and left the heads all smashed; and after a while, if anyone who didn't know any better gave me a doll, I'd thank them, and go straight behind the house and bash its head on the brick steps, to get the eyes out before my brothers did. It was okay. I only really cared about my first doll, anyway. So we had a great collection of eyes, which you could also trade at school. Once, I was offered a three-legged kitten for one green eye and a pair of blues. But we had enough cats, my parents said.

Sometimes I brought a hamster to school in my pocket, since they like to sleep all day anyway. One practical thing I *always* kept in the pocket of my school blazer was a tooth, and if I wanted to get out of class, I'd hold it up and, covering my mouth, make some sounds and head for the bathroom. That was good for fifteen or twenty minutes at least, and they never caught on, so it was well worth forfeiting the tooth fairy's reward one time for that. Of course, you had to keep track of which teachers, and roughly how many teeth can be lost in a year.

From the time I could think, I was crazy about Michael Boyer, who cared nothing at all for me. Exactly my age, and the only child of my mother's closest friends, the French actor Charles and his wife, Pat, Michael and I had been paired from infancy. He was slightly overweight and darkly handsome with a beautiful mouth and pensive, shining eyes. Everyone said he resembled his father: not the Mr. Boyer I knew, of course, but the much younger man I'd seen on television in *Gaslight*. Except Michael didn't have a charming French accent; what Michael had was a heart-stopping, anxiety-generating stutter.

The Boyers lived a couple of blocks over from us in Beverly Hills and had a beach house near ours in the Malibu Colony. Mrs. Boyer was "highly strung," with a fluty English voice that went on and on. She must have missed Mr. Boyer, who traveled a lot. Perhaps that's why she so focused on her son, fluttering over him, worrying about his every move and word, and every bite he ate. She made everybody nervous, especially Michael, but at the same time, you couldn't help feeling sorry for her.

Mr. Boyer was another story entirely. I liked him a lot—and unlike Michael, he always noticed me. Not only did he remember which of the seven I was, but he even asked me how things were going, and seemed interested while I told him. It was amazing. Sometimes he would tell me about Paris, which sounded too beautiful to exist, and I longed to see it. And what was more, he paid almost no attention to my brothers and sisters. I wished he didn't travel so much, so Mrs. Boyer would relax a little: then Michael could relax too, and who knew, one day his stutter might just disappear. I'd be happy about seeing more of Mr. Boyer myself. Because what he didn't know, what nobody knew, was that, after Eileen and my parents, Mr. Boyer was my favorite grown-up.

So I was glad when he stopped by our beach house one hot morning of my tenth summer. I hung around while he chatted with my parents, then he asked to walk me back to his house for a visit with his son, who we both knew would tolerate the encounter with polite indifference.

Together we set out along the shaded sidewalk, and as always I asked him where he'd been lately. He told me of his travels, and I watched his eyes get the far-away look. Just then, where I nearly stepped on it, a baby bird sat on the sidewalk, its mouth wide open and a little buzzing, squawky sound coming out of it. Mr. Boyer went right on walking and talking because at this point he was virtually *in* Paris, but when he noticed I'd stopped and why, his whole face changed. He leaned over and squinted hard at that tiny bird, then he reached up into the tree that hung over the sidewalk and tore off a clump of leaves. Mystified, I watched him scrub them into his hands.

"What're you doing *that* for, Mr. Boyer?"

"To take away the human scent," he said, in a new, hushed voice.

He lifted that baby bird so carefully and, on tiptoes, placed it back in its nest. I stuck my bare foot between the slats of the white wooden fence and climbed high enough to see inside: five little ones were in there, five open mouths, and now you couldn't even tell which was ours. We positioned ourselves across the street and watched for what seemed a long time, until the mother bird, a worm drooping from her beak, flew back to the nest.

"Ahhhh," he breathed softly.

Mr. Boyer and I had shared an important thing.

Again we set out, but now there was no talking. He placed his hand on my shoulder, the one nearest him. The intimacy and tenderness and enormity of all of this was more than I could understand or bear and it started my ten-year-old heart pounding. I fixed my attention on my feet as they moved automatically, one in front of the other, and I struggled toward other, more comprehensible thoughts.

"Later this summer," I observed, "my feet'll get so tough I'll be able to walk on broken glass." He didn't say a word.

When we got outside the back door of the Boyer house, he turned me toward him. He had a grip on both of my shoulders so that I felt I ought to look right into his face, and I did that, even though it wasn't easy. Then in his beautiful French accent, Charles Boyer said, "Your life will be a wonderful one, but difficult I think." Probably I said thank you or something, so as not to hurt his feelings, and I hoped with all my might he understood that this was just too much for me to begin to know how to respond. I ducked out of his grasp and ran inside, and as the screen door slammed behind me, I took the stairs two at a time and didn't stop or turn around until I reached Michael's door, which was open a crack.

Michael Boyer was lying on his bed listening to the radio, his head propped with an elbow. He went right on ignoring me.

Every room in the house of my childhood evokes a rolling of memories, and none more powerful than those of the living room because it was the room for occasions. I remember gray mornings and sun mornings and being small and scared in my navy blue uniform with a brimmed felt hat, sitting at the window seat sucking my thumb and watching for the school bus. Sometimes my father in his silk bathrobe stood next to me sipping coffee. Or Eileen sat beside me. My mother has never been an early riser.

Our living room was for special affairs. You didn't play in there. It was a spacious thirties-style room with a spotless white carpet, green striped couches, and an intense hand-painted German mural covering an entire wall, including the door that led to all the bedrooms. One long wall faced Beverly Drive through the olive trees. The opposite wall was sliding glass doors, so guests could flow easily outside onto the patio. It was a serious room, and except for the mural, which depicted a battle with horses, it was not a room for children. In the evenings, I came to the living room and stood on my tiptoes in tiny monogrammed slippers to good-night kiss my parents, and when the room was filled with strangers, loud talk, smoke, shrimps, and maids, I survived countless curtseys and how-do-you-dos.

On Christmas Eve, I spelled out my wishes and watched them lift in flames to waiting elves. I remember tree trimmings and bulbs breaking and long crimson stockings (crocheted by our nanny Barbara) now hanging empty, now bulging in front of the fireplace, and a shiny red bicycle too, and all the flutter and wonder of those first Christmases.

A less entrancing Christmas tradition was the ceremonial visit with my godmother. Louella Parsons was not noticeably talented or witty or wise, but her column appeared daily in Hearst newspapers across the country and was read by "everyone" from the thirties through the fifties, when people believed what was written, which made Louella Parsons very powerful in the movie business. She could wreck entire careers—and did. That was how things were when my parents offered the legendary columnist their first-born daughter as a godchild, and all things considered she took her role in my life surprisingly seriously. She was a devout Catholic and could be seen every Sunday at the Church of the Good Shepherd at the twelve-fifteen Mass.

Each year during Christmas week, my parents and I would dress up and drive the few blocks to Aunt Louella's house to deliver our present. We brought an important-looking package that had been wrapped in the store so I didn't have a clear idea of what was inside, but it was always big and breakable, and my father would carry it up to the door. A maid in a fancy black uniform would let us into the entrance hall; while we waited, our eyes fell on the virtual tidal wave of packages emanating from the white-frosted Christmas tree way at the end of the living room and flowing high and wide—silver, green, red, and gold—right up to the shiny black toes of my Mary Janes. And each year we were humbled into silence.

In time my godmother would emerge from the dark back regions of the house where she had her offices. She looked ancient, with a humped, neckless little body, a large head, and a vivid lopsided slash of a mouth that was pulled alarmingly toward the left (a pioneering face-lift, explained my mother, and don't stare). "Well, how nice!" she would say, in her distinctive singsong. "Thank you. Is that the dress I gave you? Don't you look pretty in it!" At this point my mother would give me a poke, just in time to stop me from saying how itchy that organdy dress is so please don't give me any more. "Well, Merry Christmas, Merry Christmas." Then we would bend down to respectfully place our gift along the shore of the sea of packages. Afterward, I always felt very tired.

In the deflated hours of Christmas afternoon, Aunt Louella would arrive in her black Cadillac to distribute her presents. We all liked her chauffeur, Collins, who doted on her and fussed over her. He called her "Missy" and "Honey," and they say that when he died he left her all his money. Collins would carry seven sumptuous-looking packages into our living room and we would savage them on the spot; but every single year it was matching bathrobes. After the flat thank-yous we would stand around fidgeting while Aunt Louella lowered herself slowly onto the gold silk cushions of the big armchair in front of our living room fireplace. All of a sudden I wouldn't be able to remember what the chair looked like without her, and I'd get a panicky feeling. For an eternity her tea would be served, then sipped, and in that strange voice she would ask us the usual questions and we would give her the usual answers. Then we would gratefully flee the living room.

Every Sunday, my father, my mother, and their seven children—boys in gray flannel suits, girls in itchy pastel organdy dresses with crinkly petticoats, straw hats, white cotton gloves, and socks neatly folded above black patent-leather shoes—marched up the aisle, far too conspicuously, I thought even then, to the very front of the Church of the Good Shepherd, where all of the Farrow children were baptized, and an entire pew was reserved for our family. We looked for meaning in the long mysterious Mass, but restlessness and boredom inevitably triumphed.

I come from a tradition of big families, and that is what has always felt most natural to me. I like the raucous vitality, the sense of being on a team or in a club, only better. But being a part of such a large whole may explain my early appreciation of solitude.

By the time I was six or seven I found myself looking for privacy so that I could read and daydream without interruption. Toward that end, I hollowed out a little chamber where the ivy was thickest against the pool-yard fence. Inside, lying on a bath towel with sunlight filtered delicate green through the ivy, in a state as close to perfection as I have ever come, I embarked on the great journeys of *The Secret Garden*, the entire *Wizard of Oz* series, *Mary Poppins*, and *Uncle Tom's Cabin*, all in the ivy chamber of our garden, and in bed by flashlight at night.

My brother Mike, six years my senior, taught me to read before I was four, kindling a passion that has never waned. I discovered that through the written word I could voyage outside the perimeters of my own awareness into other minds, other sensibilities, and into any imaginable experience. Even now when I bring home a new book, my heart beats a little faster, I am each time atingle, more eager than I want people to know.

Before long my father and I discovered our common ground, and spent silent, blissful hours browsing in the local bookshop. Then, with new books tucked under our arms, we walked home together. I liked to look at him and did my best with giant steps and little, awkward skips to match his long, oblivious strides. If he chanced to glance down at me he'd sometimes smile and in those moments I nearly drowned in such almighty happiness and gratitude and love that the only commensurate thing I could think to do was to lie down on the pavement, there at my father's feet, and offer him my entire mortal being; but of course I didn't do that, or speak of these feelings, since they would surely have been as far beyond his comprehension as they were mine. So I scampered mutely by his side.

I remember sitting under the olive trees one hot summer afternoon trying to read a passage from *Out of Africa* to my younger brother and sisters and the Roach kids, in which Isak Dinesen describes two captured giraffes onboard a boat

in the harbor of Mombasa, waiting to be shipped to a
traveling menagerie in Europe.

> In the long years before them, will the gi-
> raffes sometimes dream of their lost country?
> Where are they now, where have they gone to,
> the grass and the thorn trees, the rivers and
> waterholes and the blue mountains? Where have
> the other giraffes gone to, that were side-by-side
> with them when they cantered over the undulat-
> ing land? They have left them, they have all gone
> and it seems they are never coming back. The
> giraffes stir, and wake up in the caravan of the
> menagerie, in their narrow box that smells of
> rotten straw and beer. Good-bye, good-bye, I
> wish for you that you may die on the journey,
> both of you, so that not one of the little noble
> heads that are now raised, surprised, over the
> edge of the case, against the blue sky of Mom-
> basa, shall be left to turn from one side to the
> other, all alone, in Hamburg, where no one
> knows of Africa. As to us, we shall have to find
> someone badly transgressing against us, before
> we can in decency ask the giraffes to forgive our
> transgressions against them.

I found this passage so wrenchingly beautiful that I remember the afternoon vividly. How very far from Beverly
Drive those words had carried me, and how *important* it was,
that visit to Mombasa, in the tangled ivy outside our house,
flicking bugs off my knees, trying for all I was worth to
convey this to the kids in my gang, so that we could share
something wondrous, something better than ice cream. But
it was a tough job, trying to hold the group together for a
reading like that, and they flew apart before I'd finished.

• • •

Our shuttered, single-room cabin stood on a barren plateau and faced the sea; a ragged outhouse slouched about twenty feet away. Both constructions were of the roughest lumber, rutted and weathered gray. Ash-dry hills shouldered high behind, and at the left a narrow dirt road ribboned all the way up to the rushing Pacific Coast Highway.

It was always dark inside the cabin, and it smelled of seaweed; the walls were the other side of the same un-painted planks as the exterior. Two canvas cots were set along each side wall, with a good-sized maple table between them, on which had been placed a plain-glass hurricane lamp and a puckered, mildewed book with colored sema-phore illustrations; cracked, browning soap stuck fast in an abalone shell by the stained porcelain sink, sand and earth insects pressed into crevices and down the drain; a rusted can opener dangled from a string nailed into the wall where barbecue utensils also hung. In one corner a scrimpy broom leaned out of a bucket, and cobwebs entangled fishing rods (we were not fisherfolk), and a bag of charcoal bled its sooty contents onto the floor. Through small dusty win-dowpanes there was a startling view of the sea. This was the cabin when last I saw it. Through all these years it has held a fixed place and rank within me; in its plainness and use-fulness, its utter lack of pretense and any embellishment, in the integrity of its existence, it is a thing by which all the rest can be measured.

My mother had purchased the property at Trancas Beach with inheritance money from my grandfather. From time to time we came to visit, though never as frequently as I would have wished, because it was a substantial drive from Beverly Hills, and we had a well-equipped beach house in Malibu. But each Fourth of July, toward evening, a bright yellow school bus jogged down the steep hillside to the plateau, conveying my family, friends, food, drink, and all manner of

fireworks. In cardboard boxes we carried the things down
steep wooden steps to the beach—by July our feet were
tough as shoes.

Blankets were spread upon the sand and the women settled into soft, intimate talking and the men and boys gathered driftwood and dry seaweed to build a fire, and the kids
flew like kites on summer winds. When the signal came, we
pulled off the sweatshirts covering our bathing suits and on
borrowed bravery we waded after our father toward the rising palisades of water and followed his deep dive beneath
the waves. Out past the breakers, fear of the dark heaving
ocean and the riptides and all manner of creatures in its
chill depths kept me close to my father, and when I grew
tired I held on to his strong shoulders. Coming back
through the waves I stayed near, so when they pounded me,
churning the last breath from my lungs, he would find me
and deliver me to the welcoming of rough towels under
which I shivered into dry jeans and a white sweatshirt, with
sand in everything. Then we sat with our mothers on blankets and looked into the fire. With the warmth swelled a
sense that all was well and our thoughts returned to familiar
things.

After hot dogs sloppy with mustard and potato chips, we
waved sticks over leaping flames, blackening our marshmal-
lows, and when at last it was night, fireworks hissed and
boomed and bejeweled the summer sky. Awed, we shouted
and shook our sparklers on the Fourth of July. When it
was over our father threw sand on the dying fire, then weary
from the hard sun and wind and the demands of the terrible swim, with the night chill settling into blackness, we
gathered our things and climbed the steps to the plateau,
where the bus awaited the sleepy journey home.

Visits to that place by the sea inspired intense and inde-
cipherable feelings, a confluence of wildness and order, of
magic and the commonplace, of vitality and death, content-

ment against unutterable yearning, instantaneous and eternal.

When I was ten, and had resumed full school days, I began playing with an El Salvadoran girl who spoke little English, named Roxanna Tinocco. Soon, she was one of my closest friends, but her family was going back to El Salvador, and who knew if we'd ever see each other again? So we were shuffling morosely around the school yard, arm in arm, when Roxy invited me to El Salvador for the summer. The thought of going so far for so long was frightening, but by the time her parents made the invitation official and my own parents got enthusiastic, I could see that it would be an adventure.

My mother insisted on taking me out to buy new clothes for the trip, even though shopping was an ordeal we avoided whenever possible because I hated it so. I hated having to look at clothes and hated trying them on and invariably I became cranky and literally faint from boredom. But this time she kept the expedition brief and cheerful— soon we were sipping tea at the Beverly Hills Hotel, eating delicious cakes and chatting happily. And as we sat there, I became aware that my mother was talking to me like a friend, as if I was grown-up. In that moment some essential part of me, stirring in my most intimate, shadowy center, was acknowleged and stepped blinking into the bright afternoon light.

The departure was wrenching. The Tinoccos had to pry me off my parents and I cried all the way to San Salvador, where, within hours of our arrival, the resident seamstress came to measure me for riding clothes. Later, three sets of snow-white jodhpurs and shirts arrived, neatly folded and wrapped in brown paper and a perfect fit, for my lessons the following morning.

On a tour of the house I noted that the Tinoccos'

kitchen was bigger than our living room. One of the cooks sat talking animatedly to Roxy while wringing a chicken's neck. Their conversation, which of course I understood nothing of because it was in Spanish, continued until the hen was bald. I felt homesick.

The three younger Tinocco girls and I spent our days horseback riding and soon I picked up a little Spanish. We also spent considerable time scheming to prompt the highly strung English governess to resign. (Release a bat in her bedroom, put toads and spiders between her sheets, spread peanut butter on the toilet seat, and speak only in a language she cannot understand.) We had no sense then that El Salvador was smoldering and would soon be torn apart by terrorists representing both the left and the right, that a bloody revolution was imminent, and that the wealthy elite like the Tinocco family would flee for their lives. During that summer of 1956, everything seemed peaceful throughout the countryside, where we galloped thoroughbred horses through the immense coffee plantations and I stared back at the unsmiling workers waiting in line for a spoonful of black beans slopped onto a tortilla.

Two years later, in 1958, my mother retired from the screen. For reasons we did not understand, movie offers had thinned out for my father—he'd only made four films in four years instead of four in one year, as in 1951. Now money was a concern. I caught the strained tones and overheard snatches of conversations, and I worried.

But finally a project, *John Paul Jones*, did come together and our family moved to Spain for its filming. Mike, three months shy of his nineteenth birthday, didn't want to leave California, so we left him there in the home we loved on Beverly Drive and flew all the way to Madrid, where we loaded into the Castellana Hilton Hotel. What we didn't know, what we had no inkling of when we left that morning, was that this trip would bring about an end to the life we had known.

In Madrid we lived under life-sized portraits of Conrad Hilton and explored every inch of the huge drab hotel; we spied on fellow guests, ordered room service, attended Spanish schools, and within a month I was dreaming in Spanish. Dad gave Johnny and Patrick parts in the movie and he said I could be in it too—he even gave me a line, which was "From our petticoats, sir." "My" scene wasn't due to be shot for five months but already I was nervous. My father neglected to tell me in what context my line would appear, so I imagined every conceivable scenario and gave "From our petticoats, sir" every interpretation my twelve-year-old mind could come up with.

When Bette Davis arrived to play Catherine the Great, she brought her daughter BD, who was my age, and I was taken along on many of their sightseeing expeditions. BD was quiet, well-behaved, and pretty. Bette was energetic, blunt, bossy, vivid, and of course completely intimidating, but she was kind to me and I liked her. She, in turn, has described me as "quite mousy-looking, a lonely little girl . . . born with an old soul. She lived all alone in her own world."

Benidorm, on the southern coast of Spain, was a sleepy little village then, with burros wandering through the colorful marketplace, long pristine beaches, and a few midrange houses for the tourists, who were scarce. When Dad moved there for the final three months of the shoot, our family rented one of these houses. Our father did not live with us, but in one of the two big hotels that loomed incongruously out of the dusty town, sleek harbingers of what was to come.

But it was quiet then, nothing happening. We swam, drank lemonade, and tried to sell some to the handful of German tourists. We nursed our sunburns, argued, swatted at flies, drew in the dust with sticks, read, and I practiced my line. After dark, by candlelight we played cards, checkers, chess, argued some more, swatted the mosquitos, and sometimes we played a version of the Ouija board, using an overturned wineglass and pieces of paper with the letters of the alphabet written on them. One hot night, my mother and some of the kids and I were doing this, and asking questions, when swiftly and purposefully a seemingly self-propelled glass whirled from letter to letter, right out from under our fingertips, and spelled out MIKE DEAD. We didn't play after that.

When the day finally arrived for my film debut, I was nervous after the months of anticipation and preparation. "From our petticoats, sir" had to be the most practiced line in cinema history. Wearing a costume made specially for me, I was taken onto the set, a huge sailing ship, and placed among a cluster of women surrounding the star, handsome Robert Stack. I was shaking. There was some talk, and then suddenly Robert Stack was saying, "And where did you get the material to make this flag?" My cue, surely this was my cue. I opened my mouth to speak when, from behind me, a velvety, seductive voice was saying, "From our petticoats, sir." Stunned, I whipped around: the ravishing woman speaking my line was Mrs. Robert Stack. So it goes.

I was miserable in Spain and wrote my friend Maria, "The people here don't seem to like their dogs or their children." I missed Mike, and our dog Tuffy, and my friends, and home, and I seemed to be sick all the time. Whatever the reason, I grew listless and pale, and dark circles settled permanently under my eyes. My mother was worried: this was how I'd been in the months before my ninth birthday. The doctor couldn't find anything wrong with me, but I was so weak I could barely sit up.

Then a strange thing happened. The town of Denia, where the film was being made, put on a huge week-long festival each year, and because I was the movie director's daughter, I was chosen Queen of the Fiestas, and there was no way around it. Four long gowns had been made for me and I wore a crown and elbow-length gloves and rode in floats through the crowded streets, waving. I danced with the mayor and made a long flawless speech in Spanish to thousands of people. I visited schools and churches and handed out baskets to the poor and my mother was absolutely astonished that I could do these things, and I myself was beyond amazement. The minute it was over I again grew pale, and the circles under my eyes reappeared, and I went back to bed. For years my mother would say, "Remember in Spain how you rose to the occasion?"

Money troubles were hanging over us all the time. From the start, financing for *John Paul Jones* had come in irregularly. So we were relieved when the film was finally finished and we headed for the Wicklow Mountains in Ireland, where I rode horses all day and visited with my cousins.

In the fall we joined our father in London, where he was editing the movie, and the family took up residence in the Park Lane Hotel. Johnny and Patrick were sent to school in Bournemouth, and Prudence and I were enrolled in a convent boarding school in Surrey, while Tisa and Steffi attended a day school in London. We all survived an interminable shopping expedition at Harrods, where we bought uniforms, nightgowns, sheets, towels, hot-water bottles, and quilts, and we spent quiet, nervous hours with Barbara, our nanny, sewing name tags into every single item. Finally, on a gray September morning, a chubby, bespectacled chauffeur named Freddie drove Prudy and me out to the school. The austere brick building was set at the edge of Richmond Park. It looked a grim, forbidding place.

My sister and I were taken to separate quarters, where we cried for hours every night. I telephoned our parents begging them to let us come back even for a weekend, but they took a firm stand. It took a toothache to bring me "home" to the Park Lane Hotel.

•   •   •

"Get up Mia, get dressed." Our nanny's voice, with the firm, cheery Scottish accent, now seemed strange, muffled, cracked, as she pushed the trolleyful of English breakfasts into our hotel bedroom.

"What's the matter, Barbara?" I asked, but her lips stayed pressed together, her eyes lined pink, searching the floor. A heaviness leaned into me. I put on my uniform to return to school after breakfast. I'd been to the dentist the day before, but I wasn't thinking about cavities now.

Barbara turned to dress my little sister Tisa. I pushed around my cereal and fixed on a single tear as it slid crookedly through the lines near Barbara's right eye to hang trembling on the soft jowl below her plump cheek.

"I can't eat any more." I waited.

"Go to your mam and dad now," she said, still not looking at me.

My parents' suite was at the end of the hallway and I kept my eyes on their door, stomach turning over empty. I wanted to run—run the other way before it was too late, up the long corridor, down the six flights of stairs out into the watery English morning, where it would be seven-thirty and an ordinary day. But I put my stout black shoes one in front of the other, even when I heard the terrible sounds from deep inside my mother.

I pushed the door open and took a couple of steps into the suite. In the living room, toward the right, my father sat crookedly on the couch, bent over, silent. My mother was standing, facing him, her back to me. She threw a pillow at him hard. I shouldn't be seeing this, I thought, nor hearing these sounds.

"Mom, what happened? Mom?" She moved past me heavily, out of the living room, and I followed toward the bedroom, where she twisted slowly toward me, my serene and beautiful mother, her face torn wild, ripped apart. The scream never left my throat; I could not move nor make a sound.

"Mike's dead," she said. Then, from a great distance I heard words: plane crash, flying lessons, leaving today, Mom and Dad, California, Mike's body, a funeral, do you understand? *No, no I don't understand anything are you sure it's him maybe it's a mistake maybe it's someone else.*

"Go back to school now," she told me. Would I be all right? Would I tell Prudy? She stood apart, she didn't touch me.

"Yes, Mom, I will. I'll tell Prudy. We'll be all right . . ." I could not bridge the terrible gap between us.

"We'll be okay," I said. But I toppled hard. Never again would death catch me so unprepared. At the age of thirteen I vowed to stand ready.

Back at school the nuns had been notified and on my arrival I was taken to the Reverend Mother Elizabeth's office, where she rambled on about "God's will." I interrupted to ask if she would find Prudy, please. "I need to tell her. My mother said to tell her." It would be the most terrible and important thing I had ever done, and I would do it better than anybody because I cared more than anybody.

But when the nun returned with Prudy some minutes later it was clear that from the lips of this stranger who neither cared nor knew anything about Mike or Prudy or me or our exact and fierce love, and therefore this our own and nobody else's loss and fury and pain—my sister had been told her brother was dead. I held her, hating the Reverend Mother, who would not leave the room, and my helplessness and God himself, yes, Goddamnyou Jesuschristgod. If You exist, damn You to hell.

Did he feel pain? Was there time for fear, or just surprise? Was there a final thought? Did he love me last? Rage and grief are savage companions, but despair is the final undoing. My brother's death plunged me into the struggle of my life, drenching every bitter, brutal hour of each day and each long, foreign night. Everything was overturned, broken into senselessness.

But gradually over the next months I became aware that deep within me hope had survived. And after hope came strength, and with it a fragile clarity—just enough to reach for what was essential. So in the end I found myself at the beginning. And once again, all the world was brand-new.

And I learned a useful thing about anger—you can feel it, all of it, and then let it pass through you. It can be done —I know because I've done it countless times; the rage can just pass right through you. And eventually grief gathers tight into itself and in the most intimate, lacerating concentration of pain it takes its final, permanent place. And there is nothing to be done about it.

Chapter Three

After Mike's death, my parents moved from the Park Lane Hotel to a tall, quaint house on Swan Walk, in Chelsea. I was given the attic room, flooded with light, from which you could climb out onto the rooftop for a splendid view of the Thames. I painted the room myself, a palest shade of peach, yet I rarely stayed there; by then I preferred being at school in Surrey. Tensions between my parents had escalated. Their demons were driving them apart, and in their grief they found no solace in each other.

My father was drinking heavily. One evening, in an awful rage, he began shouting, and he chased my mother with a long knife through the ground-floor rooms of the house. I froze at the foot of the stairs until at last, knife in hand, he careened out into the night. My mother and I watched the door and after a time we made hot chocolate. But still I was shaking, so she put me into her own big bed saying that when Dad returned he'd find me there and surely then he'd soften because he loved me so. Then she climbed the stairs to the safety of my little attic room, while I propped myself up in bed, with my face right under the light, and waited.

Oh dear God, please take care of my mother, I understand something of her grief but I cannot comfort her however much I long to. Stay close to my father tonight, make him put down his knife, or throw it into the dark river but please don't let him come back here to plunge it into his sleeping child; and Lord God, be merciful, don't let him put it into himself, out there in the dark, for he is a good man and You have given him an awful lot to bear. Please, Jesus please, take care of this family, and if it be Thy will, let Dad get a movie job, I don't know what will happen to us if he doesn't, and God, one last thing, I won't ask more— if I should fall asleep, please don't let my face turn away from this light.

Winter held the Surrey countryside in gray, glassy light and the cold penetrated everything. There was no central heating in the sleeping quarters for the fifty or so girls at my convent school. I didn't much like jockeying for a place in front of the single fireplace downstairs, but after someone mentioned that wet hair would freeze in the night and break to bits, I elbowed my way to the fireside when I washed my hair to get it bone dry.

I can't remember ever being so cold. A glass of water beside the bed had a crust of ice by morning. Chilblains swelled our finger joints sore and stiff, with angry, itchy crimson lumps that didn't subside until June. Hot-water bottles were lifesavers, and although it was against the rules, beneath my navy blue woolen uniform I kept my pajama bottoms on all day. The cold, and the modesty of the convent, motivated me to perfect a technique for changing clothes with lightning speed without revealing an inch of skin.

Most of the nuns were even more severe than the sisters in California. I thought of them as not exactly human but as some sort of hybrid, short on compassion, humor, patience, and any capacity to give or receive affection. We were children without parents in an isolated and harsh environment, where the most basic kindness was unusual.

There were exceptions. Mother Lillian taught piano and art. In chapel she played the organ stirringly, and from our meager, shivering ranks she pulled together a choir that transported us beyond our capabilities and circumstances. When word of our choir spread through Surrey, we were asked to sing in local churches and hospitals and homes for the elderly. With her fine, chiseled features and long, graceful hands, Mother Lillian was as beautiful as her gentle world of music and art.

Mother Frederick had white-blond eyelashes and a round face that became flushed when she was upset. She was tall and very young. Sometimes she looked as if she had been crying. Not long out of childhood herself, it was Mother Frederick who extended a much-needed touch of humanity. When she and Mother Lillian both left the Order of the Sacred Heart of Mary, it took me twenty years to find them.

The Dickensian atmosphere of our school proved fertile ground for friendships and spiritual values. My roommates and best friends were Nancy Newton, with Spanish eyes, runaway thoughts, and a probing, promising mind; and Leslie Mullin, who had a pale, haunted, angel's face set in a short fuzz of yellow hair; at night, while everyone slept, Leslie knelt on the bare floor in her long flannel nightgown and prayed with outstretched arms. Ann Casey was a grade older than me, and I was drawn to her because she was fun and one of the most generous people I have ever met. I could always count on Casey.

Daily attendance at Mass was not compulsory, but I liked the half-mile walk through frigid winter mornings silent with nuns along dark, country roads, past the overgrown graveyard to the main school building near the chapel. At the lonely predawn Mass I took Communion and said the book prayers and made up the rest, and after school I slipped again into the quiet chapel to kneel with my arms outstretched like Leslie.

It was during the first of my two years in Surrey that I decided to become a Carmelite. The nuns at my school laughed and said I'd have to do a load of improving before the Carmelites would take me. But I yearned for the contemplative existence, to become one with the mind of God. It seemed the most pure, powerful, and significant way I could possibly spend my life.

I tried to make myself nun material. But the cards seemed to be unfairly stacked against me: I was driven by the itchy kind of curiosity that eclipsed good sense and continually got me into hot water, I tended to be forgetful or preoccupied, I found things funny when other people didn't, and in the face of wall-to-wall rules that were trivial and pointless, my instinct was to rebel.

In March 1959, my roommate Nancy made this entry in her diary: "Mia in trouble again"; and in May, "Mia—the drainpipe." I did climb out the third-floor window down the rotting drainpipe into the dewy, deery grass behind the dorm and I did, on a dare, set my alarm clock off during the Rosary, and it's true that I cut myself opening sardine tins by flashlight. It has always taken me a while to get to sleep, so when they turned out the lights, I'd wait until the coast was clear and the halls were nun-free, and then I'd get up and roam around the building, just visiting friends, having some laughs, catching up on news, and checking whether anyone had anything good to eat.

"Mia Farrow!" (Scary voice.) "What are you doing here! You have one colossal nerve!" She was crazy-eyed, but she'd said this so many times it had no meaning.

So I just said, "Yes, Mother Finbar." My thoughts were with the bag of Oreo cookies behind my back.

"Unless it is to go to the bathroom, you do not leave

your bed for any reason after lights-out. Can you get that into your head?"

"Yes, Mother Finbar, but I had to go to the bathroom." (Not true.)

"*On the second floor?!*" She was getting shrill. "*What were you doing on the second floor?*"

"I don't know, just looking around. I made it up about the bathroom. I'm sorry." (I really was.)

Back in Beverly Hills, when everyone in the house was sleeping I used to wander around and look at my family, sound asleep, and every once in a while, with my thumb, I'd very carefully open up somebody's eye, just for a second, to look at the eyeball in there.

The nuns who weren't stationed in our dormitories slept (that they slept at all was itself an odd notion) in cloistered quarters behind a thick green curtain at the end of a long hallway. One evening, while they were in the chapel, I sneaked down the corridor and with my heart doing double time I slipped behind the curtain and continued down the hall. The first doorway on the left revealed an absolutely bare room, with just a bed and a dresser. Something caught my eye that froze me in my tracks: on the white bedspread lay a crown of thorns. Underneath that, I found a black satin bag, and inside the bag was a *small whip.* You don't forget a thing like that. I was out of there in a split second.

I was careful whom I told. It took me a few days to organize guided tours, for the fee of one shilling a head. There was plenty of interest, but people were wary, and finally I only got one expedition off the ground. I was all business on that second trip behind the green door. Carmelina and Barbara were scared but it was going well. The crown and whip naturally were a great success, and soon I was feeling loose and confident enough to expand the tour a little: we were just opening the first dresser drawer when

from way down the corridor came the unmistakable clud of
nun's shoes on the wooden floor, and the terrible swoosh
and snap of long skirts and stiff, starched habits heading
our way at a good clip. I dragged the girls behind the long
drapes and slammed them flat against the window.

"*Feet!*" I hissed. Three pairs of black shoes flipped side-
ways. We didn't breathe as the nun went about some errand
of her own and left. When her sounds faded we scuttled
out of there and I never went back.

Despite our ambivalent feelings toward some of the
nuns, we remained genuinely committed to our religion and
intrigued by the lives of the saints. For penance, Nancy,
Leslie, and I rubbed stinging nettles on our arms. We made
rosary beads out of acorns, and our fingers bled with the
effort, then I buried mine in the school garden because I
thought it was impure to be so proud of them.

It was no secret that I didn't want to be in the May Day
ballet. The costumes were immodest, I felt, and the entire
event would be mortifying. So when I twisted my ankle and
a swelling the size of a ripe plum popped out, the Reverend
Mother (crediting me with more than I deserved) decided I
had done myself this injury to avoid being in the ballet.
Although she was mistaken, the idea entranced me: it would
have taken such courage, such conviction, it would have
been almost heroic. I denied it of course, but not too vigor-
ously, and when I was placed in solitary confinement for a
week, even girls I didn't know all that well risked coming to
see me; a couple of nuns visited too, and people brought
me chocolate. The Reverend Mother refused to take me to
a doctor despite the size and color of my foot and the fact
that I couldn't put any weight on it for about a month.
And she didn't get me a bandage or a crutch, and hopping
hurt so I either had to crawl or Casey piggybacked me—
but I got so much respect, it was worth it.

In the summer of 1959, after the first year at boarding
school, my family returned to County Wicklow. In the fall,

Prudy and the rest of the family went back to California, while I stayed in Surrey. That second year I won the gymnastics badge, which gave me as big a thrill as any I'd ever known. When they announced my name, I remembered trembling on my feet, and the bored face of the doctor, way back in the polio wards.

With some students and nuns I traveled to Cairo, Jerusalem, Paris, Geneva, and Rome; I got blessed by the Pope, went to Mass in the catacombs, and to the baths in Lourdes. I visited Pisa and Pompeii, where the jolt of seeing the twisted figures preserved in ash made me swallow my ring. But the most vivid memory of my travels that year was of a man who sat opposite me in the third-class compartment of an Italian train, trying to open a cheap bottle of wine bare-handed, tearing at the cap, and the bottle was covered slippery with blood.

My school in England was a world I had come to understand and make my peace with. I'd made friends and had countless laughs, and I was grateful not to be home, where there were so many problems. I hoped my parents would let me stay until my graduation, two more years, but they felt it was time for me to return to California. I was grief-stricken at the prospect of losing so much, and panicked as I braced myself for yet another life—one for which I was completely unprepared.

My brother Mike had been dead for two years when the family moved back to California into a smaller, less appealing house with no garden at all, at a much more modest address in Beverly Hills. My father had become morose, difficult, and demanding. He had not worked in over two years. He read the obituaries scrupulously, mournfully commenting "gone" at the passage of each acquaintance. He spoke often of his own death and stayed in his bedroom on the ground floor. My mother kept up a better front in the daytime—she even spoke of taking up painting, and set up an easel in a sunny alcove of her upstairs bedroom. But invariably after dinner she went to her room and the lights were out, but I knew she was not sleeping.

There were no parties now. Only the Jesuits still came. I poured two fingers of straight scotch into flat glasses and brought one to my father and each priest, officially launching their evening. Then I sat unnoticed on the stairs outside the living room, listening to the philosophical dissertations that continued well into the night. The Jesuits are the intellectuals, the core and conscience of the Catholic Church. Those long nights of theological debates and raised voices triggered in me some early questions and conclusions about the difficulty of being: responsibility, God, love, loss, and my own place in the universe. When I grew tired I crept upstairs past my mother's dark room, where she lay weeping.

It was impossible for me to communicate in any important sense with either of my parents, however much I longed to. A feeling of failure slowly settled around me. My brothers and sisters were now in trouble too. We had been through too much, too separately; and now in the isolation our grief had imposed on us, we could not reach one another.

In California my contemporaries were driving cars, dating boys, drinking beer, wearing makeup, and they had obviously thought about their hair. They were smoking Marlboros, humming hits of the day, and they could probably find the right radio station blindfolded. I was lost. My old chums Sheila, Tisha, and Kristin were now beautiful, confident, and popular. I was none of these things. I tried to copy them, even their breezy American, slangy way of talking, but I didn't fool the boys from Stanford who were understandably put off by my anguished silences and pa-

thetic attempts to communicate, and I could not successfully conceal my awful intensity. I missed my deeply rooted
boarding-school friendships, the mist-shrouded hills of Surrey, the still chapel, the spartan, spiritual, predictable life at
my school. I missed the seriousness of that place. I im-
mersed myself in books and confessed to my parents that I
hoped to enter the convent. When they seemed disturbed
by the idea, I resolved not to mention it again until after
high school.

In an effort to develop my social skills, and to help me
meet some "nice boys," they sent me to Elisa Ryan's Dance
Class. These were agonizing affairs—I knew no one, had
no idea what to talk about, my accent seemed out of place,
and even the right dress looked wrong on me. In one mem-
orably cruel exercise, the girls were lined up against one
long wall of the auditorium, while the aged Miss Ryan,
attached to her microphone, moved around goading the
boys into choosing a partner. In a state near paralysis, I
watched my worst-case scenario unfold until I was one of
the two unchosen girls facing a short, fat, stubborn-faced
boy in a military uniform. At that point I fled the room,
shot under the coat-check counter, dug out my white cardi-
gan with the melancholy orchid still attached, and in a broken run got myself home. In our garage I sat on a gasoline
can until 10:45 P.M.—coming-home time. My mother told
me again how pretty I looked and asked if I'd had fun. I
told her yes, and nothing more.

Three months after my seventeenth birthday, in 1962, I
graduated from high school, counting the days until I could
get out of the house and back to school in England, where I
had been happy. Given our money anxieties, I didn't know
whether this would be possible; so when my parents agreed
to let me go, I was overjoyed. I had by then abandoned
thoughts of becoming a nun: now I hoped to become a
pediatrician and work with children in Africa or Southeast
Asia. I loved children, and I was drawn to the idea of help-

ing them. Once this idea took root I was tremendously excited and eager to get started, but my grades had been inconsistent, and my education frequently disrupted. In need of extra credits to get into a good university and medical school, I returned to London for extra preparation for A-level exams.

By the time I joined my mother for Christmas in New York, relations between my parents had shattered completely. In a humiliating role reversal, my proud and elegant father, with his monogrammed silk shirts and handmade shoes, was left in the house that nobody loved on North Roxbury Drive to preside over the children, while three thousand miles away, his wife worked to send money home. Her paychecks apparently were not enough, and their phone calls were brief and bitter.

But my mother had entered a glittering new world. Her Broadway play, *Never Too Late*, was a smash hit and she was the toast of the town. After all the hard times it was great to see her riding high and so happy. Clutching her coattails, I was introduced to Manhattan: Broadway shows, backstage hobnobbing, stars every night crowding into my mother's dressing room, "Who's out there tonight?" Life didn't begin until after the show: there were parties, invitations, more parties, restaurants, pubs until all hours—heady stuff.

We were staying at the Algonquin Hotel, and we didn't get up until late afternoon, then we ordered a rare steak and spinach and a potato and we went to the theater. Kirk Douglas was starring in *One Flew Over the Cuckoo's Nest* across the street and he sometimes took us to dinner after the show. Often we ran into Brendan Behan, who was drinking hard and streaming strong, barely intelligible words, poetry, observations, stories, and advice. It was Brendan who bought me my very first drink, a brandy Alexander.

Since the show was clearly going to be running for a

long time, Mom rented an apartment in early 1963. I pretended not to notice that George Abbott, my mother's director, seemed to be taking more than a professional interest in her. But when my father phoned in the early hours of a January night, I could not, *could not* tell him where she was. And later still, when the phone rang and rang and rang, I pulled the pillow tight around my ears.

And when, in the hard light of day, we learned that my father had died that night of a heart attack with the phone in his hand, winds of nothingness blew cold across my soul.

There was a flatness to the day my father died, as my mother and I moved through the thick silence. She spoke briefly on the phone in a small strange voice. She took cottage cheese from the refrigerator and looked at it for a while, then put it back. In a brief exchange we agreed that, given the shortage of money, it was pointless for me to accompany her to California. He was, after all, dead. She packed a few things and went out the door.

Again I was alone, lost in the swarming of memories: my father holding his head high in the sunlight, afternoons shared at the bookstore and trying to match his long stride along Beverly Drive, and John Donne, and the doubting and trusting of the deep dive beneath the waves, and his laughter, and Saturday barbecues and the hero's medals and Christmases and waiting in my mother's bed for the knife in my chest and the years of hopelessness and anger and despair, and the final phone call that rang and rang and rang. *I couldn't answer it, Dad, I couldn't.* And I thought of Mike too, and all the sorrowing from which we never emerged, and the disintegration of my family, and my helplessness in the face of these incomprehensible things; and the unutterable pain of being here on this earth.

Chapter four

Now that our father was dead, the family's survival depended solely on our mother. She was
employed, but she was fifty-two years old, her
profession was far from reliable, and she had
four children younger than me to raise. Before
Never Too Late she hadn't worked in years. "It was
as if something died in me too," said my
mother. "A moment before I'd been drunk with
the euphoria of a big Broadway hit, and the next
moment I was a lonely widow unable to live
without tranquilizers. The only thing to do was
get out there and keep working. John didn't
leave any money. It was all a big struggle with
lots of ups and downs and there were times
when it was unbearably lonely."

Except for Patrick, who joined my mother
and me in New York, my younger brother
Johnny, and sisters Prudence, Steffi, and Tisa
stayed in California, supervised by our gentle
housekeeper, Marcel. Mom, Patrick, and I
moved into an unfurnished apartment on Fifty-
ninth Street. We purchased three mattresses,

three lamps, and three pots. I made a dressing table from an upside-down cardboard box, bought a mirror and some makeup, and began to look for an agent. It was no longer possible for me to return to school; it was time to help my family if I could, and at the very least I would pull my own weight.

I gave myself four months, six at the most, to get an acting job. I had no confidence that anyone would ever want to hire me; on the other hand, I was seventeen years old with little education—and nothing to lose. If I failed I would try something else, and someday, hopefully, I would go back to school. In the meantime, I sat in on acting classes with Stella Adler, Herbert Berghof, and Wynn Handman, and I began making the rounds.

My father always claimed he'd "never met a happy actress," and his disesteem for women in that profession was made clear to me in countless ways throughout my childhood. When I was fifteen, walking down Roxbury Drive with our dog Tuffy, a man jumped out of his car and pressed a card into my hand: he wanted me to screen-test for the movie *Lolita*. I said, Sure, and ran home to show my father the card, which he shredded into tiny pieces as he hit the roof. My success in school plays and a prize for reading from *Our Town* only reinforced his position. He hoped I would meet an English aristocrat and settle in London with chintz and china. Now, before he was cold in his grave, I was wearing makeup and looking for acting work, and thinking more than once how disappointed he would have been.

A month after my father's death and just before my eighteenth birthday, I found myself in an elevator, headed ambivalently toward a party on the top floor of the St. Regis Hotel. When the doors opened to a crush of strangers, smoke, and noise, I stood twisting my beaded evening bag until the elevator emptied and the doors shut in front of me. Before I could even feel relief, a sound startled me; I whirled around to see, for the first time, a quite extraordinary-looking man.

"Very good, very good," he chortled. I had never seen a mustache like his: several inches long, waxed and wire-thin, it sprang antenna-like from above his pursed lips into a jaunty curl at each tip. His eyes popped outrageously, and his black hair fell past the collar of a pin-striped morning coat under which glimmered a gold brocade vest. Gold too was the handle of his cane, which he raised slightly to say "Bonjour," with a short bow. Never mind that it was nine at night. "Good morning" was my reply.

When the doors opened onto the lobby, the mustache-man suggested "Encore?" with an upward gesture of his cane, and, abandoning my foothold in the real world, I nodded. There were three or four more ascents, three or four brief studies of the party, and then my companion introduced himself.

"I am Dalí. Le divine Dalí. I am completely crazy."

So I knew where I stood when I joined Salvador Dalí and his wife Gala for lunch the next day at Le Pavillon. He did not smoke or drink himself but ordered for me a fragrant liqueur called Mirabel, cautioning that it was "only for smell."

It was Dalí's custom to visit New York each fall, where he stayed at the St. Regis Hotel until St Patrick's Day when, as he put it, "everything becoming too green," and he moved on to Paris. In New York City, Dalí had accumulated an eclectic assortment of companions, including a beautiful hermaphrodite, a ballet dancer, a scientist, a woman who resembled George Washington, and a dapper little man who managed some aspect of the Dalís' affairs— el Capitán, as he was called—who had an accent, wore a uniform from no known place, and was usually accompanied by an ocelot.

From then on we met daily, sometimes with Gala, more often without. We lunched on butterfly wings and toured New York City with the garbage collectors. Speaking in a unique combination of French, Spanish, and a smattering of English, Dalí led me into the world of surrealism, cutting loose my thoughts and throwing the walls from my mind. People have said that I was looking for a father. I don't know about that. Certainly I was looking for guidance—I had lost my bearings in what seemed a sea of senselessness. But Dalí had long ago begun his celebration of absurdity and he embraced the part of me that was wildest and most frightening; he embraced the emptiness and the chaos, and the meaninglessness and nonsensicalness of the world; and his lawless interpretations transcended structure and illuminated another order that had its own shining, untrampled significance. "We are at the heart of a labyrinth and we can find our way while becoming labyrinths ourselves," he told me.

In a single, unfurnished room of the hotel, Dalí kept a large, beautiful, silver helium balloon that he visited at various times during the day, noting and delighting in its autonomous, barely perceptible movements. "I am penetrating more and more into the compressed magic of the universe," Dalí said.

When the first three-dimensional photographs emerged, Dalí was as excited as a child. He carried one in his pocket to scrutinize and show to any passing stranger, and when he noted a relationship between the photograph and a streaked fabric called moiré, a swatch joined the photograph.

A permanent fixture in that same pocket was a billfold or wallet in the final stages of disintegration. Its covering was a waffley, metal-like substance, gold and silver on reverse sides, that was peeling to bits. One day he pulled off a piece and gave it to me, saying if I kept it I would always have enough money. Dalí loved gold. He said that "bankers are the high priests of the Dalínian religion." And he once told me he would like to live in a house that was entirely made of gold, behind the wallpaper, and under the porcelain of the bathtub and under the tiles of the bathroom floor and under the wood of the staircase. That, he said, would give him profound pleasure, knowing that everything is made entirely of gold, while others were unwittingly trampling over it. He constructed a Dalínian calendar for me, using gold paint. "I never know if I am rich or poor," he said. "Gala takes care of all the money." Which was just as well, I thought, as I watched him gleefully flinging fistfuls of bills out the window of his hotel room, proclaiming, "Very important! Everything coming back one millions times!"

Whether Gala was present or not, Dalí's devotion to her was unreserved and always in evidence. "I love Gala better than my mother, better than my father, better than Picasso, and even better than money," he told me. "Without her I would no longer be Dalí. She understands everything about me, she is my protector, my mother, my queen. She calms me. She convinces me of my ability to live. She is always there to explain everything, bring me back to normal, she turns my obsessions into genius."

For my eighteenth birthday, in the lobby of the St. Regis, Dalí took a gauze-swaddled bundle from his safety deposit box and gave it to me. It was, he said, "a piece of moon," given to him by a famous scientist. It was more ordinary-looking than I would have thought, black on one side and gray on the other two. For luck, he gave me a talisman, an old print about the size of a playing card with an owl's picture and his name inscribed all over it. I put his gifts in the box I've kept since polio, a small wooden trunk I called my "magic box."

On my nineteenth birthday, Dalí arrived unannounced at our apartment and placed an object on the hallway floor. "Violence in a bottle," he declared, then turned around and left. We—my sisters, Johnny, my mother, and I—gathered around the glass jug painted in many colors but predominantly blue. The paint was still wet. Inside the jar was a rat consuming a lizard. The commotion would have delighted Dalí: my sisters shrieked, my mother screamed, "Get it out of here. *Out!*" and my brother ran outside and threw it over the wall into Central Park. Days later it occurred to someone that perhaps we should have kept it; after all, it was a Salvador Dalí painting. My brothers looked for it halfheartedly without success.

Dalí took me to a Greenwich Village party where the hermaphrodite host/hostess opened the door wearing a mink coat, which he/she stepped out of and, stark-naked, led us into the living room, where perhaps a dozen people were in various sexual tableaux. Dalí could barely contain his amusement and kept looking at me, all twinkly, checking whether I was okay. I was okay. I put off thinking about it. He never took his cape off, which was a relief, and he didn't leave my side, which was gentlemanly. We stood for three or four minutes tops, and left. He said it was "very beautiful." For himself, he said, he considered sex to be "too violent." And showers, too.

Through all these Dalínian adventures, I continued with my acting classes and auditioning for parts. It seemed that I was too old for child roles and too young for leading ladies; teen roles were scarce. You need an agent to help you get a job, and you need a job to get an agent. My wastrel existence and butterfly lunches ended when, to my astonishment, I replaced another actress in the role of Cecily in *The Importance of Being Earnest* at the Madison Avenue Playhouse. The reason I was chosen, I supposed, was because I could slide easily into an English accent.

My mother was proud of me, and I was thrilled myself. Now, every evening, we set off from the apartment to our separate theaters and met again after the shows to compare our evenings and our audiences. As for the performing it-self, the terror of my first night on the New York stage was only eclipsed by the panic of learning, one matinee, that Vivien Leigh was in the audience. To my mother, of course, she was a childhood friend from school, but to me she was Scarlett O'Hara.

Ms. Leigh showed up along with Ruth Gordon and Gar-son Kanin; even though I was racked with nerves and had to play the famous tea-party scene with a wicker chair stub-bornly attached to the seat of my gauzy dress, all three were complimentary when they came backstage. But Ms. Leigh didn't leave it at that. Because we were in the middle of a newspaper strike, there had been no reviews; so she gener-ously sent agents, casting directors, and journalists to see my performance.

Before long, I was asked to test for the pilot of a televi-sion series that the producers hoped would begin filming in the fall, in California: *Peyton Place*, based on the scandalously sexy novel. When the producer, Paul Monash, first came backstage, he asked if I could do an American accent.

I realized by then that the best way to proceed with an acting career was to stay in New York and try to work on the stage, and not be in a television series at all. But I had no other job offers ahead, and I worried that I wouldn't have any other opportunity: this might be my only chance, so I'd better take it. I shot a screen test and was offered the role of Allison, with a contract at 20th Century–Fox that included five movies. So after much agonizing and dragging my feet, I signed the contract in a coffee shop on West Seventy-second Street, together with my mother, since I was a minor, and Dalí, who remained focused on the unremark-able, brownish wallpaper, and the name of the restaurant, Oliver Cromwell. Deep in my heart I was convinced that the series didn't have a prayer.

Meanwhile my mother rented an old house by a lake, in Westport, Connecticut, and in June the rest of the children and Tuffy came east. A housekeeper named Minnie Lou was left in charge, while during the week Mom and I lived and worked in the city. But Minnie Lou didn't last long, nor did her replacement, or the one after that, though my mother was doing all she could, God knows.

Mom, oh Mom, the siblings are out of control. There are gin bottles under the beds, and someone's shooting up cooked cough medicine and someone else has got a gun and that's not the half of it, what shall we do? I'm going to the Madison Avenue Playhouse now. I don't know how to do anything more.

When *The Importance of Being Earnest* closed in July 1963, I joined an Ohio summer stock company and appeared as the ingenue in *My Three Angels.* The theater was massive, it seated four thousand people, which required quite an adjustment after the intimacy of the tiny Madison Avenue Playhouse. The first place I ever lived alone was a motel in Youngstown.

In September I returned to Beverly Hills to film the pilot for *Peyton Place.* My school friend Tisha Sterling was now living at 809 North Roxbury Drive, the house where my family had lived and where my father died. Tisha's mother, Ann Sothern, had rented the house, furniture and all. I accepted their invitation to stay for the three weeks of rehearsal and filming, and I gave no thought to ghosts.

Brought to its knees by the costly and disastrous *Cleopatra,* 20th Century–Fox had been shut down for two years, and the enormous soundstages stood silent. Shirley Temple's house, the writers' buildings, the stars' dressing rooms, the legendary commissary with its murals of famous faces of the thirties and forties, were all locked and boarded up. *Peyton Place* was the only activity on the lot.

Incredibly, just twelve months had passed since, at seventeen, I had left the Roxbury house that nobody loved to return to school in England. I had known then as well as anyone that, despite the illusion of order, circumstances can be controlled only sometimes, and sometimes not at all. Nonetheless, on that cloudless day one year earlier, as I had walked toward the car with a suitcase full of books and a mind full of dreams, I assumed that I'd be back for Christmas, and that my father and mother, and my sisters and brothers, would all be in their place as I had left them. And so my good-byes had been light as I moved toward the car.

But looking back, oh looking back . . . Why didn't I hold them there, my family, why didn't I hold them in their places, help them take up arms, to stand firm against demons, not to falter, and above all, to make no exits? Could I have pressed my own strength through their skin? Would it have helped? How did I, so feather-light, leave them that day? Was there no hint of the spiraling, breaking, dying mutations of my family?

Here now is the hard clear truth: on that clear September day when I walked out of my house, what I did was this: I did not think of them— I simply saved myself.

Now, one year later, the contents of the house were eerily unchanged. Each chair and lamp and book was in its place, exactly where my parents had left them. Ms. Sothern now slept in my mother's sorrow bed, and my old room had become a crowded beauty parlor equipped with a professional hair dryer and a big drop-backed chair, a makeup table and a mirror framed in light—Ms. Sothern was a famous television star. Tisha and I slept in my sisters' old beds. Sometimes in the middle of the night we were awakened by the sound of the heavy Spanish dining-room chairs being moved on the wooden floor beneath us, and often I went to work in the morning exhausted.

The suffering and disarray of my family had stuck to the walls, crouched in the shadows; I entered each gloomy room slowly, to allow ample time for ghostly withdrawals. With each passing day my father's presence became more vivid: memories and illusion became so entwined that I could barely distinguish them.

Ghosts, after all, do exist in possibility.

There was one room at the farthest corner of the house that I did not enter: the bedroom where my father had died with the phone in his hand. Even Ms. Sothern, who feared nothing, didn't use the room and the door was kept shut.

On the final afternoon of my stay in California, humming a little made-up tune, I crossed the large Spanish living room and stopped at the door of my father's bedroom; now in full song, I grasped the cool brass knob, and with a quick twist I stepped inside.

Tidy, hushed, lifeless, expectant—familiar details stabbed at me: the leather cup full of sharp Black Wing pencils, a yellow legal pad, a volume of John Donne, the oval portrait of my grandmother, a box of Kleenex half-full, the wooden rack men hang their suits upon, two dimes in a cup. Only my father was not in place. I touched his lovely burgundy fountain pen where it lay beside the phone, and the room thickened around me. I pressed my palms to the white bedspread monogrammed JVF, and then, perhaps, a miracle: from the depths came an urging, whispery then powerful, *"Find eternity in this and every instant of your life."*

Somewhere between birth and death, inside one pellucid moment, I stepped outside dread and imaginings, the fist of anger and guilt unclenched, and I lay down, clear as glass, on the bed where my father had died. A wound familiar as my name burst open, streaming pure and painful love and I accepted; there, finally, I embraced the essence of my father, and with him, humanity in its hideousness and its brief quivering beauty, its pig-selfishness and its willingness to give everything, in its contemptible pettiness and its most noble striving, in its utter meaninglessness and its sacred significance; and all the mysteries, hopes, lacerations, losses, and celebrations of a lifetime . . .

The contents of my father's medicine cabinet had been cleared out except for one small item: a plastic box with a transparent, hinged lid through which I read, on a shred of paper, "Mia." With my forefinger, I carefully moved the paper aside, and there on a bed of cotton lay a nest full of pearly baby teeth.

I whispered my love for my father, and in peace and fullness, I left his room, teeth in hand.

A message from Dalí was waiting when I got back to New York: he and Gala had arrived for the season. I was overjoyed to see them and told them excitedly every detail of my recent experiences. We resumed a schedule much like the previous winter's. When I confided to Dalí my concern about finding work, and my impatience because nothing was happening, he said, "If you want dramatic change, put your shoes on the opposite feet."

No sooner had I swapped shoes than I got a phone call: from Fox. In England, *Guns at Batasi*, starring Richard Attenborough, had already been shooting for a few weeks. When the young actress Britt Ekland left the project abruptly because her husband, Peter Sellers, had suffered a heart attack, a replacement was needed immediately. Within hours I was flying to Paris, where the director and producer would check me out and hopefully approve of me. I was a wreck.

Over peanuts and ginger ale in the bar of the George V Hotel, the director, John Guillermin, doubted I looked old enough to be credible as a nurse. *A nurse!* Who knew? I swallowed my peanuts and lit my first cigarette, narrowed my eyes, crossed my legs, and leaned back in my chair to say, in a low cool voice, that with makeup surely I could pass for twenty.

At eighteen, my looks were serviceable for an actress. My mother said I was lucky: I could look plain, and with help I could pass for pretty. The director and the studio were under pressure to complete filming. Right there in the bar Mr. Guillermin phoned Mr. Zanuck at Fox, and from the depths of my swivel chair, wreathed in smoke, I overheard him report unenthusiastically that I was innocuous, and he supposed I would do. Later I looked up *innocuous*.

On Monday morning I walked onto the soundstage of Pinewood Studios for my first film role, wearing my hair in a sophisticated up do, a load of makeup including fake eyelashes, and Britt Ekland's lavender skirt and top, which fit fine once I got the falsies on.

This movie was one of the last speaking roles for the wonderful Jack Hawkins, who had cancer of the throat. He wore a little green lizard attached with a delicate chain to the lapel of his costume, a military uniform. Throughout the day Mr. Hawkins was inclined to forget about the lizard and he would suddenly swat at it. Then the lizard would hang from its chain until somebody tactfully replaced it.

Richard Attenborough's performance in *Guns at Batasi* was remarkable, and he was as warm and kind as any human being could possibly be. Knowing I was alone, he invited me to his home on weekends and I was treated almost as a member of his family. He showed me stacks of books and manuscripts he'd collected about Mahatma Gandhi, and told me how he dreamed of making a film about his life.

Pinewood Studios at that time was an exciting place to be. Sean Connery was James Bond, and I watched him arrive each morning with his golf clubs. Once I saw a naked woman all painted in gold hurrying down the corridor to the Bond set. Every day was such an adventure that I'd ask the assistant director to please call me in, even when I wasn't scheduled: I loved watching the other actors working on their scenes. Soon, I felt at ease on the set, except for the day I shot the love scene. I wore shorts, and taped flesh-colored fabric to my front, and really it was just a prolonged kiss, and Johnny Leyton was as nice as could be, but still it was indescribably embarrassing. It was the first time I was ever in bed with a man.

Meanwhile, despite my predictions, *Peyton Place* was sold to ABC, and scheduled to begin shooting: I was told to return to California as soon as the movie was over. I phoned Richard Zanuck, the president of Fox, and said I'd made a mistake, so could he please release me from that commitment; but of course it was impossible. I consoled myself with the thought that as soon as I got to California, I would get my own horse.

From London I flew to Los Angeles, checked into the Chateau Marmont, and began working on *Peyton Place.* A New England town had been constructed on the Fox lot, around a village green. On weekends Maria Roach and I searched for a horse and a more permanent, less expensive place to stay. We discovered a small residential hotel called the McCarty, close enough to the studio that I could ride my new bike to work, which I did, with my deaf cat Malcolm in the basket.

Most of the cast was Irish Catholic: Ryan O'Neal, Tim O'Connor, Chris Connolly, Ed Nelson, and myself. Dorothy Malone played my mother: her blond wig was kept in the makeup room on a block with her thick, black, trademark eyelashes carefully pinned to it, so in effect Dorothy was mostly there before she even arrived in the morning. Teenagers across the country fell for Ryan O'Neal, and I was no exception—he was handsome and very funny. He was also married: Tatum was born just after we made the pilot, and his son Griffin followed. Despite the melodramatic plots and subplots of *Peyton Place,* it was a lighthearted set. We shot our New England Christmas scenes when it was a sweltering ninety degrees: plastic snow covered the town square, and we worked in coats and woolly scarves, mittens, and hats. Our hours were so long that there were times during scenes with Ryan late in the day when I laughed so hard I disgraced myself, and once I couldn't even continue the scene. I was so ashamed that the next day I sent everyone flowers.

Our shooting schedule allowed us little free time; but I found the perfect horse—trustworthy, beautiful, and big, at seventeen hands. I named him Salvador. Now I got up before dawn so I could ride in the hills behind Malibu and still be ready on the set by eight. On the weekends I rode along the beach and explored the Malibu canyons. I brought along a sandwich and Hostess Twinkies and an apple for Sal, and sometimes we stayed out until nightfall.

After the first show aired, my mother phoned from New York. Her only advice was to wear more eye makeup. "You have such lovely eyes, you should show them off." Later she admitted, "We all watched it and thought it just dreadful, we didn't know how to tell Mia." But they didn't have to tell me. I felt bad for the people I worked with, whom I'd grown fond of, and whose hopes were so high, but secretly I'd known all along that *Peyton Place* would fail. Now, I only hoped I wouldn't be singled out for criticism.

I have no memory of watching that first show. The next morning at work someone showed me the review in the *Hollywood Reporter*: the headline read MIA FARROW LIGHTS UP SCREEN. If my ring had been in my mouth, I would have swallowed it. Of course I was completely wrong about the show: people loved it, and it ran three times a week for years.

In the beginning they tried to persuade me to cut my waist-length hair into one of the styles of the day. I argued that the character I was playing wouldn't be bothered with hair. Which was true, but a strong sense of self-preservation also came into play; I didn't look good with fancy hair, and more important, those hairdos would take *time* every morning, with curlers and hair dryers, and I wanted to ride my horse. Makeup was another issue. In those days they heaped it on, with eye shadow, winged eyeliner, minnow brows, gobs of lipstick, and heavy dark base. They told me I had to match the men, who wore an even darker base, but when a ten-year-old girl joined the cast and she didn't wear makeup, I never wore it again.

Our shooting schedule was so intense that none of us had a chance to look up. We shot two shows simultaneously, and I roller-skated from stage to stage, from shot to shot. The fact that the series was watched by millions of people was not at all real to me, and except for the bags of mail that arrived several times a week, it didn't enter my consciousness until I came back to visit my family in New York for the Christmas break.

Once again I was in the bedroom I shared with Prudy and Steffi at the apartment on Central Park West, where my family had lived since 1964. It was good to feel the bite of real winter and to be with them all again. We stayed up late every night talking, drinking wine, laughing, and catching up with one another's lives. I forgot all about *Peyton Place*.

One day my brother Johnny, my sisters, and I went ice-skating in Central Park. I have wobbly ankles so I was hanging on to my brother, struggling gamely along, when I heard my name called out. I turned to see a few people skating toward me, waving white paper plates, and then I noticed more people looking at me, pointing, calling my name, coming at me, and suddenly plates were fluttering everywhere like white doves, and people were pushing, pulling, and shouting. I got separated from Johnny, I could barely stand, and I didn't know which way to go when three or four attendants got me to the rail and pulled me out. That was the day it dawned on me that I was famous.

A second occurrence that same week seemed equally strange. I had gone to Bloomingdale's to buy a pair of shoes. The salesman was as nasty as could be, so we hurried through the process and I gave him my credit card. He disappeared with it, and returned a few minutes later a transformed person, the very soul of niceness, asking for my autograph.

Peyton Place was so successful they moved me downstairs into a big dressing room that had an outer office for a secretary. The phone rang constantly and the mail was so overwhelming that finally I needed an assistant, and wonderful Barbara Daitch stepped in to take care of everything.

I rented a three-room apartment, the top half of a little house on shady La Peer Drive, for $150 a month. I bought tweedy brown furniture at Sears and put in wall-to-wall red carpeting everywhere except the bedroom, which had white furniture and a blue carpet. I got a fake rock pond with a little waterfall and fake moss all around it for my cat, Malcolm. I was thrilled with my life, and my horse, and when I was lonely, I looked up my old school friends.

Michael Boyer took me to dinner; he ate steak and, as always, barely looked at me. And not long after, Michael Boyer, whom I had loved all my life, blew his brains out playing Russian roulette.

Late on the afternoon of the funeral I stood at the back door of the Boyers' house. "Mrs. Boyer asked for you," my mother had said. "She's expecting you, no staff will be there all week, so just go on in." Even so I waited more than the appropriate interval before ringing a second time, and doubled it before I knocked. Eventually I stepped inside cautiously, calling, "Mrs. Boyer?"

Dusk had already begun to settle into the house. No one would bother to turn the lights on, not this night. Of course I already knew that Mrs. Boyer would be upstairs lying on her bed, just as I knew that Mr. Boyer would be alone in one of the darkening rooms, sitting in an armchair, a glass in his hand. So I threaded my way through the hushed house and up the curved staircase, careful to look neither right nor left.

"Mrs. Boyer, it's me, Mia." And more softly, "Mr. Boyer?"

"Mia, come in here." A voice, flat and hoarse, summoned me to the threshold of the bedroom, where, across its considerable length, within the cool beige tones, Michael's mother lay just as I had envisioned, on a too-large bed. Respect for her in this sorrow, awe of its dimensions, and fear of its strangeness forbid any further approach, so I settled at the door into awful silence. What could anyone do or give that would ease even a little Mrs. Boyer's suffering?

"I'm just so sorry" was the best I could wrench out, and it hung inadequate and reproachful in the dense space between us. I tried with all my being to lift the leaden sphere where she lay and where I stood, or to interpose myself between her and the bottomless swallowing. Feeling all this and knowing the rest, I only pressed my forehead as hard as I could into the edge of the door.

I don't know how long I stood there. Eternities. Finally I heard myself ask, "Do you want me to leave, Mrs. Boyer?" But she didn't say anything. "Or I can stay. I can stay here as long as you want." And she said, from a long way away, in a small voice, "Thank you for coming."

"Is there anything I can do for you?" I blurted. "Do you want me to turn the light on? Do you want some tea or soup or anything?" I thought she said something, maybe a word. But I didn't catch it. Then, full of self-loathing for my inadequacies, I said good-bye and crept out of the house quickly—not knowing what room Mr. Boyer was sitting in.

On Linden Drive in Beverly Hills, California, the air was

sweet and the sun was already low behind the palms. Soon it would be dark. The stars would be out.

Good night, Mrs. Boyer.

Good night, Mr. Boyer.

Fox was now booming. Marlon Brando and Yul Brynner were making a film there together, Julie Andrews and the kids from *The Sound of Music* were all over the place, and there were several other television series in production, including *Batman*. Now you had to reserve a table to eat in the commissary.

Studios have a kind of campus feel. When actors are at work on neighboring soundstages, there is a camaraderie; adrenaline runs high, and when people get restless during lengthy breaks between filming, one option is to wander over to another set. So I was delighted when Johnny Leyton, from *Guns at Batasi*, arrived for his role in *Von Ryan's Express*, starring Frank Sinatra.

I had met Frank Sinatra eight years earlier, when I was eleven, having dinner with my father at Romanoff's restaurant. "Pretty girl," he had joked, and my father returned, "You stay away from her." But I didn't suppose Mr. Sinatra would remember that. Now I stood in the dark soundstage, watching as he filmed a scene aboard a fake train with a gorgeous Italian actress, and I thought what a beautiful face he had, full of pain and somehow familiar. We didn't speak that day, but on another visit, as I was watching the filming, I became aware of Mr. Sinatra, seated off to the side, a good distance behind me, amid a boisterous cluster of men.

Suddenly a large, pleasant-faced man approached me and said, "Hi, we were just wondering how old you are?" I glanced at the group sitting in their canvas chairs watching me. My long hair was in braids and I guessed I didn't look my age, so I stood up tall to say, "Nineteen." Minutes later, I was invited to join them, and of course I did immediately, but I was so nervous that I spilled the contents of my straw bag all over the floor in front of Frank Sinatra and under his chair, and into one of my Wellington boots too. I scrambled to pick stuff up. My retainer first (the mortification), coins rolling every which way, pictures of my horse, parts of a green doughnut, jars of baby food for my cat, Chap Stick, my glasses, tampons, bubble gum, candy, keys, the full catastrophe. "Oh, excuse me," I kept saying, "I'm sorry," as he helped me.

It might have been right then, as our eyes met, that I began to love him; I felt a column of light rising inside me, pulling particles from dark dead corners. I was a little dazed when I left to get back to work. He walked me to the stage door and asked whether I'd like to see a movie with him on Friday night—a private screening of his first directorial attempt, *None But the Brave.*

"Sure," I managed. "I'd love to." It was Wednesday, and I had two days to worry about what I'd wear, and what in the world we'd talk about. I could tell he was shy, and that made two of us.

I didn't sleep very well on Thursday night. After work on Friday I met him at Warner Bros., in a screening room. I got dressed up; by that I mean I wore an olive green dress that I felt made me look older.

I'm nothing if not punctual, so right on time we said, "Hi," and not much else, and the lights went down. I don't remember much about the movie; there were the Japanese and our guys and everybody in uniform, and some skirmishes—I can't be sure, my mind wasn't absolutely with it. Somewhere in the middle, Frank Sinatra held my hand. That's what I remember.

And when the lights came on he invited me to come to Palm Springs with him that very evening.

"Palm Springs?" I repeated. He explained that he went there all the time, whenever he had time off; there would be other guests too, it was going to be fun, it was always fun in Palm Springs, so would I like to come with him now?

"Now?" I said. This was not exactly *crisp* dialogue. Then I mumbled something about my cat, "I have a cat, he has to be fed, he'll only eat baby food, and my clothes, my pajamas, and toothbrush, it doesn't make any sense, but thank you, thank you for inviting me. I'm sorry."

And I was thinking, please forgive me, Frank Sinatra, it's all my fault, I probably shouldn't have held hands with you, that was forward of me, I gave the wrong impression, I *can't* go to Palm Springs with you, or anywhere else either. I have no idea what I'm doing, I don't know anything at all, I'll only disappoint you, I have no pills or diaphragms and no clear idea of what people do since I've never done any of it myself, so please let's just forget the whole thing. I'm sorry about the hand holding.

And he said, "How 'bout tomorrow? I'll send my plane for you. You can bring your cat."

What was that? Sending his *plane* for the cat and me? Reality tiptoed out of the room. It was my turn to talk but by this time I was just swamped; so disoriented and rattled I couldn't sort out which thing to say. Maybe he understood some portion of this, or perhaps it was the awkwardness that inspired, in the middle of the swarming silence, a smile of such loveliness that I smiled a little too, then had to look away because he was watching me so. And when I could look again, behind his eyes was *no stranger*. Again the feeling of recognition took me by surprise.

Apprehension smoothed into curiosity. He was talking, I can't be sure of the words because something else was happening too—a gathering of thoughts appeared in his eyes and he pushed them into mine; but this time I held my place, I did not flinch or look away and though I sent no messages myself, the boldness and potency of all this eyeing surprised me into further silence, out of which leaped a thought, brand-new and with music and light—that it could be wonderful to be in Palm Springs or anyplace else with this Frank Sinatra.

So with fake confidence I dared to say, "Okay."

Again I didn't sleep so well, what with all the worrying and imagining, and in the morning I spent too long deciding how many jars of baby food to bring for the cat—which wasn't about the baby food, it was about whether I would be staying there overnight. I packed enough to cover Sunday, just in case, and tried not to think about the rest. Then I put a leash on my cat, and Barbara, my secretary, drove us to a special airport for private planes in Burbank.

Maybe now is the moment to mention my sense of direction because it's bound to come up again: it's as bad as they come. It's a curse. I can't find my way *anywhere* or back again, which is worse, even when *shown* patiently and in great detail, I can't do it. People get exasperated with me and sometimes I'm late because of it, which is unforgivable, and it's scary when you don't know where you're going or how you'll ever get home. Some people will understand this and most won't. Anyway, that's why Barbara was doing the driving. So we were already there when I realized that this was the same airport my brother Mike took off from and never came back.

We found the airplane—Barbara did—just where it was supposed to be, and I climbed aboard. The interior of the plane was spacious and orange wherever possible. Malcolm seemed unfazed.

Thirty minutes later we were coasting along the desert runway to a remote corner of the Palm Springs Airport, where I spotted Frank Sinatra leaning against a black car, his arms folded across an orange short-sleeved shirt. He looked handsome. As I climbed down the plane's steps clutching my cat and straw hat, he walked up to us and laughed.

During the short drive to his house he spoke about the

desert and how much he loved it there and he was sure I
would like it too.

"I don't know Palm Springs at all," I said leadenly. Then
it hit me that I'd made a terrible mistake coming to this
place.

His house was Palm Springs–casual, modern, with a lot of
Chinese things, and plenty of light. With obvious pride he
showed me a room where John Fitzgerald Kennedy had
slept, and the brass plaque that said so.

One whole side of the living room and bar was glass,
with sliding doors that opened onto a large patio, and beyond that was an oval swimming pool. He was explaining
that recently he had *moved* the pool because it had been too
near the house. I made what I hoped were understanding
noises, but after seeing the two octagonal guest houses at
either end of the pool, each with two bedrooms and *four*
bathrooms, and the helicopter port, I was well along in
being utterly overwhelmed.

Yul Brynner was sitting out by the pool wearing a white
towel robe, an attractive redheaded woman by his side. I
couldn't help but notice she was weeping. We hurried past.
Later I discovered she had originally been invited by Frank
to be *his* date for the weekend, but as plans changed (me) he
had simply passed her along to Yul, who was now doing his
best to cheer her up.

Continuing the tour we studied a very large cactus garden and I heard myself say "gosh" too many times. Along
one side of the property ran a narrow, quiet road, and the
other side was bordered by the golf course of the Tamarisk
Country Club.

Reentering the main house, I was taken to a small room
that appeared to be an office, desk and all. Except the
couch had been made into a bed.

"And here *you* are!" he said cheerfully. "Right near *my*

room," gesturing to the other end of the short hallway. We stared awkwardly into the office-bedroom. Finally I asked, "Could I please set up the cat box in here now?"

But there in the doorway he took the cat out of my arms and put it on the floor, and he put his foot on the leash and held me close against himself and I don't even know what happened then; the loneliness, fearfulness, doubt, desire, yearning for closeness and for approbation, for meaning and for miracles, and for truth too, all came together in silence beyond words.

The cat slept alone that night in the little room of the long embrace.

Chapter Five

We spent our weekends together after that and as much time as possible in between. In L.A., Frank lived in a single-bedroom rented apartment on Doheny Drive. During those first months, until he finished *Von Ryan's Express*, we were both working, most days at Fox. When he went out to dinner with his friends, he tried to get home early so that we could have some time. Although we didn't discuss it, I understood and accepted that it would be awkward for him to include me in his social life.

On Fridays, when we finished work, his helicopter would land on the back lot of the studio to bring us to Palm Springs; at other times we flew there in his plane, or he drove us in his black, custom-built Italian car. Once, when I tried to drive myself to Palm Springs, I became so hopelessly lost that I spent eight hours on the freeways—phoning him, near tears, from gas stations all over Southern California.

After a while we moved my horse to Palm Springs and I rode in the desert. I discovered an

oasis, a place that had been a water stop for covered wag-
ons, where Salvador enjoyed splashing in the muddy pond
and where I would visit an ancient Native American man
who lived in a log cabin, thickly shaded by palm trees. He
would always give me a glass of bitter, warm beer and recite
beautiful Indian prayers. I was never able to persuade Frank
to get on a horse, but when I rode Salvador in the ring and
took him over modest jumps, he liked to come, and leaning
against the rail, he'd stay there and watch as long as I cared
to ride.

Elsie was a large, maternal woman who supervised the
Palm Springs household. The professionally equipped
kitchen was her territory, except when Frank made his spaghetti sauce. Then I would perch next to him on a stool,
eating a bag of potato chips or cookies while he explained
the process. Sometimes we saw Elsie in the corner crying
because of her no-good husband.

Every morning after breakfast we sat in the living room
or out by the swimming pool, frowning into our crossword
puzzles; because Frank enjoyed them, I tried to do them
too. He introduced me to the symphonies of one of his
favorite composers, Ralph Vaughan Williams, which I loved
too, and he did his best to interest me in golf—even buying
me my own set of clubs in a white, leather bag with MIA
embossed on it in pale blue letters. But I hated the game,
and I was hopeless at it. Even more boring were the interminable golf games he would watch on television.

In Los Angeles one night, while I was driving home from
Frank's apartment, I realized I was being followed by a
couple of men in a car. When I wasn't able to shake them, I
pulled into a brightly lit gas station and telephoned Frank,
who pulled up in minutes with a loaded gun. My pursuers
took off, but Frank decided I ought to know how to protect myself. He bought a small pearl-handled gun, and in
the desert across the road from his house, he set up tin cans
and gave me shooting lessons. I was a reluctant pupil, and

even with my glasses on, a miserable shot; in the end even he agreed that it might be unwise for me to carry a gun.

In the evenings we took walks along the narrow desert roads near his house and he told me about his life, of which I knew almost nothing. He had grown up in Hoboken, New Jersey, in one of the toughest neighborhoods in the country—maybe the world. He had married his childhood sweetheart, by all accounts an exceptional woman, with whom he shared three much-adored children, two of them older than me; I wondered what they were like, and what they might think of me.

Frank's second marriage had been to Ava Gardner (I didn't say a word about Ava and my father) and there were many lovely photographs of her around the house. He looked so pained when he talked about her that it was a relief when he changed the subject. He told me how he had learned his phrasing and technique of sneaking breaths from Tommy.

"Who's Tommy?" I asked, and Frank just stared at me. At moments like this—and there were plenty—I got flustered and embarrassed, realizing that here was another thing everyone in the whole world probably knew. But patiently Frank explained that Tommy Dorsey was a very famous bandleader and trombone player who was dead, and he, the young Frank Sinatra, used to sing with his band.

"Oh I see," I'd say, "I'm sorry."

Sometimes we walked in silence holding hands and we watched bright stars take their places one by one in the soft desert sky, and in those moments I felt closer to him than I had ever felt to anyone in my life. Other times, when silence signaled his remoteness, I would lose my bearings and feel inadequate, unsure, and lost. But for the most part, those peaceful days spent discovering each other, when almost no one knew about us, were for me the happiest in our time together.

Of course Yul knew about us. He came to Palm Springs

often. Frank called him "the Chinaman," and Yul called
Frank "Charlie," I don't know why, but then I called him
Charlie too, and still do. (Frank called me "Angel Face," or
"Baby Face.") Yul became a surrogate father to me—I even
called him Dad. People said Frank must have been a father
substitute but I don't know about that. Certainly I wasn't
conscious of it. Anyway I had Yul, and in an off-the-wall
way, I had Dalí. Maybe later on in my relationship with
Frank we did slip a little into those roles, but even that's
not certain. It could also be that he was just being Italian,
and maybe that was why he became more and more protective and controlling.

Except for Yul, the only other people we saw were Jack
Entratter, owner of the Sands Hotel in Las Vegas, and his
girlfriend—later, wife—Corinne Cole.

This was a "normal" weekend, as Corinne recalled it to
me: "Inside the living room, with the air conditioner pouring out of the opened sliding door, you and I were sitting
in swimsuits trying to learn backgammon. Frank was swimming in the pool; Jack was soaking up the 'Jewish' sun,
calling in markers on the phone. Every time one of the
phones rang our hearts sank and the two of us fell silent,
waiting to be dismissed one way or the other. Then Frank
came up out of the water with only his famous face emerg-
ing, and at the top of his voice he exclaimed for all the
world to hear, 'I love you.' If anyone had been on the Tamarisk seventeenth green that second, they would have had the
scoop of the year. You nonchalantly looked up from our
deranged game and turned your attention to him. Through
the screen door you softly echoed back, 'I love you too,
Charlie.' It all seemed so normal and natural—just two
couples enjoying the Springs heat and *Tachina* flies in luxuri-
ous surroundings. In retrospect, those days of wine and
long-stemmed roses—with diamond bracelets in a box, and
walking on eggshells—were about as normal as living on
the third ring of Jupiter. You and I certainly weren't there

for the diamonds or the eggshells, but it came with the territory (jewelers hated you—you sent everything back). The wine and roses were great . . . so was the love. We thought we were the two luckiest girls in the world. We got our first choices. I also recall those weeks as a survival lesson in PR. 'Cover the fifth column, don't trust anyone, and never talk on the phone unless you want the whole world to hear you.' I wondered how the fame never seemed to bother you. You were like a swan in smooth water, and I marveled at your destiny."

Of course I realized that Frank Sinatra was a movie star and a famous singer, but it was unspecific to me: when we met, I don't think I'd ever listened to a Sinatra song or seen any of his movies. People my age were listening to the Beatles, and my parents never owned a Sinatra album: they played Gregorian chants. I grew up in Beverly Hills, where Lucille Ball picked up her kids from our school, and that was normal. I didn't know that Frank Sinatra was a *legend* who meant so much to so many people. And I don't think even he anticipated the fuss our relationship would cause.

After *Von Ryan's Express*, Frank rented a mansion on Sunset Boulevard. In the months that we had been together, except for those few people mentioned, we had seen only each other. Ours was an intimate, intense existence. A speculative line or two occasionally crept into the gossip columns, but Frank's publicist and Fox Studios effectively dispelled any rumors. I wondered whether his children knew, especially his daughters, whom he talked a lot about.

One day after work, when I arrived at his house as usual, Frank told me that his younger daughter, Tina, was outside playing tennis with a friend. Rattled, I asked if he wanted me to leave or hide or what, but he laughed and said, Sit down, he wanted Tina to meet me. I sat nervously until Tina Sinatra bounced into the room smiling. She hugged me, and said it was nice to finally meet me, and I was immeasurably relieved and grateful. Not long after, I met her sister, Nancy, and she too was as welcoming as I could have hoped. The two soon became like sisters to me.

Once a year a group of influential Hollywood wives put on a charity show in which they themselves performed, Rockette-style, and their famous husbands, singers and comedians, participated. "The Share Show" was a good-natured event and a hot ticket that drew top Hollywood stars. It also attracted major press coverage. So it was a shock when Frank suddenly informed me that we were going. I thought we were supposed to lie low. We didn't even go to restaurants. Apart from Yul and Jack Entratter, I hadn't met any of his friends.

"Are you sure?" I asked. He was. Perhaps he thought he'd get it over in one dose, give everybody plenty of pictures, and then they'd go away.

We dressed up in Western costumes and I met his buddies Shirley MacLaine and Sammy Davis, and from the stage Dean Martin toasted me, saying, "Hey, I've got a bottle of scotch that's older than you."

We all laughed, and the press took our pictures, but they didn't go away—not in the rest of our time together. It didn't help that on television I was playing a dreamy, introverted sixteen-year-old. The way people regarded Frank Sinatra was suddenly evident too: the fifty-year-old swinger, womanizer, and brawling saloon singer, together with the innocent teenage daughter of Hollywood. People couldn't seem to get a handle on it.

I kept thinking, They have it all wrong, they don't really know him. They can't see the wounding tenderness that even he can't bear to acknowledge—except when he sings. Maybe if they looked at the earliest photos of Frank, when he was a skinny kid singing in his big bow tie—if they really looked at that face, almost feminine in its beauty, they'd see exactly who it was that Frank Sinatra the tough guy has spent his life trying to protect.

"I have a respect for life in any form," Frank said at that time. "I believe in nature, in the birds, the sea, the sky, in everything I can see. If these things are what you mean by God, then I believe in God. But I don't believe in a personal God to whom I look for comfort or for a natural on the next roll of the dice. I'm for anything that gets you through the night, be it prayer, tranquilizers, or a bottle of Jack Daniel's."

Our life changed after "The Share Show." Now we went to parties and restaurants, and I was introduced to his friends in L.A., Las Vegas, and New York. I discovered that Frank could polish off a bottle of Jack Daniel's in one night, and that he had a million jokes and stories. I had no idea that his life could be so full of friends, houseguests, and hangers-on, or that hours alone together would be so hard to come by. I thought he was usually in bed by eleven.

Frank's existence was divided into three distinct worlds. The first, and most essential for me, was the time we shared alone. It was the part that made all the rest bearable, if not comprehensible. Before long I found myself missing the exclusivity of those first secret months.

Second was the social world of the Beverly Hills/Manhattan establishment. In New York there were the Paleys and the Cerfs, the Guinnesses and the Gabels, the Haywards, the Hornblows, and Claudette Colbert. In Beverly Hills it was Rosalind Russell and Freddie Brisson, the Deutches and the Wilders, the Stewarts and the Bennys, the Mays, Leonard Gershe, the Douglases, Ruth Gordon and Garson Kanin—and especially Edie and Bill Goetz.

Edie Goetz, the daughter of Louis B. Mayer, was an ambitious hostess who earned her title as queen of the A-group. The art collection in her home was legendary; it included works by Renoir, Gauguin, Picasso, Cézanne, Bonnard, and Degas, and was eventually auctioned for more than eighty million dollars. On Friday nights the biggest stars of the day trouped to the Goetzes. After dinner, prepared by a resident French chef, the Picassos rose, a screen descended, and the latest movie was projected in 35 mm, weeks before its public release. Most of the guests were friends of my parents who had known me since I was a child, which was strange in one way and nice in another. When Frank's friends came to stay with us in Palm Springs, they'd sometimes bring their offspring, some of whom had been in my school, all were older than me, and yet they would sit at "the kids' table," and I'd be at the "grown-ups'" table.

Apart from the Kanins, the only member of that exclusive crowd to whom I confided was lyricist and screenwriter Leonard Gershe. We spoke daily and in Frank's absence, and with his approval, we often went out for dinner.

Frank was adored by the A-group, and he was on his best behavior with them. They didn't know the Frank of the late-night world of Las Vegas or Miami, or Palm Springs, or that *other* New York of heavy drinking, tough talk, and "broads." As soon as he arrived at a hotel in Las Vegas or Miami, an assortment of guys materialized seemingly out of thin air. Women too. I didn't know how any of it was pulled together, or who anybody was. This was the setting for the third part of Frank's existence.

The very first night we visited Las Vegas, when I stood up to go to the bathroom, Frank handed me five dollars. "Here, baby," he said, and I didn't know what it was for. I thought maybe he wanted me to buy something, and the whole table laughed. "It's for the attendant in the ladies' room," he explained.

An average night in Vegas meant drinking and gambling and sitting around cocktail lounges telling stories until dawn. The climate was boisterous; Frank once offered a waiter a hundred dollars to drop a tray full of glasses. The waiter just stared at him, miserably computing all the possible consequences. (He didn't drop the tray; Frank gave him the money anyway.)

The women, who didn't seem to mind being referred to as "broads," sat up straight with their legs crossed and little expectant smiles on their carefully made-up faces. They sipped white wine, smoked, and eyed the men, and laughed at every joke. A long time would pass before any of the women dared to speak, then under the main male conversation they talked about their cats, or where they bought their clothes; but more than half an ear was always with the men, just in case. As hours passed, the women, neglected in their chairs, drooped; no longer listening, no longer laughing. Often I fell asleep, with my head on my arms folded on the table.

For weeks before he would begin any recording or singing engagement, Frank would stop smoking and drinking. When we arrived in Las Vegas or Miami, he would hang his tuxedo in the hotel bathroom to steam out the wrinkles, then he'd sit in his bathrobe doing crossword puzzles, trying not to talk to rest his voice. Near show time he would vocalize, then we would get dressed and go downstairs. His friend Jilly or bodyguards took me to my place in the audience.

Soon I knew every word of every song, and took each breath with him. I felt his emotion as it rose inside him and flowed into the dark theater. Part of it was mine. When Frank sang the love songs, he often looked at me, and that was an indescribable thing, to be acknowledged there, in that way, in the packed crowd where it seemed that every woman felt he was singing to her. Sometimes, I would focus on a detail: his hand, his mouth . . .

"I think I get an audience involved personally in a song because I'm involved," said Frank. "It's not something I do deliberately. I can't help myself. If a song is a lament at the loss of love, I get an ache in my gut. I feel the loss myself and I cry out the loneliness, the hurt, and the pain . . . Being an eighteen-carat manic-depressive, and having lived a life of emotional contradictions, I have an acute capacity for sadness as well as elation."

After opening night, the weeks of discipline were over and he could resume smoking and drinking. In Las Vegas he never went to bed before 5 A.M., and he slept until the late afternoon. Since I found it difficult to sleep in the daytime, sometimes I'd put on a wig and sit downstairs in the lobby to watch the people. I was glad when Nancy and Tina came to visit: then our hotel suite was like a dorm; we sat around in our pajamas chatting and snacking. As show time neared we got ready together, catching up on one another's news, trading clothes and makeup.

Occasionally my childhood friend Liza Minnelli, with whom I'd gone to nursery school, came to Las Vegas too, to perform at another hotel. Liza's career had taken flight, and it was an exciting time for both of us. Before *Peyton Place*, when the two of us were living in New York, we got our first off-Broadway jobs at roughly the same time—she was in a musical, *Best Foot Forward*. After I moved to L.A., Liza stayed at my apartment whenever she came to town. I cut her long hair short. Now, here we were in Las Vegas. I would go to see her show, then we'd join Frank. Except in Las Vegas it was never just me and him, so Liza and I huddled at the far end of the long table.

I noticed that no matter who was in a room, when Frank entered it, he became the focus. And no one was ever really at ease with him, no matter who they were or how charming he was, because there was something about him that made people uncomfortable. He was absolutely without falseness, without artifice, in a world of pretenders. He had a child's sense of outrage at any perceived unfairness and an inability to compromise. He was tough in his judgments of others, and of himself.

Ava Gardner once said Frank was "so wild, so full of love and energy, that he is like three men rolled into one. But behind the front of a big drinker and party giver, he is highly sensitive and intelligent, and he has a heart of gold." What with Ava's relationships with my father and Frank, our history was an unusual one; but we got along so well together that once, in a jumble of warm emotions, she declared that I was the child she and Frank never had.

In August 1965, Frank decided that we were going on a boat trip. We would get some friends together and sail along the coast of Cape Cod. He studied maps and planned it all carefully. My television series at first seemed an obstacle, but we had the same bosses at Fox, so the *Peyton Place* writers obligingly put me in a coma.

We set sail from New York City on a ship 170 feet long. Claudette Colbert was onboard, and Roz Russell too. Yet with their combined lifetimes of movie stardom, they were unprepared for what came next. Even Frank, after all his experience with paparazzi and always expecting the worst from journalists, failed to anticipate the pandemonium that boat trip would trigger.

Within twenty-four hours you couldn't see the ocean for the flotilla of paparazzi, and you couldn't hear yourself think for the helicopters, and you couldn't watch television without seeing yourself and hearing about how ancient Frank Sinatra was, and how young I was, and how we were going to get married, and how many beautiful girlfriends he'd had, and famous fights, and the rumors about Mafia connections, and outrage at the size of the boat.

We read this, and we watched it on television, and even though it quickly reached the point where we didn't dare to step outside, the strangest thing was that Frank and I never said one word about what was going on. I didn't know if he was angry, or hurt, or embarrassed, or what he was feeling.

Each day the situation worsened, but Frank Sinatra is a stubborn man, and the consummate host, and he was absolutely determined that everyone would have a good time. He would never call it quits, and nobody was about to argue with him, so we kept right on sailing through a sea of cameras.

We visited the Kennedy family in Hyannis, where I met Rose, and Joe in his wheelchair, and Teddy. Things lightened up when the Kennedy sisters Jean, Eunice, and Pat (whom the press mistook for Jacqueline Kennedy, fanning the fire further) came aboard with their husbands for an evening. Behind closed curtains we played charades and drank our share. The Kennedy group seemed so young and exuberant; and they *were*, compared to our crowd, who were at least fifteen years older than Frank, and he, as *everyone* knew by then, was fifty.

Claudette recalled to me that "the press was abominable, everywhere. You looked like a little girl, honestly, about thirteen or fourteen. I guess Frank just decided to try and tough it out. Every day we thought it might blow over. And actually, as long as we stayed inside, we had a good time." But I found it impossible to ignore the commotion and the confinement, and worst of all, Frank's remoteness.

When we reached Martha's Vineyard, Roz and Claudette tried to defuse the situation by talking to reporters, attempting to add a tone of respectability as "chaperones" and friends of my mother's, which indeed they were. They also insisted that no wedding was planned. This speculation was particularly embarrassing, since Frank and I had never even discussed marriage.

In the middle of the night, the phone awakened us. As he pulled on his clothes, Frank told me that one of our crew members was lost overboard after a dinghy had capsized in the choppy harbor.

For two days we heard the foghorns and watched them drag the harbor. Everybody felt terrible. Roz and Claudette played backgammon. I don't remember what I did. Nobody said much. Then, to everyone's relief, Frank called it quits. "We stayed two days while they dragged the harbor," Claudette remembered. "Frank finally decided there was nothing that could be done. It served no purpose to stay there."

A few weeks later the crewman's body washed up on-shore.

Back in *Peyton Place*, the bags of mail were multiplying, expressing approval and disapproval of my relationship with Frank. People wrote to me about all kinds of things. Younger people frequently saw me as a soul mate and they confided their most secret feelings. Eventually we had to hire a "fan mail service," as there were just too many letters, and any single one of them could upset me for the whole day.

It amazed me that girls my own age so often wrote about my hair, which in those days of "flips" and "bubbles" hung loose to my waist, solely because I was lazy and had never given much thought to it. The sudden focus on my looks and all the attention my hair was receiving was not entirely unpleasant, and that in itself made me wary. The horror of vanity instilled in convent school—the same fear of pride that had led me to bury the rosary beads I had made from acorns—compelled me to cut my hair.

I waited for a moment in the *Peyton Place* story line when it would fit; Allison's nervous breakdown was perfect. I didn't ask for permission because I knew I wouldn't get it: they would certainly oppose my changing any ingredient in a successful series. So one morning before work, in the makeup room, I picked up a pair of scissors and cut my hair to less than an inch in length, laid it in a plastic Glad bag, and turned to the mirror. It looked fine to me. But the hairdresser was aghast, and the producers were upset, and people with wigs were summoned, and there were stern lectures about responsibility, and I apologized a lot, but privately I couldn't see a problem.

There must have been *nothing* going on in the world that week, because my haircut got an absurd amount of press coverage. There was wild speculation as to why I'd done it: some said it was to spite Frank, and back in New York, Dalí, never one to minimize, labeled it "mythical suicide." But there was no drama, no fight with Frank, he loved my hair the minute he saw it, so I kept it short for years.

That first Christmas we spent together I was hoping for a puppy, and I was sure Frank would come through—I'd been hinting broadly for weeks. When I asked him, Animal, vegetable, or mineral? he had answered, Animal, with a twinkle.

George Jacobs, Frank's houseman, took a picture of us on Christmas Eve, kneeling by the tree in the Palm Springs living room: there are lots of presents under it, and in the picture, we are laughing. Frank is wearing a red sweater, and I am in a brocade floor-length silvery pink hostess gown, and I have just opened my present. The box I am holding contained a diamond koala bear. Secretly, I was disappointed.

On Christmas Day we both flew to L.A. While Frank visited his children, I went out to Malibu to see my brother Patrick and Susan, his wife, and newborn Justine, blond and serenely beautiful in the antique wooden cradle that was my gift. They lived on a cliff overlooking the sea. Each ornament on their tree had been homemade, and Susan had stitched the patchwork quilt on their bed, and a little one for the baby; yarns in earth colors stretched across her loom. Industrial-sized wooden spools were stacked and used as shelves for books and for Patrick's sculptures, and a wood fire warmed the room. At the time they had no consistent income, and yet they had all the essential, enduring ingredients right there in that room. I didn't mention the diamond koala bear.

Once, while Susan was pregnant, they came to Las Vegas as Frank's guests. In that context, they appeared even more extraordinary—utterly unadorned, pure of face and of purpose against the glittering casino, they stood side by side at the roulette table watching Frank bet away twenty thousand dollars.

Frank loved having houseguests, *lots* of houseguests. When the two octagonal guest houses were insufficient, he built another two-bedroom bungalow and a huge projection room/game room, then a tennis court, and a white clapboard New England—style four-bedroom house with shutters and a big living room and kitchen. Now he could host twenty-two guests at a time. No wonder they called him the Innkeeper.

Frank personally stocked each medicine cabinet with cotton balls, eye pads, mouthwash, toothpaste, toothbrushes, tampons, shaving equipment, shampoo—more stuff than hotels. Once, when guests were expected and one of the dwellings had only just been completed that afternoon, Frank had the local art gallery bring over their *entire* stock of paintings. A whole truckload of art arrived, and he helped the man hang paintings for three or four hours.

In the evenings guests were advised of the next morning's activities: breakfast is served from eight on, golfers leave for the course at ten. Everyone joins up for lunch at the adjoining country club at one. The afternoon was left open for swimming, tennis, and relaxation of choice—cars were waiting in the garage for anyone who wanted to go shopping. All were invited to gather for drinks at the bar from five until seven-thirty, when we would either leave in a convoy for a restaurant, Ruby's, or dinner would be served in the dining room, after which a movie was screened. Then came the time for shooting pool and hanging out at the bar. Things were so well organized, I'd get a migraine.

Over lunch one day at the golf club, Ruth Gordon ordered a slice of onion for her hamburger. With a strange expression, Frank asked if she liked raw onions and Ruth said, Yes, sometimes a slice on a hamburger. The onions here are nothing special, he said, you gotta try Maui onions. Ruth had never heard of them. Frank said, Oh for crying out loud, and left the table.

A day or two later, during our free time, I took Ruth and Garson to see the oasis where I rode my horse. As we drove along listening to the news, the announcer suddenly said, "If you happen to like Maui onions, it's a good thing to know Frank Sinatra. It seems one of his guests expressed the desire to have some, so Mr. Sinatra phoned Hawaii, and we've just learned that the pilot of flight number such-and-such is delivering the onions to Palm Springs." The next day at lunch, everybody had Maui onions.

It had been one of those interminable Vegas nights. Frank and I were safely in the golf cart, returning to our part of the hotel and to our waiting bed. He was wearing a shoe box on his head to keep the sunlight out of his eyes. Back at the casino, he had been angry. But things finally got smoothed over and nothing had come of it.

Suddenly, without any warning, he turned the golf cart around and pressed the gas pedal down as far as it would go; we were headed straight for the shiny plate-glass window. I couldn't see his eyes on account of the shoe box but I knew it was pointless to say a word. By what series of decisions, I wondered, was I here, now, in Las Vegas, in this golf cart, at five in the morning, with a man wearing a shoe box driving full-speed toward death by glass?

Should I have done something differently? No, I decided, as we raced toward the window; there was nothing to be done differently, not then or now. All the occurrences of our common time, tender or troubled, were linked as surely as the beads on a rosary.

In the final instant, we swerved and smashed sidelong into the window. With a little leap of surprise, I realized we were both unharmed. He was already out of the cart and striding into the casino as I trotted after him, clutching my little beaded evening purse. He threw some chairs into a heap and with his golden lighter he tried to set them on fire. I watched the rising commotion as people gathered around and casino guards rushed over. When he couldn't get a fire started, he took my hand and we walked out of the building.

The details of our first breakup were absurdly insignificant, even then, but they reflected the chasm of insecurities we had each brought to the relationship, and our startling ineptitude when it came to discussing our differences. It came without animosity, just the numbness and resignation we were neither of us stranger to.

I began to spend time with someone else, a delightful man who was not at all frightening. Like his friends he was young, brilliant, and funny, and it was surprising how little they all drank. On my Easter holiday from *Peyton Place*, my friend and I went to Rome and Venice.

The night I returned to L.A. I was awakened at two or three in the morning by a phone call from Frank in Las Vegas. Someone had been trying to reach him at the casino, giving my name, and he was calling me back. I had been in a deep sleep, so I'm not sure how the conversation inched into the other zone, but the next evening I was waiting for his plane at the airport and we began, for the first time, to plan a future. Difficult years had shaped us both. Our needs were enormous and not simple. We understood ourselves and each other so little, and whatever comprehension we may have had, we could not convey. Blindly we sought completion in each other.

It was not a surprise when, one Palm Springs morning, Frank led me outside, and with my two hands in his, asked if I would marry him. In the closing space between us, I placed all the hope of my lifetime.

High above the clouds in his Learjet on the way to New York, Frank was as usual coaxing me to eat. "Try some dessert," he said, but hidden under the cake was a little box. In it was an engagement ring with the biggest pear-shaped diamond I ever saw. He told me which finger to put it on. I thought, This is a ring I'd better not swallow.

Our engagement was announced, and Frank went on to London to shoot *The Naked Runner*. My apartment in L.A. was suddenly covered in photographers. I remember waiting until dark to crawl around the floor beneath the windows, opening the refrigerator from the bottom and pulling down a cold pizza. I phoned Frank from the floor and told him things were getting crazy again, I didn't know what to do. He said, Let's get married right away, we'll meet up in Las Vegas.

I had a white suit, so the next day I put it on, and the Goetzes picked me up and we flew to Las Vegas in Frank's plane. It occurred to me how hurt my mother was going to be, but Frank said I couldn't tell *anyone;* even Nancy and Tina didn't know. So I wondered how all the press found out. When I walked into the suite at the Sands, Frank was already there, wearing a dark suit, and smiling. He looked handsome. We laughed at all the excess feeling, and then we couldn't look at each other.

The ceremony was brief. There was a cake that nobody touched. The Goetzes were there, and Jack Entratter, and Red Skelton, who had just shot his wife. Champagne was uncorked, and we both had a sip for luck. Frank decided we had better step out and let the press take some pictures, so we did. The photos show a dazed but happy-looking couple. Once we got to Palm Springs, we phoned our families. We didn't turn on the television, of course. Photographers were outside the house all night.

The Goetzes threw a big wedding party for us, and my brother Patrick and his wife came, and Prudence, Maria, and Lenny Gershe, and my godfather, George Cukor, brought Katharine Hepburn; Spencer Tracy arrived separately. Edward G. Robinson was there, and Dean Martin, Ruth and Garson Kanin, Richard Attenborough, and the Billy Wilders. There was a huge wedding cake.

We were not quite back on earth as we headed to London two days later. Frank had an apartment in Grosvenor Square that was decorated in shiny green silks with lots of tassels, little glass-top tables, and jade ashtrays. While he was shooting, the wives of his London friends tried to look out for me. They'd just show up—there was no stopping them. Once they took me shopping, and I fainted at Harrods from boredom. Usually, when they dropped by, I'd hide in the bedroom while Barbara, my secretary and friend, would make excuses.

The press was still a problem. Of course one mature way to handle it might have been to walk out the front door and smile, and hope that eventually they'd lose interest and go away. But Frank was too outraged at their predatory behavior, and incensed at their continual invasions of his private life. So he spent much time and energy to avoid giving them a picture. When one evening we went out to dinner, he spent hours making elaborate plans to foil the paparazzi. Three cars were used, and he left the apartment with pockets full of cherry bombs. We hid with the garbage, and sneaked around corners, but we made it to the restaurant.

When we got back to California, Frank took me house
hunting. We looked at Beverly Hills mansions worth millions of dollars. I couldn't picture myself in any of them
and the more we saw, the more I felt like crying. Frank was
running out of patience, and I couldn't articulate what was
wrong. In time we were shown an English Tudor–style
house that wasn't too big or swanky; we both liked it, so
Frank bought it. Edie Goetz chose a decorator, and while
the house was being renovated, I went to London to make
A Dandy in Aspic with Laurence Harvey, who assured me that
I'd only have to be in London for ten days, and three days
in Berlin. It sounded like fun, and Frank didn't seem to
mind, although he wouldn't come back to London with me.

The first ten days went according to schedule, and then
we went to Berlin. The director, Tony Mann, was a kind
and thoughtful man in his mid-sixties. Larry Harvey, Tom
Courtenay, Lionel Stander, Peter Cook, and I were all staying at the Kempinski Hotel in Berlin, and shooting around
the city. I don't know why the film fell behind schedule,
and the promised three days exceeded a week, but Frank, on
the phone, was fed up.

One particularly frigid and windswept day we were
shooting on a race track outside the city. It was so cold the
actors chewed ice before they rolled the cameras, to reduce
the vapor coming out of our mouths. Although we were
freezing, Tony, the director, was in a good mood because
his young wife was flying in from London that day.

Back at the hotel in the evening I had a long hot bath to
thaw out before joining the rest of the cast in a restaurant
at nine. Tony said he'd be there with his wife but he was
late. In the middle of dinner we got a phone call. Come
quickly, said Mrs. Mann, something's happened to Tony.

We all rushed out of the restaurant. When there weren't
any cabs, we ran through the streets back to the Kempinski,

and upstairs, and we burst into the room where Tony was lying on the bed, completely dead.

Larry Harvey was trying to help Mrs. Mann, and calling the concierge or somebody. I went up close to Tony. I had never seen a dead person before. I sort of hugged him and Tom Courtenay yanked me to my feet and said, Don't be morbid.

Then a woman doctor arrived and after one second she said, He's dead, which we already knew. Larry and Mrs. Mann were talking about how the movie would get finished, and I'm thinking, Who cares about the stupid movie? Then a waiter walked in with a silver tray: instead of an undertaker, the concierge had sent room service. Nobody spoke any German, so we just pointed at Tony, and the man ran out of the room. Poor Mrs. Mann talked and searched through papers and opened closets. As hours passed, I began to feel quite comfortable, as if I'd been sitting all my life in that hotel room, with those people talking and Tony on the bed, dead. It was no stranger than anything else.

Larry Harvey directed the rest of the movie.

Chapter Six

What with one thing and another, *A Dandy in Aspic* had resulted in absences from my new husband that were long and stressful for both of us. Now that it was over, we were looking forward to a period of free time at home. In a few months we planned to work together in *The Detective*, back at Fox. Already I was wondering what it would be like to be in scenes with Frank, and worrying that I would disappoint him. Lee Remick, an actress I admired very much, was also cast.

It was at this moment that Paramount offered me *Rosemary's Baby*, a film to be based on the then-current bestseller by Ira Levin. Roman Polanski, thirty-three years old and internationally respected, was set to direct. It would be my first opportunity to star in a feature film, but more important, to prove myself as an actress. If the project succeeded it might place me in a position where I could choose good projects and roles. My goal was to make just one worthwhile

picture a year. Then I would have plenty of time to be a
wife and maybe even someday a mother.

But the timing of this offer was terrible, and I was in a
quandary. Frank and I discussed the pros and cons at
length. *Rosemary* was scheduled for a twelve-week shoot, and
I asked if he could weather a few more months of my being
at work. It seemed like the chance of a lifetime. At least, I
reasoned, I would be right here in L.A., home every night.
There was just one week in New York at the outset, and
three days at the end of the shoot.

Frank tried hard to be understanding but continued
to have reservations about the project. Finally, one air-
conditioned Palm Springs night, lying on his side of our
bed, he read the script. When he finished, his only comment was that he couldn't picture me in the part. I could
see his point. Suddenly I couldn't picture myself in it either.
I half-hoped he would take the matter out of my hands and
just tell me not to do it, but in fact he was reserved and
sympathetic, and tried to be supportive.

Riddled with ambivalence, self-doubt, and anxiety, I accepted the role. On an empty soundstage at Paramount
Studios, in a confounding maze of tape marks (intended to
represent walls and furniture but that I never could make
sense of), we began the two weeks of rehearsal, while the
actual set was being assembled on another stage. Then, in
the summer heat of New York City, in front of the Dakota
apartment building—now known, tragically, as the place
where John Lennon was shot—we began filming. Our family's apartment, conveniently, was right next door, on Central Park West and Seventy-third Street.

Off the set Roman was shy with me, but when we were
working he communicated clearly. He had an infectious enthusiasm that few could resist, and a real knowledge of
what would work professionally. When Roman wanted me
to eat raw liver, I ate it, take after take, even though, at the
time, I was a committed vegetarian. While we were shoot-

ing on Park Avenue, he had the idea that I should absent-
mindedly walk across the street into moving traffic, not
looking right or left. "Nobody will hit a pregnant woman,"
he laughed, referring to my padded stomach. He had to
operate the hand-held camera himself, since nobody else
would. I took a deep breath—an almost giddy, euphoric
feeling came over me. Together Roman and I marched right
in front of the oncoming cars—with Roman on the far
side, so I would have been hit first. "There are 127 varieties
of nuts," he told a journalist. "Mia's 116 of them." I'll take
a compliment any way it comes.

Except for the phone booth scene, all the interiors were
shot back at Paramount in L.A. Although I only weighed
about ninety-eight pounds when we started, Roman told
me to lose weight for the scenes when I'm sickly pregnant,
and we'd shoot that part last.

Roman preferred to film long scenes in one shot, moving
actors and the camera with precision. Because of the inherent technical demands, and Roman's perfectionism, he frequently shot as many as thirty or forty takes. This method
of working drove John Cassavetes nuts. John was a wonderful actor, as well as a respected and innovative director and
writer of his own highly personal films. But his approach
could not have been more different: his films had a raw,
improvised quality, while Roman, who had adapted the
script from the book himself, expected the actors to utter
every word precisely as written and, of course, to hold up
through as many takes as he wanted to shoot. John felt that
this killed all the life in a scene. I was too inexperienced to
have an opinion, but my commitment was to Roman, and I
felt embarrassed and upset when the two men openly dis-
agreed and grew apart.

One workday, while we were waiting to shoot, Roman
was discoursing about the impossibility of long-term mo-
nogamy given the brevity of a man's sexual attraction for
any one woman. An impassioned John Cassavetes responded

that Roman knew nothing about women, or relationships, and that he, John, was more attracted than ever to his wife, Gena Rowlands. Roman stared at him and blinked a few times, and for once had no reply.

During the shooting, one evening Frank and I took Nancy and her beau out to dinner. As we sat at Trader Vic's in the light of two stubby candles, I sipped a sweet drink and poked at the gardenia floating on top. The talk flowed easily and all was well—until the evening swerved. This had happened countless times before: after dinner and enough Jack Daniel's, Frank was likely to suddenly decide not to go home, but to Las Vegas instead, or Miami, or New York. He would feel the pull of that other world—the third part of his life—and it would be pointless to object. By now I was used to these abrupt departures alongside my husband, who was soon to metamorphose into a virtual stranger and would forget many things, including me. My stomach knew to turn over.

That night I couldn't go with him: I had to be at the studio early the next morning. So after alerting Don, his pilot, Frank drove me home, sweetly kissed me good night, and continued on to the airport. Later he woke me by phone to say that he had safely arrived in Las Vegas. I heard no more, nor did I expect to, until the morning, when he reached me on the set at Paramount.

His speech was unclear but I soon made out that there had been a fight, the caps had been punched clear off his teeth, some other guy had been hurt, headlines were sure to follow, and his dentist was on the way with new teeth. It didn't much matter what started the fight: they always had to do with his powerful Sicilian sense of propriety, which by four in the morning could get a little cloudy. He sounded bewildered and upset as he said he loved and needed me, and with my whole being I loved and needed him too. And when he told me not to leave him ever, I promised him that. Life was not easy for Frank Sinatra, or for anyone who stood beside him. Although the armies of his heart and mind did frequent battle and left him isolated and restless, in matters of conscience and of human hope, they were one.

At Paramount Studios we were falling behind schedule. I appeared in every single scene of the film, except when, during a rape sequence, a body double was used in my place. But I didn't entirely miss out on the scene: one day I found myself—me from convent school, who prayed with outstretched arms in the predawn light—tied to the four corners of a bed, ringed by elderly, chanting witches. The Pope brought over his big ring for me to kiss, while a perfect stranger with bad skin and vertical pupils was grinding away on top of me. I didn't dare think. After finishing that scene the actor climbed off me and said politely, in all seriousness, "Miss Farrow, I just want to say, it's a real pleasure to have worked with you."

The sixties were in full bloom. Roman was humming, "If you're going to San Francisco, be sure to wear some flowers in your hair," and I painted the walls of my dressing room with rainbows, flowers, and butterflies. When I was done painting, they brought in a Ping-Pong table and I pestered everybody to come play with me. Except for the days Ruth worked, I was the only female on the set and the guys treated me like a kid sister. Ruth Gordon had been my friend long before we made the movie, and nobody was better company. Her energy and enthusiasm were unmatched. She was sharp and quick and unfailingly saw right to the heart of everything.

Filming seemed to be going well, but very slowly. Across town *The Detective* was shooting on schedule, and my start date was drawing close: I was expected to report for work there in mid-October. Frank was baffled and outraged by the pace of our filming. When he went to New York for a few weeks of filming on *The Detective*, I joined him on weekends, trying to hold things together. As the date neared, it became clear that Frank expected me to meet my commitment even if it meant abandoning *Rosemary's Baby* before it was completed. I began to understand that my whole marriage was at risk. The ultimatum was clear. But if I left *Rosemary's Baby*, certainly my career would be finished. I thought of the months of long days and countless takes and everyone trying so hard. I thought of the people whose trust I'd earned, and I thought of my own work, which for the first time in my life might have some value. To lose Frank was unthinkable, but I didn't believe he would leave me. I also realized that in this decision I would define myself. If I walked out on this project, in time even he would see that I had done a less than honorable thing, and he would respect me less.

I pictured myself in Las Vegas sitting with the hookers as I had so many times before. It is 4 A.M. Frank and the other men are telling jokes and laughing loudly. A jaded piano plays the cocktail songs. The women are apart, we are wearing our best dresses, our faces are fixed right. We chat about cats, and we wait.

In dread I continued to report for work each day and prayed that he would change his mind. Jacqueline Bisset was cast in an abbreviated version of my role in *The Detective*. There were rumors of an affair between Frank and Lee Remick. Then, without warning, on an afternoon in November, Frank's lawyer, Mickey Rudin, appeared on our set carrying a brown envelope. He pulled out documents that I looked at just long enough to see they were made out in my name: they were an official application for a divorce from Frank Sinatra. I remember the unprofessional look of surprise as Mr. Rudin realized I had not expected his visit, nor did I know anything about the papers he carried. This was the first mention of divorce. I held myself together and signed all the papers without reading them. If Frank wanted a divorce, then the marriage was over. I told Mickey Rudin that I would do whatever they wanted. I would have no need for any legal counsel myself. After he left, Ruth and Roman tried to patch me up and get me back on the set, but I needed some time, and closed the door.

All the detail, illusion, and embellishments of my mortal self—all that was nonessential—was singed to gray ash and blew away where I stood, a bare, scorched human stalk, bent into the wind. The familiar bulwarks held fast; pain, doubt, hope, and something else too; a large internal eye, blankly hanging in the space of me, restlessly scanning the depths of my being, beholding nothing.

I applied myself to the remainder of the movie with a fervor usually reserved for prayer. The days were long and difficult. I was still living in the Tudor-style house, and speaking with Frank in New York whenever he called. Neither of us mentioned Mickey Rudin's mission. On weekends, the rented house in Malibu that Roman shared with Sharon Tate was filled with friends and laughter. Like the princess in a fairy tale, Sharon was as sweet and good as she was beautiful. Generously they invited me into their lives, and since I now had none of my own, I gratefully spent my weekends with them.

Relations between John and Roman, however, had broken down. While mapping out the final sequence of the movie, John became openly critical of Roman, who yelled, John, shut up! and they moved toward each other. Every time in my life when the commonplace has veered into the netherworld, it is as if I am watching television and I can't change the channel. It was Ruth Gordon, with consummate professionalism, who said, "Now, come on, let's get back to work," and saved the day.

Back in New York, Ruth and I filmed our last scene on Fifth Avenue in front of Tiffany's. I stood for a moment on the sidewalk, watching everyone pack up and scurry back to their lives. It was Christmas. I returned to Frank's orange apartment on the East Side and packed up all my things.

Then I sat down by my suitcases, trying to decide where to go. At that moment Pamela Hayward breezed in. She had been worried about me. She was heading to Palm Springs that day to spend Christmas with Frank. I heard her on the phone telling Frank how pale and thin I was, and the next thing I knew, we were landing in the Palm Springs desert.

Frank was waiting on the tarmac, we hadn't seen each other for over a month, and despite the tender greeting, his overall mood was withdrawn and stern. Still, I was grateful to be there, and anxious not to do anything wrong. We didn't talk about any of it—not *Rosemary's Baby*, or *The Detective*, or Ms. Remick, or the papers I had signed, and, above all, not the future. And each night, in our old bed, sleep found us entwined in hopeless silence.

From the beginning, a short life had been predicted for our marriage, and now, with two Hollywood studios involved in the endgame, the tabloid headlines rang with reports of every kind. Nonetheless, life went on as usual at the Palm Springs compound. Just as before, Frank asked me to arrange the seating for each night's dinner, with the instructions that under no circumstances was I to seat a certain woman next to him, because she was so boring. Each evening I dutifully reshuffled the twenty-two guests around three tables, careful to place the offensive guest anywhere but next to her host. Frank tolerated this woman because her husband was so amusing, and they were established members of the A-group. On the fourth night I was in the living room alone after dinner when the woman's husband came toward me. I smiled, but his words were already flying at me, shrill and furious. "We've been here four days," he began, "and not once have you seated my wife next to Frank. She is upset and embarrassed and insulted. I think you are a stupid, rude little girl—you will *never* be a hostess!"

I was so unprepared and thoroughly terrified that I didn't say a word, not to him or to Frank. I knew that the

man would never in a million years have dared to attack me
had he not assumed I was on my way out of Frank's life.

This couple, friends of Ronald Reagan, were eventually
instrumental in securing Frank's support for Reagan and
the Republican Party. Back in 1966, the war in Vietnam
had polarized our positions and joined the list of things it
was not safe to discuss. And to my dismay, over the next
years, Frank, an old liberal in the best sense, moved steadily
toward the right.

My gift to him that Christmas was a real London taxi
purchased while I was making *A Dandy in Aspic*. It had taken
months to have it converted to U.S. specifications, and in
that time a lot had happened. Nonetheless, Yul had
planned a grand presentation ceremony and even rented
snappy livery uniforms for himself and for George, the
houseman: at five that afternoon, when everyone was sitting
around the bar and living room, Yul was going to toot the
horn and I would get Frank and everybody outside, where
Yul and George, with as much fanfare as possible, would
present the taxi.

I was beyond excitement by the time five o'clock rolled
around and the horn sounded, and the guests who were in
on the secret and the spirit of the occasion trooped out the
front door, followed by Frank, who was grumpy—he didn't
like being told what to do—and me, tugging his arm. But
the second we stepped out the door, Frank said it was cold:
I'd have to go back inside and put on a sweater. A *sweater?*
Now? That's okay, I'm not cold, just please come on. But
he was getting mad, and he wouldn't budge, and neither
could I, until I put on a sweater. By now all the guests had
gone quiet and they were turned around facing us. I could
feel my face all hot and my smile was stuck to my teeth. So
I ran back, dug a sweater out of my bottom drawer, and
dashed back with it around my shoulders and everybody
was still there trying to keep the ball in the air. Frank said,
No, put the sweater *on*, so I quickly put my arms into the

sleeves, and he waited, and everybody waited, until I buttoned every single button. *Then* we went down the path and the guests moved aside. Yul was smiling in uniform, bowing, presenting papers rolled up like a scroll, and George was beaming and saluting like crazy and everybody was clapping, they were so relieved, and Frank and I just stood there, locked into that moment, with the bones of our relationship completely exposed, as we stared at the shiny London taxicab.

That New Year's Eve, the whole gang, dressed to the nines and already tanked up, climbed aboard private planes headed for a party in L.A. I was worried because, as I said, we had never discussed what was going to happen after the holidays. Alan Lerner and Joshua Logan came up to me at the party: they'd seen parts of *Rosemary's Baby* and they paid me lavish compliments, even asking me to be in their movie *Paint Your Wagon.* This was remarkable, just the way they were looking at me and talking to me. Frank said nothing, and soon my circuits jammed, and I was quiet too. Before midnight Frank said he was leaving, and I asked, Can I come too? and ran along after him. He drove me to the house in Bel Air and there he said good night and that he was leaving for Acapulco.

I laughed into the pale face in the mirror—he was right, my arms were thin, even I could see that now. The telephone was ringing. I delicately unwrapped a Wilkinson razor that was lying by the sink, then I couldn't think why I did that and neatly I refolded the paper around it. I couldn't concentrate for long. The house was just space and a lot of unrelated, meaningless objects. In my mind nothing was recognizable. I didn't know how to proceed. There was nothing to move toward, nothing to return to. Here was a mess of my own making.

Without warning, one evening Frank arrived at the front

door wearing a dark suit and shiny shoes and he smelled of
the aftershave lotion that reminded me of my father. (I can
say it now, they had the same identical smell.) I wished I
had known he was coming so I could have put on nice
clothes or something, my eyes were all puffy. But he was
smiling and had brought me a present, a really wonderful
one, not jewelery or anything, it was the nicest thing I ever
had—a beautiful antique music box. He showed me how to
crank it, and we listened to the seven songs. Afterward I
offered him Sara Lee chocolate cake, although I knew he
wouldn't eat it. I didn't know what else to do. I wished he
didn't have to leave.

Word was spreading beyond the gates of Paramount that
Rosemary's Baby was going to be a hit, and a dream movie
career was being handed to me, with respected directors,
interesting scripts and roles, exotic locations, pots of
money, and costars of legendary proportions. Even John
Wayne, on whose tall chair I had been stranded as a little
girl, now wanted me to do *True Grit*. But at twenty-one I
had lost my husband, my anonymity, and my equilibrium,
and it was peace I yearned for.

Every hour seemed like dusk inside the Bel Air house of
our highest hopes. Exhausted, I lay on the practically new
king-size bed. There was a fireplace in our bedroom but we
had never got around to lighting it. The logs were fake—
who even knew how to turn it on? I tugged the Porthault
sheets tight around my chin. Tiny yellow flowers were embroidered all along the border. The house was cold. The
housekeeper or the Japanese cook who looked at me
strangely would know how to turn on the heat but I
couldn't bring myself to ask. I hated that they were there. I
was never remotely comfortable with them, not in my high-
flying times, and certainly not now. At night I crept down
to the refrigerator for Sara Lee chocolate cake, passing

Frank's favorite room, the one with the big television and a bar, and five tall stools with orange leather seats, and a custom-made backgammon table and three squishy couches, also orange, like the carpets.

" 'Evening, Mrs. S.," said the guard, no matter what. He had a gun.

When certain guests came over—those who were older than Frank, or with whom he didn't feel comfortable—he put on a tie and we would sit with our drinks and cigarettes in the formal living room, which was actually not orange but white and yellow and had a lot of antiques in it. Every single thing in every single room had been chosen by the decorator, except for the encyclopedias, which were my anniversary present. It felt like somebody else's house. I was careful never to break anything.

I had come to Frank Sinatra as an impossibly immature teenager without any person or system I could rely upon. With the best of intentions, Frank brought me into his own complex world and I, with the best of mine, gratefully clung to him there. I loved him truly. But this is also true: it was a little bit like an adoption that I had somehow messed up and it was awful when I was returned to the void.

My life had fallen away, and I could not envision a future. Work and religion suggested themselves, but extended thought about either left me in a tangle of confusion and suspicion. It seemed to me that my brief acting career had summoned all the selfishness, arrogance, and shortsightedness inherent in me, and these unworthy elements had conspired to destroy what I needed and wanted most. I was *not* a pediatrician in Southeast Asia, or a Carmelite nun in England: I was a lightweight—a Hollywood starlet on the verge of divorce.

Take all the pictures you want (*flash*). Be my guest, no problem. Pardon me? Oh yes, I was married to Frank Sina-

My mother, Maureen O'Sullivan, and her father, Charles.

My mother and grandmother, Mary Frazer O'Sullivan, in Ireland, 1958.

The oval portrait of my father's mother, Lucy Farrow, in the year of her death at the age of nineteen.

TOP LEFT: Maureen O'Sullivan, as "Jane" in one of the Tarzan films.

©1932 *Turner Entertainment Co.*

TOP RIGHT: John Farrow, newly arrived in California.

Maureen O'Sullivan and John Farrow.

My parents in Canada in 1940, during wartime.

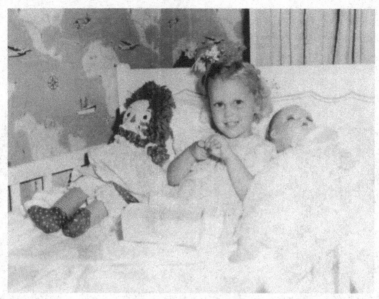

Me at four with Raggedy Ann and Mickey.

The Farrows in 1949: my father, my mother with baby Prudence in her arms, Mike, Patrick, me, and Johnny.

A shared fifth birthday with my father.

Mike, me, and Patrick in a boat in our Beverly Hills swimming pool.

Johnny and me in
Malibu, 1955.

The day of my First
Holy Communion,
with Billy
the dog.

OPPOSITE: My father
brings me home.

INSET: A polio ward in
the 1950s.
*(Courtesy of the Francis A.
Countway Library of Medicine,
Harvard University)*

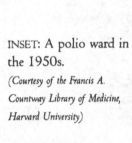

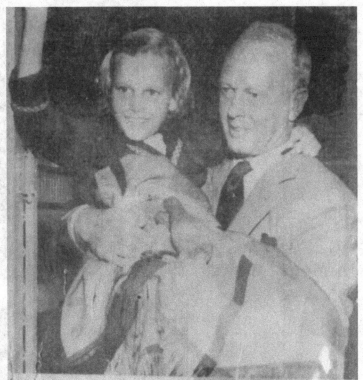

MARIA GOES HOME—Maria Farrow, 9, daughter of Film Director John Farrow and Actress Maureen O'Sullivan, is carried by her father from the polio ward of General

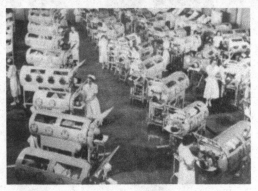

O'Sullivan Child
Leaves Hospital
Polio Ward

Maria Farrow, 9-year-old
daughter of Actress Maureen
O'Sullivan and Film Director
John Farrow, yesterday left
General Hospital

Maria Roach and my brother
Johnny at the Candy Cane Ball.

Queen of the Fiestas in
Denia, Spain, 1958.

Mike with Dad.

Mike

Michael Damien Villiers Farrow
Born May 30th, 1939
Died October 29, 1958

Our Father who art in heaven,
Hallowed be thy name.
Thy kingdom come,
Thy will be done . . . .

Eternal rest grant unto him, O Lord,
and let perpetual light shine upon him.

My favorite picture of Mike.

My father in his bedroom.

JANUARY 29, 1963

John Farrow

Film Writer John Farrow Dies at 58

Actress Maureen O'Sullivan flew home Monday from New York to arrange funeral services for her husband, John Villiers Farrow, 58.

The colorful film writer-director was found dead late Sunday in their Beverly Hills home by his son, Patrick, 20, eldest of the couple's six children.

Farrow lay fully clothed on a bed in his study in the home at 809 N Roxbury Dr. His hand rested on a telephone as if he were about to make a call.

Massive Heart Attack

Dr. William Weber Smith, the family physician, said he died of a massive heart attack. He had some heart trouble long ago and a circulatory disorder more recently, Dr. Smith said.

Funeral arrangements are pending at the Cunningham & O'Connor Hollywood Mortuary.

Farrow, winner of the Motion Picture Academy's 1956 best screenplay award for "Around the World in 80 Days," was born in Sydney, Australia, in 1904.

Short story writing led Farrow to Hollywood, where he was employed as a scenarist by Cecil B. DeMille in 1927. His greatest success began 10 years later, however, when he wrote and directed "My Bill" for Warner Bros.

In Canadian Navy

In 1939 he joined the Canadian Navy, seeing action with the anti-submarine patrol in convoys in the North and South Atlantic.

Farrow's long list of film credits includes such pictures as "Wake Island," "Bill of Divorcement," "Five Came Back," "Two Years Before the Mast," "Hondo," "California," "Botany Bay," and "Back From Eternity."

Tragedy visited the Farrows in 1958 when the eldest of their seven children, Michael D. V. Farrow, 19, was killed in an air collision near Whiteman Airpark, Pacoima.

Others of the surviving six children are John, 16, Prudence, 15, Stephanie, 13, and Tisa (Theresa) Farrow, 11.

With Ryan O'Neal in
Peyton Place.
(Courtesy of 20th Century–Fox)

Dalí and me.
(Photo by Philippe Halsman,
© Halsman Estate)

Riding Salvador.

Graduation in *Peyton Place*.
(Courtesy of 20th Century–Fox)

My first film, *Guns at Batasi*.
John Leyton is
on the left and Richard
Attenborough to the right.
(Courtesy of 20th Century–Fox)

Frank with our dog Samantha.   Malcolm and me.

The Share Party, 1965: my first time out
in public with Frank.

The boat trip.

Roz Russell,
Claudette Colbert,
and me with the
boat behind us.

With Bill Goetz.

Edie Goetz and Yul Brynner.

Just married, 1966.

tra, and while I'm smiling let me say that I'm happy to write my name on your menu or your arm or wherever, and I don't mind at all being dragged over to meet your family —it's mother's milk to me. Except it was a *mistake*, becoming famous—so I'd be grateful if you wouldn't get excited or think I'm anything special when I'm not.

Supposing you make a mistake at a very early age, and the mistake sets in motion certain mysterious forces that should never have been fiddled with in the first place. As a result, the fragile and complex connections between you and everybody else get screwed up, as people respond to illusions, artificial images. It's scary to think that nobody can see *you*. How is it possible to know anybody if they're busy reacting to a thing that isn't you? Frank says if you just keep moving . . . But by becoming famous, I have bombed the very bridges I needed most, to cross the gulf, to connect with other people. Isn't that, in the end, what redeems us?

I could change my name. Dye my hair brown. Get fat. Move to another state. I'll pick a spot on the map, pack the music box and encyclopedias, or actually Barbara could do that and she'll take me and the encyclopedias and the music box to the airport, and then I guess I'd say good-bye to Barbara because I wouldn't need an assistant anymore. So I arrive there, somewhere, I rent a Hertz car, load up the encyclopedias, check into a motel, people do it all the time, and look for a sweet little dream house to buy (remember to call my business manager, find out how much money I have). Actually a whole different country might be best. Spin the globe. A bicycle repair shop in Peru! Dogs asleep on the dirt floor. I can even speak Spanish, sort of. There are countless options. What were they again? Change names. Dye hair. Get fat. Move to Peru. Fix bikes. Have I thought of everything? I wonder how long you can live on Sara Lee chocolate cake?

A phone call in the night. My sister Prudence, in Boston, unmoored in some nightmare of her own, was talking about transcendental meditation. Without understanding any of it, I filled a duffel bag with books and walked out the front door; I waved to the gardener, who was standing near the pink roses. I got into the car and Barbara drove me away from the house in Bel Air and all its contents, away from the gleaming grand piano, and the deaf cat watching from the window, my music box, and even my encyclopedias. Without understanding a thing I boarded a plane to Boston.

Prudence and I made our way through Boston's snowy streets to a crowded auditorium where Maharishi Mahesh Yogi was speaking. "The mind can transcend all limits of experience and thought," he said, "and is left in a field of pure Being—the source of all wisdom, creativity, peace, and happiness . . ."

Inside the numbness came a newborn nuzzling of hope. After the lecture we shouldered through the photographers and reporters.

"Where's Frankie?" someone yelled.

"Hey Mia, look this way!"

"Is your marriage really over?"

My sister and I were haunted, shuddering specters in the flashing light. But Maharishi said, Come to India, Come to a teacher's training course there, and Prudy and I accepted. I said, Yes, I will learn to meditate, and seek enlightenment and peace at the foot of the Himalayas!

A world away from the leafy stillness of Bel Air, I groped numbly through New Delhi's anarchic streets. A swirling cacophony of Indian pop songs blared tinny out of countless unseen radios, as cars driving crazily played on horns; smells of spices, sewers, and piles of rotting garbage. There were cows with red spots painted on their foreheads and bells on their feet traipsing right through the middle of everything, and everybody swarmed in all directions, shoving and spilling out of buses and rickshaws. Vivid saris fluttering, purple, sapphire, turquoise, and gold, unreadable watchful dusky faces, vendors of all kinds, fortune-tellers, snake charmers, magicians, flies, and flocks of ragged children, begging. From the gutter, a dead dog's eye stared back at me. It was a collision of magnificence and wretchedness.

We journeyed north. Winds howled raw at the foot of the Himalayas, where saffron-swathed monks were wading serenely in the icy Ganges. By the bridge at Rishikesh, lepers begged with fingerless hands.

The ashram was a fenced compound consisting of six *puri* —single-story, concrete, barracks-style structures, each with ten simple rooms facing a single wan sapling in a sandy courtyard. A gravel path connected the buildings, then wound beneath tall eucalyptus trees toward the kitchen and dining area and beyond to the lecture hall where Maharishi addressed the meditators and responded to questions every evening. All these buildings stood on a hillside that descended steeply to the Ganges.

Patches of snow lay on the ground and the rooms had no heat. Each morning a bucket of steaming water was placed inside my door by a young Indian man with large, mistrustful eyes. I liked the austere little room—its hard bed, chest of drawers, and dim lamp met my needs perfectly.

We were a reverent, drab group of fifty or so men and women of various nationalities, ages, and professions. All spoke English and the course was conducted in this language. Maharishi suggested that we meditate for twelve hours of the day, taking short breaks as we needed. During these hours, when meditators, often wrapped in the heavy brown blankets from our beds, encountered one another along the gravel paths or beneath the trees, we exchanged other-worldly smiles and the Sanscrit salutation *"Jai Guru dev."*

On the much-anticipated day of my initiation into meditation, I presented Maharishi with a bunch of cut flowers, as is customary, and sat cross-legged facing him, a little nervously. Then at last he gave me my mantra—my own secret, magical sound—and just as he said it, soft like he did, I sneezed. So, I'm not positive, but *maybe* I didn't quite catch it—his voice was so low, and the word or sound was strange and brief, and he had a beard, and he said it right in the middle of my sneeze, so after a moment I said, Excuse me, I don't think I quite heard you. But he would not say it again—ever. So I couldn't be one hundred percent sure I was doing it right. And when I brought it up, which I did from time to time, he would just wave it off. But when I was meditating, the thought would edge back into my mind that maybe I was doing it wrong, and that's what was keeping me out of the "field of pure Being."

I tried to meditate for the recommended twelve hours a day, but I rarely came close. At least I wasn't throwing up anymore, and my concentration had improved to the point where I could read again. With a book in hand, I would clamber down the hill to read or just to watch the Ganges rushing past. Sometimes I wandered across the bridge into the town of Rishikesh. When I brought back an emaciated, flea-ridden stray puppy, Maharishi named him Arjuna, after the warrior, and said he could stay with me at the compound.

All that I read, and most of my thoughts, were parts of a single process. My religion, as it had been presented to me and as I had interpreted it, was no longer helpful, satisfying, or even acceptable to me—nonetheless, since childhood my orientation had been to a higher order. I could not be a nihilist. Separation from my faith had left me with a sense of incompleteness that went far beyond missing Frank. I felt that I had lost what was at the heart of my existence: my bond with everything that is. With the help of the books I had brought with me, along with a few I found at the ashram, I began to redefine my relationship with Christianity, Catholicism, and Being.

In the Bhagavad Gita I read that the Divine Being is the very substance of the universe, but that everything we experience with our senses is merely illusion: "Water cannot wet It, nor can fire burn It, wind cannot dry It, and weapons cannot slay It. It is the all-pervading, omnipresent, divine Being . . . Hard it is to pierce that veil divine of various shows which hideth me; yet they who worship me pierce it and pass beyond."

The teachings of Buddha tell us that the Self is the greatest obstacle to true understanding: "The worldling will not understand, for to him there is happiness in selfhood only, and the bliss that lies in a complete surrender to Truth is unintelligible to him."

Thomas Jefferson wrote extensively about Jesus Christ, and guided by his work I began to discriminate between the core of His teachings and the dogma that has been attached to it. "We must reduce our volume to the simple Evangelists," he wrote. "Select, even from them, the very words only of Jesus . . . There will be found remaining the most sublime and benevolent code of morals which has ever been offered to man . . . Among the sayings and discourses imputed to Him by His biographers, I find many passages of fine imagination, correct morality, and of the most lovely benevolence; and others again of so much ignorance, so much absurdity, so much untruth, charlatanism, and imposture, as to pronounce it impossible that such contradictions should have proceeded from the same being. I separate therefore the gold from the dross . . . When, in short, we shall have unlearned everything which has been taught since His day, and got back to the pure and simple doctrines He inculcated, we shall then be truly and worthily His disciples: and my opinion is that if nothing had ever been added to what flowed purely from His lips, the whole world would at this day have been Christian."

Tolstoy said much the same: "Nothing needful can be poured into a vessel full of what is useless. We must first empty out what is useless . . . True Christian teaching . . . tells us nothing about the beginning, or about the end, of the world, or about God and His purpose, or in general about things which we cannot, and need not, know; but it speaks only of what man must do to save himself, that is, how best to live the life he has come into, in this world, from birth to death. For this purpose it is only necessary to treat others as we wish them to treat us . . . Belief that the Gospels are the inspired word of God is not only a profound error, but a very harmful deception . . . Jesus himself did not write a book . . . The reader must remember all this in order to disengage himself from the idea, so common among us, that the Gospels in their present form have come to us directly from the Holy Spirit."

In his essay entitled *How to Read the Gospels and What Is Essential in Them*, Tolstoy wrote that "to understand any book one must select the parts that are quite clear, dividing them from what is obscure or confused. And from what is clear we must form our idea of the drift and spirit of the whole work . . ."

These insights illuminate, far more eloquently than I could, the shape and distillations of my befuddled thoughts. And so I lifted the words of Jesus out of the New Testament and wrote them out in my clean, lined notebook; and in taking them to heart, the confusion that had previously besieged all my efforts to define my position fell away, and was replaced by plain understanding.

From the chaos of the recent years, and the personal failure and forgetting, emerged a powerful remembrance from the polio wards of my childhood. As a member of the human family, I rediscovered my sense of responsibility. Now I would begin to search for a mission that could breathe meaning into my existence.

Nearly every afternoon Maharishi sent for me to come to his bungalow for a private talk. From the start he had been especially solicitous and attentive to me, and I had responded with wary resentment. "Not only does he send for me every single day, and not the others," I complained to my sister, "but also, he is giving me mangoes. And to the best of my knowledge, he has not given a single mango to anybody else . . ." Prudence said the problem was me.

The ashram, up to this point, was a strange, cold, colorless place where meditation was the sole focus: we moved as if in a dream and spoke only when necessary, in the respectful, hushed tones of visitors to a graveyard. So it went, quietly and evenly, until one afternoon when, out of the blue, the Beatles arrived.

Right on the heels of their groundbreaking, earthshaking *Sgt. Pepper's Lonely Hearts Club Band*, all four Beatles and their wives descended upon the ashram. Maharishi managed to keep the press outside the compound, but even there, at the edge of the earth, there were photographers in the trees. Nonetheless, with their cheerful chatter and guitars and singing, the new arrivals brought an element of "normalcy" to the ashram—a sort of contemporary reality, which at first seemed jarringly out of place. After a short time Maureen and Ringo Starr left because of the flies; and they missed their kids. Ringo and George were the most accessible of the four, but I liked them all. Now the Beatles too came to Maharishi's bungalow in the afternoons.

"Whenever I meditate," John said, in his irresistible Liverpool accent, "there's a big brass band in me head."

"Write it down, write it down," recommended Maharishi.

I think of John, so off-center and quick, peering out from behind his glasses; he made me laugh, which I hadn't done in a while. And at evening assembly he used to turn his chair completely around, and look at everyone. John seemed to see everything on a mystical plane, and he thought of Maharishi as a kind of wizard.

George was gentle and kind, with a radiant spiritual quality—he would go to the elderly women meditators to play his guitar and sing for them. It was his serious commitment to meditation that had motivated the other Beatles to come to India. He was interested in playing the sitar, he said, not just to entertain, but so that he could play the ragas—rhythms passed through holy men from the Vedas —because it is believed that they alter the consciousness and can influence people for the good.

I didn't get to know Paul well, but I was friendly with his girlfriend, Jane Asher, a freckle-faced, redheaded actress who, like Patti Harrison and Patti's younger sister, Jennie, was roughly my age. They were not noticeably serious about meditating; and for me, a slight de-escalation of the intensity of the previous weeks came as a welcome relief.

Now, on the rocky Ganges shore, the Beatles played their guitars and sang, and we talked, and for some extended moments the heaviness that had settled around me lifted. They were in the land of light, and of youth, strength, and certainty; they seemed beautiful and fearless. Not since high school had I spent time with people my age. It was 1968, an exciting time to be young, but the feeling persisted that I was on the outside, always either too old or too immature. Chilling were the times when I caught myself pretending to be my own age.

The flat roof of our *puri*, in the hours when it caught the late-afternoon sun, was a good place to get warm, and read, talk, or meditate, and for George to practice his sitar. I had given up trying to meditate for twelve hours a day and was pleased when I could manage six. But Prudy was meditating continuously, and no longer appeared at meals (we left a plate outside her door) or at the evening lectures. Finally, she did not leave her room at all. Even in our setting, this was extreme.

The ashram seemed a cheery place now, in the spirit of the flower-child sixties. The Beatles were everywhere and so was their music. They even brought their guitars to meals and improvised songs. I heard no complaints from the meditators: our eclectic group had bonded, Beatles and all. Then a self-important, middle-aged American woman arrived, moving a mountain of luggage into the brand-new private bungalow next to Maharishi's along with her son, a bland young man named Bill. People fled this newcomer, and no one was sorry when she left the ashram after a short time to go tiger hunting, unaware that their presence had inspired a new Beatles' song—"Bungalow Bill."

In response to several frightening, emotional eruptions that occurred during the long hours of meditation, Maharishi appointed sets of "team buddies" to look out for one another. Prudence's "buddies" were George and John, and they took their responsibility seriously. Every morning and most afternoons they met in Prudy's room, where they discussed their respective lives, the meaning of existence, and who Maharishi really was.

"I just wanted to meditate as much as possible," Prudence told me. "It was a special time, and such a holy place. One night when I was meditating, George and John came into my room with their guitars, singing, 'Ob la di, ob la da, life goes on, naninani.' Another time John, Paul, and George came in singing 'Sgt. Pepper's Lonely Hearts Club Band,' the whole song! They were trying to be cheerful, and it was so sweet of them. I was grateful, but I wished they'd go away. At first I don't think they realized what the training course in meditation was all about. They were just having fun. They didn't quite understand until later."

No one is ever indifferent to Prudence. When the

frames on her glasses broke—"It's like I'm underwater without them," said Prudy—Paul spent a long time fiddling with a piece of wire and managed to fix them. And when, a day later, they fell apart again, again he wired them together. This went on for some time; Paul's commitment to my sister's glasses was admirable, but it seemed that no matter how he bent that wire, the glasses ended up in pieces.

Before they left the ashram, Paul and John wrote the song "Dear Prudence" for my sister: "Dear Prudence, won't you come out to play, Dear Prudence, greet the brand-new day . . ."

"I guess I thought it was really nice, but I didn't know they were going to put it on an album or anything," said Prudy. "I didn't really think about it; it wasn't anything in my mind. Then much later, after India, I heard people saying there was a song. I was really grateful that it was something so nice."

"Now we will meditate in my 'cave,' " said Maharishi, and I followed him down steep wooden steps into a dark, humid little cellar room that smelled of sandalwood. It was my first time in his cave: there was a small shrine with flowers and a picture of Guru Dev, Maharishi's dead teacher, and a carpet on which we settled ourselves in the lotus position to meditate. After twenty or so minutes we were getting to our feet, still facing each other, but as I'm usually a little disoriented after meditation, I was blinking at his beard when suddenly I became aware of two surprisingly male, hairy arms going around me. I panicked, and shot up the stairs, apologizing all the way. I flew out into the open air, and ran as fast as I could to Prudy's room, where she was meditating of course. I blurted out something about Maharishi's cave, and arms, and beard, and she said, It's an honor to be touched by a holy man after meditation, a tradition. Furthermore, at my level of consciousness, if Jesus Christ Himself had embraced me, I would have misinterpreted it.

Still, I flung the essentials into my faded cloth shoulderbag, stuffed passport and money into a pouch hung around my neck, and without a plan, and nothing to lose, I dashed out of the guarded gates headlong into the spreading Indian twilight.

The next weeks had the quality of a long hallucination —sometimes blurred, sometimes jaggedly sharp. I walked and rode and hitched, I traveled in buses, cars, trains, an elaborately hand-painted truck, a bullock cart, rickshaws, a steamer, and an airplane. I crossed bridges and waded through streams, I wandered along peaceful country roads past rippling mustard yellow fields, and through the slums of Calcutta; I slept in hotels, huts, and dives; I rode an elephant, killed cockroaches the size of mice, and kicked a rat clear across a room. I saw the lacy Taj by moonlight, and by day I explored countless temples, monasteries, and palaces. At ninety-five pounds, with my cropped hair, I dressed and looked like a boy, and that seemed a useful thing throughout my travels. I wasn't afraid, but I was lonely; and when I begged my brother Johnny, who was back in California, to come on a great adventure, he did.

It wasn't even light when I jolted awake, feeling something fumbling at my neck. The woman who had given me bread the night before was now laughing into my face. Quickly, I traced the outlines of my passport and traveler's checkbook still inside the pouch. The woman was making signs that she only wanted to touch my hair, unusual blond hair, but I was already backing out of the hut; it wasn't until I noticed her fingers missing—not in a neat, clean way—that I began to run. The river was shockingly cold. With my bar of Ivory soap, I scrubbed the leprosy off.

In southern Goa, the white sand beach was completely

deserted except for a barefooted, bearded young man who was walking toward us wearing faded, sawed-off jeans and a T-shirt, and carrying an empty bucket. We recognized, in a flabbergasting coincidence, our brother Patrick's closest friend. Along with another neighbor from Beverly Hills, he'd been living on this beach in a lean-to made from palm fronds. At their invitation, and lacking any better plan, we decided to stay awhile, and assumed our share of the household chores, which included walking a couple of miles into town to buy food and sodas in the marketplace, cooking supper on an open fire, washing our clothes in boiling seawater, drawing fresh water from the town well, and a brand-new skill, rolling fat hashish joints.

We went through our daily routines with little if any conversation, to the tuneless, woody wails of our host's flute. The weather was hot, the water was warm, and the days passed in a haze of hash, until one morning when my brother and I were out swimming just beyond the surf, a large fin sliced the water between us. Like cartoon whirligigs, we churned through the surf until we were safely back on the sand. As we sat, panting, I glanced at Johnny and saw (as I had a thousand times before) our father's ocean blue eyes fixed upon the waves. After a long moment, my brother quietly said, "I want my razor-sharp mind back."

The next day, we left our friends in Goa. I didn't have the slightest idea where to go, or what to do, or how to go about it. But it was time to make a decision. I considered staying in India, but as much as I liked it, I did not feel at home there.

So thinking, This is only temporary, I telephoned my agent, who'd been trying to contact me about a movie to begin shooting immediately in England. In a Calcutta hotel room I read the script, dawdled awhile, then phoned my assent, knowing that with this job, a busy and protected life would take shape around me, albeit temporarily, and this time it would be in London.

Chapter Seven

The movie was *Secret Ceremony*, directed by Joseph Losey. Elizabeth Taylor and I were set to play a delusional mother and daughter, and my father's old pal, Robert Mitchum, was cast as my father. Peggy Ashcroft and Pamela Brown played the batty aunts. The movie people dyed my hair soot black, hoping to create any slight resemblance between myself and ravishing, raven-haired Elizabeth Taylor. When that failed to do it, I wore a long dark wig.

Frank, who was in Miami, had invited me to stay in the vacant flat in Grosvenor Square. The idea made sense, and was appealing because I imagined I'd feel less cut off from him. But in fact, staying in the apartment where we had lived as newlyweds returned me to Frank's world, and I began to miss him even more acutely.

I had been in London for nearly two weeks but we had not yet begun filming. I couldn't sleep at night despite the prescription sleeping pills and I spent my days in bed. Although I

often felt claustrophobic, I couldn't bring myself to go outside. The plump English doctor gave me stronger pills. The
disorder in my mind, and mounting depression, reached a
crescendo, and finally that same doctor was standing beside
my bed asking what "a rolling stone gathers no moss"
meant. When I had no reply, he checked me into a clinic. I
spent three days there, heavily medicated, before Barbara
arranged my escape: I pulled my coat off the wire hanger,
slipped into my shoes, and as a nurse dropped her trayful
of tea, we climbed out the window and down the fire escape.

"If you kill yourself," said Barbara, "I'll never forgive
you."

Within hours, I was in Miami. It was a hot and humid
night as the taxi drew up to the Fontainebleau Hotel. A
giant sign said FRANK SINATRA in lights, and all the way out
on the driveway I could hear the band playing, "It's my
kind of town, Chicago is . . ." He was standing in that
familiar smoky light with his tuxedo and microphone and
hair and black tie.

Through a restless night we dredged up our regrets and
loosed them on each other. The old dreams roused themselves too, and choked the sky with their changing forms.
By morning we had spent everything, and we fastened ourselves together with shaking promises.

The next day or the day after, I went back to London. We
agreed we'd finish our respective movies. Then we would
see. I moved out of the London flat and into a rented
cottage in the country, near George and Ringo. Frank and I
spoke regularly on the phone, and we wrote to each other,
and I turned my attention to work.

The mere presence of Elizabeth Taylor and Richard Burton in London was creating a stir. In a studio adjoining
ours, Richard Burton was making *Where Eagles Dare*, and the

two companies had synchronized the couple's schedules. They were living in a sizable section of the Dorchester Hotel, while Elizabeth's numerous little dogs, who were not permitted to enter the country because of quarantine laws, could be visited on the Burtons' yacht, moored in the Thames for that purpose.

Workday lunches with the Burtons took place in a restaurant near the studios and generally lasted about two hours. Without fail, Elizabeth saw to it that I was invited to lunch and any other event she thought I might enjoy. "I feel protective of you," she recently told me. "I always have."

I was night-shooting the week my mother came to visit me in the country cottage. So I wasn't there when two men came and broke our windows, and turned the house inside out. They tied up my mother, and pulled the rings off her fingers, even the engagement ring from my father that she never took off. The next day I took her to Cartier, and while she cried I bought her a new ring. It had been my ring the thieves were really searching for, the diamond engagement ring Frank had given me; and my mother hadn't known it was right there, in the case with my glasses. Soon after, I sold it and the diamond koala bear and the rest of the jewelry and gave the money away.

Secret Ceremony also took us to Holland, where we filmed in an immense, decaying seaside hotel. In the off-hours I rode horseback on the beach, and Bob Mitchum wrote beautiful little poems on shreds of paper. Every evening we all gathered in the lounge where Richard Burton recited his many favorite verses in a golden voice. As he drank, he became more and more disrespectful toward his wife. But Elizabeth always held her own, and even when he turned mean, she was so good-natured that she kept the rest of us laughing. At the start I was in awe of Elizabeth—I'd seen every film she'd made since *National Velvet.* Now, working with her, I experienced her legendary loyalty, her generosity, and her down-to-earth humor. Bob, Elizabeth, Joe, and I became friends and shared good times, and in the process I grew stronger.

My friendship with Joe Losey continued through the years; he was the most tortured man I'd ever met, and one of the most sensitive. After we finished *Secret Ceremony*, I reconnected with my old friends: Maria Roach, Dalí, Ruth, Liza, Lenny Gershe, and Yul. After a few months, although I loved Frank no less, I began to believe that we should not be looking for a future together.

I wish I could tell my children that throughout the sixties I was busy fighting bigotry, but it wouldn't be true. Events in Montgomery, Birmingham, and Jackson were a long way from Beverly Hills. My all-white consciousness began to awaken after I read *Letter from the Birmingham Jail*, Rev. Martin Luther King Jr.'s eloquent expression of his moral philosophy. Dr. King's dream and the civil rights struggle roused my own slumbering social conscience.

During the summer of 1968, while I was filming *Secret Ceremony* in London, *Rosemary's Baby* was released and became the number one movie in the country. Its success, and my own too, were abstractions that translated into surprisingly little satisfaction.

I managed to dodge my divorce from Frank until August 1968; after I returned to California, his people arranged for the proceedings in Mexico—I don't know why. On the morning of the seventeenth, Mickey Rudin and I were the only passengers aboard the Learjet. I sat as far away from him as the compact plane would permit, but when our eyes met by chance, I smiled so as not to hurt his feelings. He shuffled through papers or lay, moist and heavy in his seat, with his tie loosened and his eyes closed. I fiddled with a large hole in one of my sleeves. The sun and salty sea of Goa had faded the once-yellow cotton shirt to a wheat color. My worn-out sandals had taken me clear across India and through the damp months in England. But shopping never got any easier, and I wore a thing until it was in tatters. It crossed my mind that maybe people got dressed up for divorces—I didn't know.

At the Juárez airport, a fast-talking little man in tinted glasses and a shiny suit sprang out at us. After flinging a perfunctory nod in my direction, he then referred exclusively to Mr. Rudin.

As if it were an emergency divorce, we flew into town and came screeching to a halt in front of a nondescript office building. From the paparazzi outside I could tell this was the place. Once inside I asked, Where's the bathroom? and I threw up. I was then taken to a fair-sized room crammed to the ceiling with the press and their artillery. A well-lit desk held center stage as if sitting, illogically, in a boxing ring. I was cowering, backing up, even as someone pushed me into the room toward the desk. For scariest occasions I don't wear my glasses; now I also flipped my eyes out of focus. Fuzzy cartoon papers materialized on the table in front of me. A pen leaped into my hand. The walls were a tangle of metal, glass, lights and flesh that whirred, clicked, flashed, and hurled bold questions in foreign languages. The floor shook so badly I could barely form a signature.

And that, more or less, was that. The day had the hurried, rancid flavor of a backstreet abortion or a high-stakes cockfight, and it left an imprint of deep personal shame. Apart from the bathroom request, I don't think I said anything at all on the Juárez trip. Mr. Rudin didn't try to talk either. The last time I laid eyes on him we were reentering L.A. from the airport. By then he was chatting a blue streak to the driver: traffic was bad, practically at a standstill (*galloping hooves, the rush of wings*). On the freeway, I stepped out of the car, closed the door politely behind me, and hitched a ride to Frank's.

By the time I got there Mr. Rudin had called and put a

negative spin on how I had gotten out on the freeway and disappeared into some stranger's car. Frank was so mad he seemed to have forgotten all about the divorce, so finally I said, Well, we're not married anymore, so I guess I can hitchhike if I want; which calmed him down and after a while everything was okay. Still, I was careful not to stay too long.

I was living, for the moment, in the crumbling, single-room coffeehouse formerly occupied by my brother Patrick and his family. My encyclopedias were stacked in boxes on the wooden floor and covered with a madras bedspread to make a table. Like the beach cabin of my early summers, this house too was on a cliff and it faced the sea.

Again I was without moorings in an unfamiliar world, but by then unfamiliarity had itself become the familiar, and the late sixties was unlike any other time. In the inflamed idealism of my generation, things almost made sense —pieces came together to form one vaguely comprehensible whole, and in response to it, fragments of myself were drawn together too, and the heavy numbness began to lift. Light and feeling flooded the dormant parts as they struggled to become one.

This new me celebrated spring and sought the center of each moment. I marched against the war in Vietnam, and sang new songs, and went wherever anyone was kind enough to invite me. Along the way I met writers, artists, rock stars, movie stars, revolutionaries, folksingers, and regular folks. I saw them all as teachers who awakened a vision of countless thousands of golden threads streaming, spinning, weaving through time and space, connecting all of humanity, creating a shimmering cloth, a fragment of Being, through which we could transcend our separate selves to touch an infinite whole.

If at times I was restless or lonely, I would also have said, without knowing why, that these were among the most important days of my life. Sounds of Joni Mitchell, Judy Collins, the Mamas and the Papas, the Beatles, Bob Dylan, and Leonard Cohen floated over the Malibu cliffs and mingled with wind chimes, and scents of sandalwood and marijuana. But when the people left and I was alone, my music was Mozart and Bach, Beethoven and Mahler, especially the slow movements. In Mozart I found all the perfection and purity I ever hoped existed.

With Roman Polanski and Sharon I went to Joshua Tree in the desert, to Big Sur on the northern coast, Paris, London, New York, Texas, and Acapulco. In Switzerland I visited with Yul and his family, and, with my first boyfriend after Frank, I explored Rome, Florence, and Naples.

When a random turn or two brought me more than once to the edge, I did not topple into the tangled mysteries below. But on that glassy threshold, the great strengths of my life pressed themselves into being—my illusive tools for survival, gifts from some primeval ancestor, passed in secret along the chain of my forebears. In the end, mine is a navigator's sense of place and the strength again to hoist the sails, the will again to catch the winds; and even when the land and all I ever loved are lost to me, and the stars are shrouded, and I am sore with losses, and afraid—even then, the miracles all around will leap to celebrate themselves, and I will celebrate them too. And even then, I'll trust that a new shore will rise to meet me, and there, in that new place, I will find new things to care about.

Martha's Vineyard had been a scene of my nightmares ever since "the boat trip," as Frank Sinatra always called it. But the Kanins loved the island and they were sure I would love it too. So when the time came for their annual fall visit, they were adamant that I come along. I woke up so hungover after a party in Malibu, where I was living, that I almost missed our flight. For all her moxie, Ruth Gordon had to be the most skittish passenger on the airplane that day. I nursed my hangover as she clamped my arm painfully through the takeoff, turbulence, and landing in Boston.

At Logan Airport, an unimposing, white-mustached figure in a rumpled, blue-and-white striped seersucker suit bounded toward us with his arms outstretched. Nearly concealed behind the ample shape of Thornton Wilder hurried his diminutive sister, Isabel, pressing a little straw hat into her brown curls. To spare Ruth a second plane trip, the Wilders were going to drive and ferry us to Martha's Vineyard. Isabel peered resolutely over the enormous steering wheel as she chattered away, bringing to mind a Disney chipmunk.

The four old friends shared a long and impressive history. Their pooled ingredients and delight in one other's company made a treat of the journey, which included a side trip to Quincy, where Ruth had spent her childhood, a lobster supper overlooking the harbor at Woods Hole, and the ferry ride across, in a wind of crying gulls, to the Vineyard. Inside the warm circle that seemed to hold them and now me so securely, their talk was of local characters, lobsters, and berry bushes; theater, from Sophocles to Strindberg, the Broadway they'd loved and contributed to for forty years, roles I ought to play, and the merits of Shaw's *St. Joan* versus that of Anouilh; Thornton's winter visits to Vienna and Paris, Brecht, "dear Gertrude" (he meant Stein), and a recent, remarkable production of *The Ring*. Thornton told a story that still had the power to amuse all four, of Sigmund Freud's efforts to persuade young Thornton to marry his daughter, Anna.

Clearly, Dr. Freud was wasting his breath: I quickly realized that Thornton Wilder did things his own way. When the Kanins launched into a heartfelt lecture on the lunacy of their seventy-year-old pal driving around in a rattletrap relic of a Pontiac, and his insistence on picking up any hitchhikers along the way, Thornton ignored them cheerfully, and pointedly changed the subject, while behind the big wheel, little Isabel shook her curls and sighed loudly, Dear, dear, dear.

Nonetheless, when confronted with something she did not know, Ruth always said, "I'll look it up in Thornton," for there was little to which Thornton Wilder had not given thought. He was a talker, and his words tumbled out like fast-popping corn. But equally, he was a listener: genuinely interested, enthusiastic, insightful, frank, affectionate, and wise. I was instantly nuts about him, and before the week was over he was referring to himself as "your Uncle Thornton," and "your old Thornyberry."

We spent the next day, a crisp autumn spectacular, poking around the island. By five or six that afternoon, although the average age of my companions must have been seventy, no one felt the least bit tired. Rather, it seemed we were under a spell when we left the paved road to follow a dirt track through dense pines and dappled emerald light, until the woods abruptly broke open onto a lake that wrapped widely around us on three sides. At the end of the track, on the point where we stood, a single, gray-shingled cottage was shuttered tightly against the silver stillness. A mile or so up the left shore, the sea danced in the day's last, low light. To our right, ducks bobbed obliviously in a sandy cove where pines and beach plums cast perfect, fringed reflections. No breeze stirred the branches. Even Isabel fell silent.

"Imagine!" I cried. "Who could possibly live here?" It happened that nobody lived there. The place had been built by an Edgartown bishop as a summer cabin for his children, who had long ago grown up and left the island.

Two months later, while north winds clawed the frozen lake, shivering the pines, I stamped the snow off my shoes, turned the key in the stiff lock, and with a carton of ency-

clopedias heavy in my arms, I stepped into my Wooden
House on Lake Tashmoo.

My brother Patrick and his wife Susan, pregnant with
their second daughter, were moving in with me, an arrangement we hoped would be mutually beneficial. Following
three-year-old Justine as she raced through the icy rooms,
we got our first look inside the house. Only then, hearing
the wind squeeze angrily through cracks in the pine walls,
did we realize that the cabin had neither heat nor insulation. We lit a fire and spent those first winter weeks in our
California coats, stapling bags of insulation onto the walls
and ceiling. At night I lay in my new Sears bed, studying
the enigmatic inscription on each insulation bag, "CERTAIN
TEED SAINT GOBAIN," and I felt at peace with life's mysteries
and grateful to have finally found my home.

That winter I returned to New York to film *John and Mary*.
Despite my admiration for Dustin Hoffman, the project
turned out not to be a particularly rewarding one for me
artistically, but the Wooden House on Martha's Vineyard
was everything I'd hoped for, and more.

What I recall most about the making of that film was
that during it a relationship was forming, via telephone,
with André Previn. We had had mutual friends in California and I'd seen him there occasionally, along with his wife.
But when we bumped into each other by chance at a party
in London, circumstances had changed: I was no longer
with Frank, and he was, for the most part, living and working there, as conductor of the London Symphony Orchestra. When he visited New York I introduced him to Dalí,
but my unpredictable old friend didn't like André, and André didn't much care for him either. On all matters, including this one, I sought Dalí's approval. Nonetheless, the
minute *John and Mary* was completed, I joined André in Ireland, where he had rented a cottage in the hills near

Clifden; he had wanted to take me on a holiday, and I suggested Ireland, since I hadn't been there in eight years.

It was the first time we had spent more than a couple of days together and he was wonderful. A raconteur second to none, he had, it seemed, read every book ever written. He loved modern art, which I knew nothing about, he was a jazz pianist and a classical pianist, a composer and a conductor. André was so quick, he arrived before he even left. And he was more interested in me than anyone had been in my life. I kept thinking how much my father would have liked and enjoyed him. In the west of Ireland we walked along country lanes and across damp fields, and we took a trawler to the Aran Islands. Within two purely delightful weeks he had ruined his shiny, pointed green shoes, but we were making plans for a lifetime.

I had returned to Martha's Vineyard, and André was back in London, when I discovered I was pregnant. I'd always imagined I wouldn't be able to have babies——that to hatch an actual child inside the body I had closely observed throughout my life would surely be beyond my powers of will and personal magic.

"I hear you knocked up my sister," said my brother to the telephone. André was calling from England.

"Get out. Out!" I chased him out the door. And the phone said, How terrific, I will love you more than ever, more than anyone ever and forever. And hearing that, I loved him too, even though I barely knew him.

As a kid, I feel I threw up my fair share; still, nothing prepared me for the great throwing up of that pregnancy. What I remember most vividly about that time is hanging over a toilet watching the watery remnants of a Ritz cracker swirl into the vortex.

It was also during those months that Sharon Tate, eight and a half months pregnant and as pure and sweet a human being as I have ever known, was murdered by strangers. "Why?" Roman kept asking as we walked around and around Elaine's restaurant.

Months before it made sense I bought tiny clothes, read and reread every book available on pregnancy, childbirth, breast-feeding, and babies. I memorized Dr. Spock, ate chocolate, and named and renamed the baby. All this time André was in England, and since our two weeks in Ireland, I had scarcely seen him. I was lonely and I began keeping a journal.

September 4, 1969
Martha's Vineyard

To My Child,

It is late at night and I am in bed, in my little pine house at the edge of the woods, on Lake Tashmoo. My brother Patrick and his wife Susan and their two daughters are asleep in another part of the house. Foghorns roll through silence. Your father is working in England. We are in the midst of *such joy* because you are coming. You are only three months along—just a little firm bulge, but already I love you. I think of you all day and eat healthy foods and I have stopped smoking, and with all my heart I hope there will someday be for you a world of peace and understanding.

October 12, 1969

André is doing concerts all over the world. He writes almost every day, and it's wonderful that he calls so often, but I wish I could share this time with him, and all these new feelings and thoughts . . .

October 19, 1969

Twins! I can scarcely get my mind around it
—when they told me, I had to sit down! Already I look like Tweedledum, and there are five
more months to go. I'm glad it's twins and not
—I don't know, a seal, or several very large
mangoes. With Susan's help I made a beautiful
patchwork quilt, and now *two* little crib-sized
ones. André calls every day from London but I
wish he could be here. I'm reading Jane Austen,
which is *perfection*. I dream of babies, and count
the days till I can hold them . . .

November 28, 1969

André says that once he is established as a
conductor, he won't have to travel so much. But,
obviously, if we are to have a life together, I will
have to move to England; that, after all, is where
his orchestra is. The thought of leaving the
Wooden House is more upsetting than it ought
to be.

André bought a house for us in Surrey. I
haven't seen it, of course, although in the picture
it looks pretty. He is so excited. At this point
how can I say, I wish I could have helped to
pick out the house; or, I was hoping it would be
near water, even a trickle of a stream; or, This
house here on the Vineyard means so much to
me, I don't know how I will leave it.

I try to tell him everything, but maybe the
phone is the reason I don't seem to be able to
convey it as clearly as I feel it. Or maybe he isn't
quite listening, or perhaps my hormones are
clouding my perspective and I have no real point
to make, or I've just been by myself too long
with no one to talk to. This is ABSURD. I love

him, I miss him, and I want to be with him, and
he said we could come back to the Vineyard
every summer. So after Xmas I'll move to London and have the babies there. *Of course the house
doesn't matter.* What's *wrong* with me? We will be
happy together.

January 4, 1970
London

I am in the flat André rented on Eaton
Square. It is full of somebody else's ugly stuff.
Even though the place is suffocatingly over-
heated, I put my patchwork quilt on the bed to
make myself feel better. It looks beautiful and
out of place. André is on a U.S. tour. A live-in
housekeeper, Rossario, came with the flat. She
scares me.

I stay in the bedroom anyway. The doctor
says I have to be in bed until the babies arrive,
and if they haven't come by February 26, he's
going to induce them a month early: by then
they will be big enough, he says—and so will I.
I WEIGH A HUNDRED AND TWENTY-SIX POUNDS.

January 6, 1970

We had hoped to be married by Christmas,
but André's wife, Dory, doesn't want a divorce,
which I completely understand, most of the
time. But still—a real wedding on the Vineyard,
by the edge of the lake, with all my brothers and
sisters, my friends and my mother, that was the
dream. I even got a burgundy velvet-and-lace
dress that accommodates my stomach. But I
shouldn't complain about *anything.* André and I
are happy, and we *feel* married, and someday we
will be. Nothing else matters.

January 10, 1970

The time is passing unbelievably slowly. I am so huge that hardly anything is worth getting up for. André had to take his orchestra on tour for three weeks. Like all his dates, this one was fixed years ago, so he had to go. But it's hard here without him. I feel so out of context. Rossario is a powerful presence. But A's letters are everything, and the thought that he will be back for the babies' birth. Then we will begin the rest of our lives.

January 12, 1970

Barbara arrived from L.A. in a wacky orange hat with big holes in it. I feel *much* better, even Rossario seems less intimidating now. What a good and funny and comforting soul Barbara is. Nothing ever seems to scare her or get her down. I want to be like that. How does she do it?

The new house in Surrey becomes ours on the sixteenth. On that day Barbara and I will pounce on it and try to make it livable in time for the babies' arrival. I shouldn't have worried about not liking the house, it needs some fixing up inside—bathrooms, etc., and we don't have *any* furniture, but it will be wonderful. It's on fifteen acres of woodland, and there are hundreds of oak trees, and it's at the edge of the Ashdown Forest, which is owned by the Queen, so no one can ever spoil it.

February 4, 1970

Barbara has organized everything. Painters are at work on the house and someone is making curtains, and carpenters are putting in book-

shelves. André has lots of paintings, which are
still with Dory. He says he's going to put paintings on "every square inch" of the walls.

February 20, 1970

The English press are the pits. People are
camped outside the flat. I feel depleted and
trapped. I dream of babies and wait. André is
back, but he works eighteen hours a day, and
when he isn't actually conducting, he's studying
scores into the night. So I hardly see him. Sometimes when he walks through the door, I feel I
don't know him at all, which is scary. Our time
together in Ireland seems so long ago.

When he was fifteen, André was accompanying Frank
Sinatra on the piano, and already on his way to becoming a
respected, much-recorded jazz pianist. That was about the
time he began working at MGM. It didn't take him long to
become a successful movie composer—his arrangements for
Porgy and Bess, Irma La Douce, Gigi, and *My Fair Lady* earned
him Academy Awards. Then, at thirty-nine, André confounded everyone: turning his back on Hollywood, he set
his sights on becoming a world-class orchestral conductor
—a formidable challenge, even for André Previn. And it
was at this transitional point in his life that our paths con-
verged. Now, when he was not rehearsing or practicing piano, or appearing on his own television show, or giving
concerts or touring the world, André was poring over
scores, keeping a step ahead of the massive repertoire.

I understood some of the challenges he had before him,
but I had no concept, nor am I even certain that André
himself knew, how completely consuming his professional
life would continue to be. Of his marriages I knew little,
only what he told me—there were two young daughters,

Alicia and Claudia, from his first marriage to a singer, Betty Bennett, and none from his second marriage to Dory, a songwriter. He had conducted a discreet, separate life for some years, but did not seek a divorce until he met me. Dory Previn experienced things quite differently, and made that clear publicly through her songs. I am sorry to have contributed to her pain.

On the day my twins were born, I got up before dawn, showered, put on just a touch of mascara, and sat on the end of the bed to wait. That's how little I understood of what lay ahead. I remember every detail—a day like this is lifted from the rest; it stands alone, etched in light. My suitcase had been packed for weeks, each tiny nightgown and blanket washed and neatly folded inside a plastic bag. What slipped my mind was that things so eagerly awaited almost always come with a hitch.

It was obvious almost immediately that inducing labor had been a terrible idea. "Never mind," I yelled, "I'll come back another time," as I tore at the IV, and tried to haul myself off the delivery table. But they fought me back down. "She looks like a child," observed a nurse, as if she were watching the news, while I moaned and raged, huge on the operating table. Eight hours later someone was slapping me into consciousness, pushing a tiny, furious baby in my face. By then I was beyond caring.

"I think she's had enough," I heard the doctor say, before dispatching me into darkness, but raised voices found me there, and before I woke I was sure that the second baby would be dead.

When the doctor leaned over the operating table to say he was just leaving for a couple of weeks, golf, I think he said, in Scotland, I said, Thank you, and I sincerely hoped he would have a terrible vacation.

I was blinking into André's face, trying to hold it in place as he was telling me, It's two boys, we have two sons, with no mention of a dead one.

By the time they wheeled me in to see the babies it was the middle of the night, and the nursery lights were dimmed. It would have been quiet except for one infant over in the corner under the bright light, screaming bloody murder. André pointed to a nice-looking baby and said it was mine. I stared. My sleeping son. He didn't look familiar. They were already pushing me toward the corner—toward the noisy baby with the reddish purple blotches on his face. They didn't need to tell me he was mine.

"Why does he look like that?" I asked. "What happened to him?"

"Nothing, dear," said the nurse with the chipper voice. "He wasn't breathing on his own at first, so he just needed a bit of help. The doctor had to breathe into him and his face got a bit bruised, that's all. He's fine."

"How long?" I asked. "For how long didn't he breathe?"

"It was . . . let's see . . ." She found it on the chart. "Nine minutes."

We had to stay in the clinic for ten days. The babies weighed five pounds, fifteen ounces each, that's about the size of a shoe box. All of it, the whole thing, was immense, overwhelming. Two small strangers, and a large one, had suddenly claimed one hundred percent of my life.

When the twins were a few weeks old we moved out to the country, to the house we called The Haven. I banished from my mind the first feelings of disappointment that it was right on the road and without so much as a fish pond. After all, it was lovely, a seventeenth-century tavern with half-moons carved out of the door frames where the barrels had been carried through, and there were beamed ceilings and beautiful, creaky floors and fireplaces you could sit in, and the woods were magnificent, giant oaks by the thousands, and the bluebells were already coming into bloom.

> April 7, 1970
> The Haven

I've just fed the babies. As I write, André is practicing the piano—Mozart—for next month's concert. It's great to have him home. Spring has arrived—is it always so glorious? The daffodils are out and a million new living things. Deer come right up to the house. The horse in our neighbor's field is very pregnant and looks happy, I remember the feeling. Our own babies are a daily wonder, each fiercely intense, each quite different.

> June 1970

I miss André. But I can't take the babies on tour with him the way we planned. And I won't leave them. They're tiny and they cry easily and they're up most of the night. I'm exhausted all the time. It doesn't help that I'm anemic. Having twins is no joke when your starting weight is ninety-two pounds. Barbara is living in London, but she comes here almost every day. There are still a million details to finish up on the house, she deals with the carpenters, plumber, electrician—she keeps everything going.

> June 1970

André says Barbara has to go. It's awful. She's been with me since I was nineteen. Through *everything!* He says it's unhealthy for me to be so dependent on her—he says I don't know how to do anything. Which I guess is true, but I don't want her to leave.

June 1970

Every week I dress up the babies and take lots of pictures that I send, along with a detailed account of the many good things in my life, to my family, and to my friends Yul, Liza, and the Kanins, Lenny, Maria, Thornton, and Nancy [Sinatra]. *I send no pictures to Dalí.* He thinks the proportions of babies are grotesque, and he still insists on referring to the twins as "embryos."

The nanny and a chirpy New Zealand couple live in a separate wing of the house. All of them have false teeth. I keep to myself.

September 1970

We were married in a Unitarian church. I didn't want our wedding to be in an office. Mom was there, and Steffi and her husband Jim and André's mother, no one else. André has a beard.

September 1970

All year we had been planning and looking forward to André's two weeks off. We rented a VW bus and drove through Scotland, just stopping wherever and whenever we wanted, sleeping in the bus. It was cold, especially in the early mornings, but Scotland is beautiful in its bleak way, and a place we both wanted to see. It was a swell time. It's the first time I've been apart from baby Sascha, but he gets upset easily, he doesn't like strangers, or having his routine disrupted, so we brought only Matthew—what a serious, dignified little citizen he is. He has an unblinking, most unbaby-like intensity. I think one day he'll be a judge. Or a customs inspector.

Except for André's concerts in London, I didn't go anywhere. I didn't even drive in England. André had a driver. I missed Barbara.

We'd made a couple of friends; the Kanins introduced us by letter to Joan Plowright and Laurence Olivier, who lived in Brighton, about forty minutes away. They were excellent company, and they had young children, so we were encouraged to bring our babies along in their baskets when we went to dinner. When the Oliviers came to our house we had chicken because it was what I could cook. Invariably Larry told his chicken-carving story: how his father, the parson, "could carve a chicken to feed twenty people." Larry always did the carving.

With the Oliviers we went to dinner at 10 Downing Street. It was a stiff crowd—except for us and Leonard Bernstein, with whom I had a depressing conversation about the death of symphonic music and civilization in general. Larry, sitting next to me, was Lord Olivier from the moment he arrived. At the dinner table the Queen Mother was on his other side. She asked me about the babies and I said they were fine, thank you, and then, because of the silence, I asked, What, in your view, is the most important thing I can teach them?

"Let me think for a moment." Her Highness looked thoughtful.

"Ma'am, I think Mia means—" Larry interjected, flashing a look that jogged a vague recollection that you're not supposed to ask queens questions.

"I *know* what she means. I'm just thinking—" She cut him dead. Then, with her eyes shining, she said beautifully, "I think it's . . . *manners.*"

"Really?" I squeaked. "You *think?*"

"Yes," she said decisively. "I believe that manners can get you through *anything.*"

November 27, 1970

The doctors have said that one of the babies has "autistic tendencies." He is nine months old and has never looked at me, not even once. He sometimes screams for fifteen hours at a stretch, as if electric shocks are going through him. Nothing seems to reach him. I can't comfort him. I can't get through to him. By the time he was two months old I knew there was a problem, but the doctors wouldn't listen. I was just a young, inexperienced mother, so they tried to convince me I was imagining it, or even that I might be *causing* the problem by being worried. But now that he is nine months old, it is obvious even to them. At Great Ormond Street Children's Hospital they did frightening tests, injecting dye into his brain. At least now, with a diagnosis, maybe someone will help.

December 1970

It turns out nobody knows a thing about autism. There is no treatment. No advice. They just prescribe tranquilizers for me and for the baby (for whom they had the reverse effect), and they have given me the name of a residential school I can contact when he is five. If I wait that long I will surely never reach him.

February 1971

I found a doctor, *finally*—Dr. E. at the Anna Freud Clinic in London—who says he will try to help. He is American. I am hopeful.

May 1971

For thirteen Saturdays I have picked up Dr.
E. at the Reigate train station and have taken
him to our house, where he watches the baby for
two hours, takes copious notes, eats the cheese
sandwiches I make, and says next to nothing. He
is polite, but in my hardly expert opinion, he
seems not entirely human. Certainly he is not
any help. I'm wondering if we are part of some
sort of research that he or the Freud Clinic is
involved in.

May 1971

Today when my mother came to visit, the
baby looked at her! For not quite three seconds.
We jumped up and down.

I barely slept that night from excitement, and trying to
devise a plan. But had it been a fluke? Would it ever happen
again? It was so fleeting, we could have imagined it, from
wishing so hard. But if it *did* happen—why, when he has
avoided eye contact with all of us for fifteen months? What
was different about my mother? The only thing I could
come up with was her bright pink lipstick.

The next day I took the baby to a damp, monk-bare
room upstairs in our chilly thatched guest cottage. My
mother's lipstick was smeared on my lips, as bold as pink
could ever be, but his faraway eyes floated over to the sunlit
window.

So I bought big sheets of white poster board that I
tacked over the windows. Then I, pink-mouthed, babbled
into my son's wandering face . . . and he looked! For the
first time in his life, he looked at me—at my bright pink
lips.

In the white room, over weeks and months, buoyed by
minuscule but ongoing successes, I tried whatever entered

my mind to catch his eye and hold it; I bought lipstick and
eye shadow in every color, I painted dots, stripes, patterns,
all over my face, I covered it with tin foil, then with Saran
Wrap, I blew smoke out of my mouth, blew bubble-gum
bubbles, crinkled cellophane between my teeth, ate carrots,
potato chips, I wore gloves, I lugged in pots of water to
splash in, I sang, whistled, tickled, and clucked. I had seen
my baby son smile at crinkling cellophane, and at the
crunch of autumn leaves underfoot. Finally, now, he smiled
at me.

October 1971

WE PLAYED PEEKABOO!

During the second year of my marriage to André, if you
connected all the days he wasn't somewhere else, we spent a
total of fifteen days together. It was not an atypical year.
Whatever strength or confidence the early bloom of our
relationship had lent me began to evaporate in the isolation
of the drafty Surrey house. The pregnancy and the birth of
the twins had left me with a fatigue I couldn't shake.
Worry over the baby, and day-to-day life without a soul to
talk to, in the expanding space of André's absences,
amassed into wordless, familiar loneliness.

But I was absorbed with my children and they brought
pure delight to each day. I don't know whether I missed
acting or not, for there was another unexpected factor: piece
by piece, comment by comment, over the first year of our
relationship, I had assembled the dimensions of André's
contempt for the movie industry and anyone connected
with it. Given the fact that I had had a father who had
"never seen a happy actress," and a first husband whom I'd
lost partly because of my determination to work, I feared
anything that might jeopardize my marriage to André. We
agreed then that I would accept a movie if it permitted me

to come home every night—home to The Haven in Surrey, England.

Sometimes, when I felt homesick for the Vineyard, I would call the Wooden House, and listen to the phone ringing through the rooms; I imagined the mice scurrying and the sound touching the furniture, books, the lamp with the painted-glass shade, all my things, just as I had left them, in the stillness, with the ringing phone. It was the next best thing to being there.

Through it all, Nancy Sinatra remained close, and Frank and I stayed in touch too, although our contact was less frequent now. Sometimes I missed him more than was appropriate, which André knew, because I told him everything.

But the good times were still good. I loved going to André's concerts, and the music became important to me. I took pride in my postconcert tasks of packing my husband's drenched white tie, the cummerbund, his ruffled nylon shirt and black tails in the navy garment bag, and laying the still-warm patent-leather pumps in their separate, soft brown sacks with the tube of batons at the bottom. André and I didn't ever fight, and our small sons were the light of our lives. We even hoped to expand our family.

In 1971 and 1972, in London's parks, I marched, pushing a twin stroller alongside Vanessa Redgrave, to protest U.S. military involvement in Southeast Asia. The senselessness of André and I having another baby when already there were so many children in the world needing homes was dramatically underlined by the war, as it stretched on interminably. Every morning's newspaper brought fresh documentation of human suffering. It was in this climate that we decided to adopt a Vietnamese war orphan.

Two years of delays, disappointments, and frustration followed, but led us finally, in May 1973, to an airport hotel in Paris, where André and I toasted our *three* children in a champagne supper, and through a sleepless night we held hands and watched the skies, waiting for our baby daughter, due at dawn.

By the time the plane from Saigon landed it was nearly noon. André and I stood by the entrance to the terminal dizzily searching the weary passengers as they trudged past, some holding babies. Countless, countless times I had studied the tiny black-and-white photo we had been sent from the orphanage, but *which* baby was ours? An airport official advised us to sit down, the orphans from Vietnam were not among the other passengers, they would be brought from the plane in a special minibus. We then sat, staring through the window, down the runway at the airplane in the distance. After what seemed an eternity, we saw the minibus slowly approaching.

More than a dozen men and women wearing medical coats came through the terminal doors, each carrying a child. Last to enter was a small gray-haired woman. Smiling, she walked toward us and placed in my waiting arms a little plastic baby seat; way down at the bottom, not a third of the way up, enormous, shining black eyes peered with interest into my flowing ones. The woman handed me a nearly empty bottle and a Vietnamese passport and then disappeared into the crowd.

We brought our daughter home—home to The Haven, where her brothers, now three and a half years old, were waiting excitedly. At three months, Lark Song weighed only five pounds. She was asthmatic, and already the fragile survivor of two bouts of pneumonia. She was the most exquisite little girl we had ever seen.

Lark's adoption also brought home an awareness of the desperate conditions of the orphanages in Vietnam. I learned the facts and got hold of photographs. I contacted anyone I ever knew even remotely and sent them the information along with lists of items the orphanages needed so desperately. Everyone, I assumed, could send *something*. And they did. To my surprise companies responded too—with disposable diapers, baby formula, and vaccines; Air France even transported everything to Saigon for free. The president of Fisher-Price Toys, Mr. Henry Coords, agreed to sell us their almost indestructible toys at cost, and every toy we bought, he matched with another, and arranged for their shipment to Vietnam.

The Great Gatsby, filmed in England at Pinewood Studios, about two hours from The Haven, was one of the few acceptable projects. It was during this film that I became pregnant with our third son, Fletcher. Consequently, what I remember best about *Gatsby* are my earnest and mostly successful efforts not to throw up on Theoni Aldredge's gossamer costumes. I also remember the Watergate hearings, which riveted Bob Redford and me to the television set in his dressing room, and provided us all with an endlessly fascinating topic for discussion. Nor will I forget Bob's good heart, and the pleasure of his company.

Because my hair was short when we began shooting, I wore a wig in the film. The hairdresser had bleached it snow white the night before our first day's shooting, so it permanently felt and looked like cotton candy. Nobody else cared or even particularly agreed with me, so the bad wig stayed throughout the filming and, I felt, undermined "Daisy" as I had wanted her to appear.

Nor was producer David Merrick's presence on the set helpful, especially to Jack Clayton, who was best known for his sensitive small films. Ultimately, *The Great Gatsby* was a victim of overhype; the market was flooded with tie-in promotions, from Ballantine's scotch to "Gatsby cookware." This delicately balanced script was blown up into something it never was meant to be, and released as if it had been *Gone with the Wind.*

•   •   •

In the years between 1971 and 1977 I made several films, but my focus during those years in England was my family, and my primary work took place on the stage. Through J. M. Barrie's odd and intense *Mary Rose*, which I played in Manchester and London, I met the composer John Taverner, and found a lasting soul mate. García Lorca's *The House of Bernarda Alba* was an opportunity to explore as an actor, and its favorable reception gave me a fleeting boost in confidence professionally, but its most enduring benefit was my friendship with the play's translator, Tom Stoppard.

In September 1974, I was admitted into a London hospital with severe pain in my lower-right abdomen. The examining physician had diagnosed it as acute appendicitis and immediately scheduled an operation. I was nursing Fletcher, my six-month-old son, so I brought him with me to the hospital, expecting a stay of three or four days at most.

But things went another way. The surgeon came into the room looking important and distracted. He gave my stomach a little token push or two and concluded the problem was not my appendix but some other thing, "possibly a tubular infection." Whatever that may be, it was not the problem: my biggest problem turned out to be his misdiagnosis. A ruptured appendix had been the cause of the pain and fever, but they didn't discover that until the operation nine days later, by which time peritonitis had turned my guts to gum.

My baby was taken home around the time of the first surgery—I, who took the quickest baths in the Western Hemisphere so as not to leave him for long; I, who had never missed a night tucking my children into their beds or telling them a bedtime story; I, who planned to breast-feed the baby for as many years as he wanted; I, who, with my secret ration of personal magic and with all the powers of my will, could not turn this unthinkable progression of events around. The medications had "poisoned" my milk, they said, and anyway, by then I was too weak and in too much pain to even lift the baby. There was nothing I could do—I was losing ground, moving inexorably into a sphere where all thoughts, even that one, would be crushed from my mind, where there was only pain—pain to the farthest reaches of consciousness. No other self exists there. I *was* pain.

The morphine-heroin concoction they injected into the tops of my thighs at three-hour intervals didn't cover it—but more would kill me, they said, and gave no options. My mother flew in from New York and moved into the hospital. There were three major abdominal surgeries. Days and nights fused molten red. I was fed through a tube threaded up the vein in my arm, around my shoulder, and into the large artery near my heart. A half dozen other tubes streamed in and out of me.

There came a day, during the second month of my hospitalization, when I awakened into a zone of hyperawareness. The pain had receded somewhat and in its stead a curious lightheadedness was superseded by a sensation of tremendous acceleration—as if I were hurtling at top speed toward the shiny wall that came no closer than the foot of the bed. I could barely catch my breath—breathing became the task at hand. I was not afraid. Inside an exquisite clarity, it was very simple—no welcoming light, or waiting loved ones, no gathering of angels, just one breath. And not the next.

"What's going on?" André in the far far distance entered the room then slipped away. Simplicity and silence—then three, four shocks—people swarming, garbled talk, urgent and loud, but really it was my decision. I *willed* myself to take the breath. And the next . . .

Later the doctors said that was the day I almost died.

After eight weeks I left the hospital. I came home differ-

ent. It was hard to talk. I stuttered. Anyway, what was there
to say. Nothing seemed familiar. I couldn't remember what
foods I preferred, which colors I liked, or how I felt about
anything. I cried without knowing why. My mother, who
had never cooked in her life, astonished us both by making
sensational meals that she carried upstairs to my bed on a
tray. She stayed, taking care of me until I was well.

Although our nanny was wonderful, in my absence little
Fletcher, who was now eight months old, had withdrawn
into an infant depression. He slept fitfully or not at all, and
he would not take baby formula, but with his bottle of
apple juice he gathered into himself and rotted the first
baby teeth right out of his mouth. When I first came home,
the older children were overjoyed to see me—but Fletcher
would not even look at me those first days. And then he
could not let me out of his sight without coming undone,
until he was five or six years old.

I could not have known it then, but Tom Stoppard was
at the hospital nearly every day. He set up a work space in
the waiting room and told André to pay no attention to
him, he had plenty to do. But if André needed anything,
Tom was there. Tom is godfather to my second daughter,
Daisy.

In 1974, we had written to the director of the orphanage
in Vietnam, hoping to adopt another child. But then South
Vietnam was invaded by the North, and unforgettable images of panic and pandemonium were transmitted around
the world—the swarming Saigon airport, the evacuation
from the roof of the U.S. embassy, men dangling from
crowded helicopters, and the infamous crash of the "orphan
airlift" that killed seventy-eight children and seven adults on
takeoff.

In rural England, with the daffodils just coming into
bloom, I was watching all this on television when a telegram, impossibly, arrived from Saigon saying that a baby
girl had been chosen for us and put on the airlift—look for

her at Presidio Air Force Base in California. Her identification number was H-2. I phoned through the night trying to locate H-2 in the chaos of the base. I was also in continuous contact with Jacqueline and Yul Brynner in New York City. A baby for them had also survived the crash—a new sister for Rock, Victoria, and my namesake, "little Mia," who had arrived from Vietnam one year after Lark.

Under these dramatic circumstances I became the mother of a frail, seven-month-old, six-pound baby girl. At UCLA Medical Center we were told that she had suffered from malnutrition to such a degree that her liver was "palpable" and her intestinal lining had come away, distending her abdomen and making it impossible for her to digest normally: she was fed through tubes going into her temples. Even after her hospitalization she was too weak to hold up her head without support. Her scabby limbs fell like limp vines from my arms, and her cry was barely audible and without conviction. But she was luminously beautiful, and there was something in the quality of her gaze that let me know everything was going to be okay.

Within a year Daisy matched perfectly, both in size and abilities, her silver-haired, blue-eyed brother, Fletcher, who is six months older. The two became inseparable companions—my second set of twins. When they were about five years old, the pair came running, flushed and breathless, into my room. They had dressed themselves identically in blue mechanic suits, hand-me-downs from their older twin brothers, and they were wearing ski caps that covered their hair. Two radiant, gloriously different little faces declared ecstatically: "Look at us Mommy! *No one* can tell us apart. We even have the same number of pennies in our pockets!"

Between 1974 and 1977, I appeared in five plays—*The Three Sisters, A Midsummer Night's Dream, The Marrying of Ann Leete, The Zykovs* by Gorky, and Chekhov's *Ivanov;* the last three were with the Royal Shakespeare Company. It seemed that every night someone terrifying was in the audience—Paul Scofield, Laurence Olivier, Joan Plowright, Ian McKellen, Irene Worth, Peggy Ashcroft, Eileen Atkins, Vanessa Redgrave, John Gielgud, Ian Holm, Noël Coward. Before the curtain goes up, the evening ahead looms like Mount Everest, or as a series of hurdles, which, when it is going well, you soar over effortlessly: emotions, thoughts, and words come spontaneously, and everything feels true, real. When it goes badly you feel leaden, false, uninspired, and wretched.

By 1976 André and I had gone through our jagged patches but we supposed they were behind us—that we had really settled in for the long haul. Our five children generated such radiance within our home, surely it would be shielded from harm. We decided to adopt another daughter, and this time our request was for an older child, because we were aware how very difficult it was to find families for children past infancy. Once again we waded through the daunting piles of paperwork, the months of interviews and home studies, and all the official back-and-forthing between our U.S. adoption agency, immigration officials in the United States, Great Britain, and Korea, and social welfare officials in Korea and England. Eventually we were approved, and a little girl abandoned that month in the streets of Seoul was assigned to us. Her precise age was not known, but estimated to be around five; there was no other history. She could not understand or speak enough to answer any questions. She did not even know her name. The orphanage named her Soon-Yi.

At that point we ran headlong into a federal law that limited to two the visas an American family could obtain for the purpose of adoption. We had our quota. Forget it, the agency told us: to change the law would require an act of Congress.

But we had already been sent a blurry black-and-white two-by-two-inch head shot of a child who looked neither happy nor sad, with a shaved head and sores on her lips. This was my daughter. She had already taken her place in my heart, and I would not walk away from her. I had Soon-Yi transferred to another orphanage, the best in Seoul, and I began making phone calls. My old friends, Bill and Rose Styron, sought the help of Massachusetts Congressman Michael Harrington, and he agreed to sponsor the bill that was necessary. More than a year went by with me relentlessly phoning people and Soon-Yi still in the orphanage. Finally, in 1977, Congress passed the bill. Soon-Yi could come home.

I didn't have to travel to Korea; the agency usually arranged for escorts to bring babies to their families. But Soon-Yi was not a baby, and I felt it was important to go there and bring her home myself—I wanted her to know me in advance of the long journey, I wanted to see the orphanage where she had spent more than a year, to meet her friends, and to take plenty of pictures for her scrapbook. I wanted to understand what little I could of her life there, with the hope that it would help us to build our relationship and make the transition easier for her. In my knapsack I brought two pretty little dresses and a pink candy-striped nightgown. Each was wrapped with the nicest paper I could find and tied with a pink ribbon.

When I arrived at the orphanage, a dozen or so little girls combed and clean were lined up on the pavement in front of the entrance. Standing behind the children was a nun who must have pushed Soon-Yi toward me. Out of respect, and not to frighten her, I knelt down, took her hand, and smiled. She left the orphanage without a sound or a backward glance. Only at the revolving door of the hotel did she stiffen. I carried her into the elevator and when it began to move, she threw up. This was my own child.

She seemed delighted with her presents and sat on the floor holding them for the longest time until it occurred to me that she didn't know about unwrapping and opening gifts, so I ripped a little corner to show her inside, but that upset her, so I waited awhile, then, careful not to rip the paper, I unstuck the tape and pulled out the candy-striped nightgown. Soon-Yi loved it. I held it up in front of her and carried her to see how good it looked in the mirror over the bathroom sink. Seeing the mirror, she jackknifed with a sound of pure fear and kicked it so hard we both fell backward nearly into the bathtub. On that day, it must have seemed that anything was possible—even a duplicate world where another strange-eyed, pale-haired woman was holding another terrified child who was holding another nightgown with pink candy stripes.

Soon-Yi didn't know about mirrors, or revolving doors, or carpets, or elevators, or ice, or eggs (I picked the shells out of her mouth), or grass, or flowers, or in fact most of the things the rest of us take for granted. Whatever caught her fancy—paper clips, peanuts, money, flowers, rubber bands, chewing-gum wrappers, Cheerios—she stashed in her underpants. And the only place she could fall asleep was on the floor next to my bed. When I went to Egypt to film exteriors for *Death on the Nile*, I brought the two children who were most dependent upon me, Fletcher and Soon-Yi.

It would be hard to come up with any better way to sail the Nile. I explored the temples and tombs with my incomparable companions Maggie Smith, David Niven, Peter Ustinov, Angela Lansbury, Jack Warden, and Jane Birkin. And Bette Davis and I found ourselves together once again, in another distant land, and this time I too was an actress. But by 1977 the long years of hard battle had taken their toll on Bette. Fragile and frightened in her hotel room in Aswan, wearing a lace nightcap (excessive wearing of wigs, she explained, had left her nearly bald), she sat in the big bed, surrounded by too many impractical-to-pack silver-framed photographs of her children and grandchildren. Obviously, her family was a great source of joy, but she was mordant about the rest of her life. When I asked if she had a boyfriend, she groaned, "Oh God, no! I'm through with all that."

Surprisingly and heartbreakingly insecure about her work, she fretted constantly about the job at hand. Always, she confided, she had depended upon strong directors: she desperately needed guidance. Gone was the indefatigable sightseer on whose enthusiasm two apathetic twelve-year-olds were propelled through countless museums, churches, and palaces across Spain. The beauty and mysteries of ancient Egypt held no interest for this Bette Davis, who did not leave her hotel room except to film her scenes.

"In my day we'd have built all this at the studio—and better!" she snapped, as we gazed across the Nile toward the Valley of the Kings. The magnificent structure that had been Bette Davis—the illusion of size and power she had projected so valiantly for so long—had imploded under the weight of her disappointment and honest fury.

Bette was not gentle in life, nor had life been gentle with Bette. After completing our film she was attacked by cancer, and then strokes that paralyzed half her face. But it was my old friend, her daughter BD, who dealt the most devastating blow in her book about her childhood.

By 1978, my marriage was beginning to come undone. It was no one's fault. We had spent too much time apart; by then we had different expectations, concerns, goals, friends, and, finally, different lives. What power had drawn together our myriad pieces and shaped them into one? Why did it fail to hold? My thoughts continually returned to Ireland, to Scotland and the VW bus, and to holding hands as our son was born, and waiting for Lark while we watched the skies through the long Paris night, and the thousand golden moments—how cavalier we were with time, as if it were not irreplaceable.

I accepted work without regard for where it took me, and in the summer of 1978, the children and I trouped to Bora Bora, a tiny dot in the South Seas. My father's stories about Polynesia had enthralled me since earliest childhood —and in reality, the islands were even more remarkable. On silver beaches my children played with their native companions and swam in the turquoise lagoon. They fed fish the colors of plastics, climbed coconut trees, and learned to whistle crabs out of their shells. In the South Seas you can read by starlight.

I had come to Bora Bora to make *The Hurricane* with the Swedish director Jan Troell and to work with a superb cast: Jason Robards, who played my father, Max von Sydow, and Trevor Howard. The renowned cinematographer, Sven Nykvist, became a close friend. But it was *Notes from Underground* that rearranged the landscape of my mind. In that paradise on earth, while my marriage crumbled, I descended into Dostoyevsky's dark, uncompromising world. *The Idiot, The Possessed, The Brothers Karamazov*, and *Crime and Punishment* gave a dangerous shape to my own inner life of turmoil, fear, loss, loneliness, and disillusionment.

I didn't go back to England when the movie ended. Instead I returned with my children to my beloved Wooden House on Martha's Vineyard. The children settled happily into the local Montessori school, and with snow on the driftwood I read works by Kierkegaard, Hegel, Kant, Nietzsche, and I reread Kafka and Camus. A first encounter with Sartre sent me scurrying back to Plato, and when I looked up, it was spring. During that time, except for visits from André, and occasionally from Sven, or my neighbor and good friend Carly Simon, my only sightings of another adult occurred when I went to the market, or collected the children from school.

The children and I kept a large saltwater tank with sea horses, starfish, anemones, and many fish, all named Gladys. We were happy on the Vineyard, but it was time for me to get back to work. A funny and wonderfully written play by Bernard Slade invited me to Broadway. So we arranged to move back with my mother, to the same apartment on Central Park West.

Chapter Eight

We made provisions for the fish named Gladys, and with two dozen mousetraps neatly baited with peanut butter, and the encyclopedias dusted on their shelves, we locked the door and drove down the windy dirt road. The children were wildly excited but I was quiet. Who knew how long the play would run, or when we might be back, or what was ahead of us? With my home once again slipping away, dread echoed in emptiness.

We moved into the same apartment I had been returning to since I was eighteen. But this trip was unlike any previous visit to the city: I was no longer a teenager under my mother's protective wing, there was neither a movie company watching over me nor a limousine waiting; I had not come to hit the nightspots with Frank Sinatra, or to tag along while André Previn gave concerts. This time I had come to New York in the comfortless light of an ordinary day to earn a living.

In truth all I wanted in this world was to

turn back the clock and be with André, safe in the green hills of Surrey. But a new girlfriend had already moved into The Haven, and I had already been to Santo Domingo to sign divorce papers. On principle, I had retained no counsel and neither sought nor received any alimony. Through it all André and I managed to remain close: we had spent several weeks together that summer, and we spoke on the phone almost daily. We still thought of ourselves as a family, so from the beginning André had been in on the discussions about my adopting another child as a single mother. He was supportive, but when I told him that this time I wanted to adopt a child with special needs, he advised me to "be sure his hands are all right, so he can play the piano."

The agency presented me with a choice between a little girl who had been badly burned, or a little boy with cerebral palsy: both were in Korea and both were under two years old. I asked which child would be more difficult for them to place; the little boy, they said. Cerebral palsy scares away adoptive parents, and his prognosis was unknown. After discussing it at length with the other children, we applied for the little boy; he might not play the piano, but he was the right child for us. The kids could not have been more excited, especially Fletcher, whose brothers were considerably older, and he felt covered in sisters. Now we began the wait, hoping he would arrive by Christmas.

Romantic Comedy opened strongly, and we settled into the Barrymore Theater for a run. Tony Perkins, playing opposite me, was brilliant in his role, and we got along fine. His two boys and one or another of my kids could usually be found backstage. Soon Holly Palance, who played Tony's wife, moved downstairs to share my too-large dressing room, and our company became a happy family. Meanwhile my mother opened to wonderful reviews in *Morning's at Seven*, and we cabbed each night to our respective theaters, as we had done sixteen years earlier; but now we were both on Broadway, just two blocks apart. Apparently it was the first time a mother and daughter had starred in concurrent Broadway shows.

Most nights I was out of the theater ahead of the audience, and in bed before eleven. I had to be on deck at seven to get the kids up, dressed, brushed, breakfasted, and walked to school. Only very occasionally, when someone I knew appeared backstage, I would consider going out for a drink, or even a late supper. It was in this way that, to my great delight, my dear friend Ann Casey from convent school reentered my life.

I even found our old Irish cook from Beverly Hills, Eileen. Once again, in the afternoons, I had tea with Eileen, but now we both drank from grown-ups' teacups. She was old and frail and had been working for a decade as housekeeper in the enormous mansion of Benjamin Sonnenberg. Now she was ready to retire. I helped her move into her own little apartment on the Lower East Side. She told me that after a lifetime "in service"—living in other people's houses, taking care of other people's things, and making no judgments—when the time came for her to buy a couch, or a lamp, or dishes, she discovered that she had no tastes or preferences.

The night Michael Caine, an old friend from Fox Studios, came to see the play, he asked me to come along to Elaine's restaurant afterward, where he would be joining Mick Jagger. It was Wednesday and I was already tired from doing a matinee and an evening performance, and Elaine's was way uptown on the East Side; it would be jammed, too noisy to talk, and it takes forever to get served. I was looking forward to getting home, raiding the refrigerator, having a bath, and getting into bed with Henri Troyat's biography of Tolstoy. On the other hand it had been a year since I'd seen Michael, and it would be fun seeing Mick Jagger, and really

I *ought* to go out every now and then. It was a flip-of-the-coin decision that landed me in Elaine's that night.

As we threaded our way toward our table, where Mick was waiting, Michael stopped to say hello to Woody Allen, who thanked me for the fan note I had written him about his movie *Manhattan*. I was stunned that he remembered. "It made my day," he said, without smiling.

Less than a year earlier I had saved the picture of him from the cover of the *New York Times Magazine*. He was standing under an umbrella on a gray day. I tore it from the magazine and put it in my giant dictionary for safekeeping, because there was something so interesting and appealing in his face or expression I thought I might want to look at it again. When, over a glass of wine, I confessed this to Michael, he dashed back to Woody's table and returned with a compliment for me.

Within weeks a printed invitation to Woody Allen's New Year's Eve party arrived at my apartment.

My sister Steffi, now divorced, was living with her young son, only a block away from me in New York. That New Year's Eve, following the performance of *Romantic Comedy*, we made our way over to the Harkness House, a great old mansion off Fifth Avenue. I presented my invitation to one of the women seated behind a table in the marble foyer and then Steffi and I were directed toward a staircase where Woody Allen stood, greeting his guests, New York's most starry figures, as they moved past him up the stairs. A lovely, dark-eyed young actress smiled by his side. Upstairs, hundreds of people—movie stars, icons of Broadway, socialites, politicians, and basketball players—milled together through the huge rooms. There was unlimited caviar, shellfish, and every other kind of food. Two bands played on different floors. My sister found some friends of hers and stayed on. I left before midnight. The following day I sent him a book, *The Medusa and the Snail*, with a note of thanks.

My son Moses Amadeus Farrow, whom we called Misha at first, after my brother Mike, arrived in 1980, the week before his second birthday, January 27, which he shares with Mozart. When he was just a few days old, he had been left, wrapped in a pink blanket, in a phone booth in Seoul. His right side was afflicted with cerebral palsy. He had no speech yet. He was a beautiful angel.

I spent the remainder of the winter getting to know my new son, tending to the rest of the brood, and doing eight shows a week. During intermissions I knitted many small, red mittens and hats and a seventh Christmas stocking. I also embroidered a "tooth pillow," as my children were suddenly losing teeth at a wondrous rate.

Ours was one of the few buildings on the Upper West Side that was not co-op, which meant we didn't own our apartment, we rented. When my family moved there in 1963, you could buy or rent on the West Side for peanuts by today's standards. Under the law, they could only raise the rent by some three percent every few years. Hardly a week passed without Mom or I noting how lucky we were to have the place.

It was a gorgeous building, built near the turn of the century, when ceilings were ten or eleven feet high. The nine spacious rooms of our apartment retained all their original moldings, paneling, and floors. Our kitchen was big enough for ten people to sit comfortably at the long butcher-block table. The dumbwaiter in our larder wall was only a spooky, spidery hole now, but a half century earlier it brought hot food up to the apartments from basement kitchens. Just off the lobby, where Lee Strasberg's library is now, was the old dining room. I imagined the carriages and coaches drawing up at the rear doors, and people, beautifully dressed in formal wear, laughing softly under crystal chandeliers. I'm told that on Friday and Saturday evenings there was chamber music in the dining room, all those years ago. Some nights as I lay in bed, beautiful music drifted up the stairwell and almost reached my ears before the noise of traffic drowned it out.

The room where I now slept had been my mother's, when I was a teenager. It was she who trained the ivy to weave through the black curls of the heavy wrought-iron screen that divided the room. The space that had been her office was now a cheerful nook for my youngest son. I tied wooden toys, stuffed animals, and colorful origami shapes to his side of the screen, and I covered the walls with quilts and children's paintings. When he awakened during the night, I lulled him back to sleep in the same chair that I had rocked his brothers and sisters in, back at The Haven. I don't know many lullabies, so I sang Christmas carols.

In April 1980, a phone call from Woody Allen's secretary made my stomach jump. She asked if I would have lunch with Mr. Allen. We set the date for the following week, April 17, at one o'clock.

"You never heard of Lutèce!" Tony Perkins was incredulous. Every night we waited in our positions onstage for five or so minutes before the curtain rose and the play began. That was the time when we exchanged our news. "It's only the *most* chic restaurant in New York City! What are you going to wear?"

"He doesn't care about clothes, does he?" I asked, thinking of Diane Keaton's thrift-shop ensemble in *Annie Hall*, and his own casual rumpled look.

"Are you *kidding*?" snorted Tony, who knew Woody Allen.

I was a little fidgety on the morning of the 17th, so I set out on foot, with my hair still wet, at 10:30 A.M. For a

second the clothes thing threw me, but in the end I dressed
warmly in a skirt and an Irish sweater, with sensible shoes,
leggings, and socks. It was a brisk, windy day.

At one on the dot the maître d' led me to the table
where Woody Allen waited, wide-eyed behind black-
rimmed glasses. He was handsomely dressed in an unrum-
pled tweed jacket and tie.

The wine was 1949 Château Mouton-Rothschild. As it
sank in its bottle, we traded fragments of our respective
histories. He asked many questions, and before I knew it we
were talking about Mozart, and Mahler's slow movements,
Schubert, the Heifetz recording of the Korngold, Plato,
Christianity and Jefferson, Walter Kaufmann as a guide
through existentialism from Dostoyevsky to Sartre, the poems of Yeats, my children, and my lifelong passionate albeit
imaginary relationship with James Agee, who died before I
could meet him but whose wife had actually been named
Mia. Floodgates opened; it had been so long since I had
shared these sorts of thoughts. He too loved Yeats and
Mahler's slow movements, and I hadn't known he played
the clarinet, and I had never heard of Sidney Bechet or Jelly
Roll Morton or Johnny Dodds, but I couldn't wait. And so
it went.

When we left the restaurant it was dark outside. A
chubby uniformed chauffeur named Don was opening the
door of a white Rolls Royce. Woody offered to take me
home. During the ten-minute drive, he said he would be in
touch when he returned from Paris the following week, if I
liked. I told him yes.

Less than a week later, his secretary called to propose a
dinner date for Sunday, when there was no performance of
the play. This set the pattern for the next months; each
week his secretary would call to confirm the date and time.
The fact that he never phoned me himself made things a
little strange. But instead of talking on the phone, we left
notes and small gifts with each other's doormen. Two

records arrived with a note explaining that the Bach, second selection, and the second movement of Stravinsky's Concerto in D for Strings, contained his favorite slow movements. Another time it was the *Apollo* Suite, with the notation "great." There were antique postcards, a slide of a frog's foot, and a poem by E. E. Cummings:

somewhere i have never travelled,gladly beyond
any experience,your eyes have their silence:
in your most frail gesture are things which enclose me,
or which i cannot touch because they are too near . . .

In the beginning his name felt awkward to me: "Woody." It seemed extreme, and it didn't feel quite real, perhaps because it wasn't. His actual name was Allan Konigsberg. So I asked him, "What do I call you?" hoping maybe he would want me to call him Allan or something. But he said, "I would be pleased if you would call me 'Woody.' "

He thought my name was awkward too. Sometimes I heard him refer to me by my name when he couldn't make the point with "she" or "her"—but he never ever directly called me Mia.

It was hard work keeping *Romantic Comedy* fresh for so many months, but all in all I was enjoying the run. Woody had a soft spot for thirties-style comedies, so he came to see the play and liked it very much. The whole company knew I was nuts about him.

Sunday nights flew by too quickly. When the waiters began loudly turning chairs up onto the tabletops, we took our cue to leave the restaurant.

I can't wait to see you! I wrote to him.

One summer night, as I stood in the wings of the Barrymore Theater waiting to make a second-act entrance, my dresser, Madeleine, rushed up. "It's from Woody Allen!" she whispered excitedly, putting an envelope into my hands. "His *chauffeur* is here." On a plain white card Woody wrote that Sunday was too long to wait, and he asked if I would join him after the following evening's show. It promised to be a clear night and we could go up on his terrace and look at the stars. Yes, I scribbled back.

With that we began seeing each other more frequently. We went to museums and movies and the opera. We walked all over the city with the white Rolls Royce to meet us at our destinations. He showed me the New York he loved: high on a clock tower with a heart-stopping view, he took two wineglasses and a bottle of Chateau Margaux out of a paper bag. It was as if I had stepped into a Woody Allen movie. He was more serious, less humorous, far more confident than in his films; but, I thought, more attractive, more interesting.

My new son Moses was an eager, affectionate, cheerful little fellow with an irresistible smile and a passion for bugs. Before he could be fitted for a brace or begin physical therapy, he needed to have an operation on his leg—the first of two—that he endured without complaint, along with months in a cast, and six years of physical therapy and speech therapy. Woody had not yet met any of my children.

In August 1980, I was the one in the hospital—for major abdominal surgery, my fourth, for complications resulting from the peritonitis in 1974. My stomach pains forced Woody and me to leave Rao's restaurant before we had finished our dinner. Later that night I checked in to the emergency room at New York Hospital.

During my second week in the hospital Woody came to see me and, for the first time, he telephoned me. After that, while I was convalescing on Martha's Vineyard with the children, he called two or three times every day. While on the phone to Woody, I suddenly became aware of the din around me, something I was normally oblivious to. I was, of course, acutely aware that he had lived his forty-five years entirely without children. He had never dated a woman with even *one* child. As he put it, "I have zero interest in kids." And if that wasn't clear enough, he talked about his sister, who also lived in Manhattan, with whom he had shared an unusually close childhood. He spoke to her on the phone; he loved her, and he helped her financially, but he avoided her company. He described her as "pushy," and as an example he told me about her unwelcome and futile efforts to involve him with her children when they were younger.

The previous year on Martha's Vineyard had given me time to reflect, in every season and in every conceivable frame of mind. As each attempt to rehabilitate my marriage had failed, I was left with few illusions. I was a single mother with seven young children; wonderful as they indeed were, I understood it was unlikely that I would ever again meet a man who would want to become seriously involved with me. That is not to say I was without hope—but hopes are not expectations.

The children and I returned to my mother's apartment in the fall of 1980. I'd played out my run in *Romantic Comedy*, and even though it was difficult to leave my home on the Vineyard, I went back to New York because of my feelings for Woody.

He lived in a penthouse on Fifth Avenue directly opposite my apartment, less than a mile across Central Park. We blinked our lights at each other, waved through binoculars, and shook towels out the windows. This relationship, I remember thinking, will be the best of my life. We will be together forever.

My children met Woody on an Indian-summer afternoon in late September 1980. The kids and I were returning from the playground, just entering the lobby of our building, when he arrived early to take me for a walk; they were holding dripping chocolate ice cream cones, and they all had on hats. Somehow it seemed as if there were more of them when they were wearing hats and eating ice cream. Seven small faces stared up at him: Matthew and Sascha were ten, Soon-Yi was seven going on eight (her age was finally determined through the standard method of X-raying her wrists), Lark was seven, Daisy and Fletcher were six, and Moses, covered with ice cream in his stroller, was two and a half. By then even the littlest kids knew Woody meant a lot to me, so they were curious and sweet and shy with him.

He said my kids were "very cute," and before spring arrived we were all staying at his place on Friday and Saturday nights. At first we carried our stuff back and forth across the park with us: sleeping bags, stuffed animals, pajamas, dolls, toy cars, stamp collections, videotapes, Lego, board games, puzzles, art supplies, books, and snacks. In time, shelves appeared in the back bedroom, then a bunk bed, and we began to leave things there. The kids brought their friends along for sleep-overs. My robe hung in his bathroom. He gave me my own drawer. My hairbrush, soap, and shampoo took their place alongside Diane Keaton's (his girlfriend from more than a decade earlier), which I never presumed to touch, in the cabinet above the sink.

On Saturday and Sunday mornings, at around seven-thirty, Woody and I would go for a walk. When we returned, I would get the kids ready, put the room where they slept back in order, and then we would go back to our own apartment, where I would make pancakes for breakfast. Woody wanted to be alone to exercise, see his analyst, write, and practice his clarinet. The kids had their play dates, piano lessons, cheeseburger lunches on Columbus Avenue, and excursions to the playground or the Museum of Natural History.

Woody was never comfortable with the children, but in his way, he tried. He traded his white Rolls for a black stretch limo big enough to transport us all. On weekend afternoons throughout the fall and winter, he had movies screened for them at his Park Avenue editing rooms. While they polished off deep bowls full of candy left for them by Woody's assistant, they watched the movies of Bob Hope, Jerry Lewis, Abbott and Costello, Chaplin, Cary Grant, Frank Capra, John Ford, and every science-fiction and kids' classic right up to the latest Disney and Spielberg. I once left Daisy and Fletcher with him at his apartment while I went to the doctor. When I returned less than an hour later, he was throwing his hats and gloves into the fire. The kids were ecstatic. "I ran out of things to do," he shrugged.

A postcard, circa 1935, arrived from across the park. It pictured a man in a bowler hat with five small children. Over the top was printed, YOUR FUTURE HUSBAND—YOUR FUTURE CHILDREN.

A French cook named Colette worked for Woody full-time, but he preferred to eat out, except for Mondays, when he played clarinet at an East Side pub, and Sundays, when we had Chinese take-out together with the children in my kitchen. He never ate our food or used our plates or utensils because of the cats, who had been known to jump onto the table. He couldn't stand the cats.

I missed our first, long dinner dates in quiet restaurants, when we talked until the waiters dislodged us. Now, as had been his custom for years before we met, we joined Jean Doumanian and her boyfriend for dinner. Woody had met Jean in Chicago when he was a stand-up comedian playing nightclubs; she and her then-husband were fans who kept returning to catch his show. I had been aware of her importance in Woody's life, and I was curious to meet her, but that didn't happen for the first six or more months that we were dating. In those early days we kept to ourselves, steering clear of high-profile restaurants like Elaine's. So nothing appeared in the gossip columns until the night a photographer came blazing into La Grenouille restaurant. That was when I swallowed my ring.

Although we had dinner with Jean several times a week for almost a dozen years, I never became comfortable with her. Not that she wasn't nice to me, but she had been close to Woody for so long, they talked on the phone several times a day, and she was older than Woody, who was himself a decade my senior. The whole package was intimidating: her breezy, seamless confidence, well-timed remarks, chic all-black wardrobe, perfectly styled black hair, dark eyes, and thin lips on a chalk-white face. Her show-business anecdotes were the latest, her other interests were exercise, health food, massages, and acupuncture. I didn't know what to talk to her about.

When Woody suffered from a kind of chronic sty that none of his doctors could cure, Jean brought her herbalist up from Chinatown to the Fifth Avenue penthouse. The old fellow produced a cat's whisker and stuck it into Woody's tear ducts: it had no effect at all on the sties. This departure from traditional medicine aside, Woody Allen was connected to his doctors like no one I ever heard of: he had a doctor for every single part of his body. He carried around his doctors' home numbers, he rushed to the doctor before a twinge could reach symptom status. If he felt the least bit unwell, he would take his temperature at ten-minute intervals. He kept his own thermometer at my apartment. In his pocket he carried a silver box full of pills for any conceivable ailment. Whenever one of his movies came out, he'd have a screening for his doctors and their wives. It was called "the doctors' screening," and the room was always full.

•   •   •

On the weekends Woody and I went to the screening room, where we watched movies old and new, and drank red wine before dinner, a single bottle of which might cost as much as five hundred dollars. I got to see *The Bicycle Thief*, which was every bit as great as Frank had told me. The last scene of that movie was the only time that I may have seen Woody shed a tear, although it's possible that his sty was itching.

Sometimes we brought one, two, or three of the children along with us to dinner. They were made much of wherever we went. In time the Russian Tea Room became their favorite restaurant and a tradition for birthdays. Our booth was in the left corner, by the maître d', under the picture of Ruth Gordon.

Now our walks around the East Side were filled with talk about the film he was writing for the summer of 1981. When one day he asked if I would like to be in that movie, a wild banshee jumped into my mouth and said loudly that I wasn't much of an actress so maybe I'd better not. Woody looked surprised, but he was reassuring. "In the past," he said, "actresses who have worked with me have tended to come off very well." I agreed, but my thoughts flew in all directions. I wanted to work with him, I had been hoping to work with him: it was what every actor in the world would wish for and I was no exception. I should be thrilled. Except now that he had asked—it felt strange to be offered a role because I was "the girlfriend." And what if I didn't measure up? What would happen then? I couldn't imagine what it would be like doing scenes with him, *and* with him as the director-boss and boyfriend. Life was complicated enough.

Maybe it was automatic after two broken marriages, that a sort of generic fear would set in: fear that comes from feeling unsafe, fear that his feelings were nothing like mine —it was hard to know what he really felt—fear of something in him, or something not there in him, fear of surrendering my last shred of power. So I would draw myself up to my full height and be the first to declare my ineligibility. Get a jump on things.

Wait a minute. He's wonderful, and he loves me. Only the other day he complimented me on my male logic and said ours is the best relationship he's ever had. It's a miracle, don't screw it up. From here it seems possible that we could love each other forever. Anyway, *I'm qualified to work with him!* I have *prizes.* I was a member of the Royal Shakespeare Company. I'm a "wonderful actress," he said, and Judith Crist, a critic friend of his, has been telling him for years to use me, so one day we might have worked together anyway. That's what he said. So. It will only be great. And fun: we'll get to be together all the time and we'll grow even closer. I will do the best work of my life and the kids will be proud of me, and he will be proud of me and therefore love and respect me more. And besides, I have to work—if I took a job someplace else, *that* would hurt the relationship.

A Midsummer Night's Sex Comedy was filmed on the Rockefeller estate about an hour outside the city. Except for the nearly steady air traffic, it was an ideal site for this turn-of-the-century piece. It was summer and the children usually accompanied me to work, quickly disappearing into the woods and along the stream on business of their own.

The film was shot almost entirely outdoors with the incomparable Gordon Willis as cinematographer. Our days were spent waiting for moments of perfect light. Meanwhile I was in the camper (Woody and I shared one through thirteen films), wearing a robe, with my hair tightly wrapped around cone-shaped curlers, my torso compressed into a killer corset. Bleary-eyed from a pulverizing headache (the curlers, the corset, the heat, the humidity, the nerves), I just wished I could be my sister out there looking adorable in her jeans and baseball cap and straight hair, lounging in the tall grass, strolling under the trees, talking and laughing with Woody.

Weeks before we started shooting, Steffi had asked to be my stand-in on the movie. My nerves were already knit into concentric circles and this idea brought me to a halt. I thought back to when my brother Patrick had briefly worked as an extra on *Peyton Place*, and how awkward and out-of-whack things became in that context, with me playing a role, and tons of people being so attentive to me, and a chair with my name on it, while my big brother was herded around with the other extras, who almost never got treated very well. It was upsetting, and made it harder for me to do the work. And now my sister needed this job—so I asked and she got it, even though Woody thought it was a bad idea: he said he wouldn't have *his* sister on the set no matter what. Then it took my breath away how quickly and unreservedly he accepted Steffi. It seemed so out of character. In no time at all he had asked her to come with us on a three-day trip to Rome and Paris. Which she did.

At times during the shooting, I was overpowered by such a paralysis that I couldn't understand who the characters were supposed to be or what they were doing. Woody, now my director, was a stranger to me. His icy sternness pushed my apprehension toward raw fear. I was no artist, only the most inept poseur. This seemingly straightforward material was beyond my capabilities. I remembered the movie *Pat and Mike*, in which Katharine Hepburn, a professional athlete, was unable to do a thing when Spencer Tracy was around. My instincts, an actor's lifeline, screamed to head for the hills. By midmovie I had an ulcer and was taking Tagamet four times a day. I was so apprehensive, dispirited, and humiliated, and so convinced I had failed Woody, that I asked if in the future, if there was a future, I could be his assistant, so I wouldn't have to act. He looked at me doubtfully and said, "It's hard work being an assistant."

"I tend to be maybe a little abrupt sometimes," he told

his biographer, Eric Lax. "So I calmed her but I was not completely sympathetic, because I didn't realize the dimensions, the gravity. I knew she'd be wonderful in it. It never occurred to *me* she'd disappoint me."

I wasn't the only one who was having difficulty. José Ferrer, after numerous failed attempts to do a scene, finally blurted out angrily, "Now I can't do it. You've turned me into a mass of terrors."

Woody's comments to actors could sting. "I don't believe a word of that," he would say quietly, but very intensely. "Human beings don't talk that way." "That was pure soap opera" was one of the comments that upset Geraldine Page while they were doing *Interiors*. "You could see that on afternoon television," Woody told her. Maureen Stapleton, who worked on the same film, said, "He's not shy, he's antisocial. That's a different ball game."

"There are certain directors," he has said, "who have affectionate relationships with actors, but I've never been able to work that way. I give as much contact as is required professionally." But that didn't stop actors from wanting to work with him for a fraction of their usual salary. "I think they do that because there's an appreciation of what my films try to be."

Woody usually shot his films in the fall, but for obvious reasons *Midsummer* had to be made during the summer; since that left the fall free, he decided to make *Zelig*, another small film, back-to-back with *Midsummer*. But both films took longer than anticipated and overlapped with *Broadway Danny Rose*, which in turn ran into *Purple Rose of Cairo*. There were days when we shot scenes from two or three different films.

The children and I visited Martha's Vineyard rarely now. Going there for longer than a week without Woody, who wouldn't go, was out of the question, and to go for less than a week was costly and impractical. We had to take two taxis to the airport and get eight seats together on the shuttle; in Boston we hurried over to the Air New England terminal with our fingers crossed; if the flight wasn't canceled from fog, we boarded the little plane, grateful to be bounced over to Hyannis, Nantucket, and at last the Vineyard. Just getting there was such an accomplishment we couldn't think about leaving.

When we got to the house, we turned on the water, electricity, and heat. We threw out the dead mice, and then everybody piled into the jeep to buy food at the market. It was only then that it hit us, as we walked up and down the aisles, that we were actually back. We said hi to familiar faces as if we'd been there right along. If eight people each want a sandwich, that's sixteen pieces of bread. Everyone wants eggs and toast, that's another loaf of bread and sixteen eggs. Or a couple of boxes of cereal a day.

Departures began with a trip to the dump. I loved the dump. All the weathered, forsaken things, and especially the seagulls—armies of giant gulls claiming their desolate mountains of garbage and the air above it. The dump was a wild, beautiful, thrilling place.

But all things considered, the Wooden House, place of my dreams, didn't make sense for us anymore. I put it up for sale and began the depressing search for a house I was certain couldn't exist—a place as nice as the Wooden House within a three-hour radius of the city.

"Get one on the beach," Woody advised. "The open sea. Crashing surf. There's nothing like it."

But my budget was limited to what I obtained from the sale of the Vineyard property. A house on the open sea with room enough for all of us, within a reasonable distance of New York City, would cost a lot more than that. Anyway, crashing waves don't seem so wonderful when you're minding little kids, and I don't like the beach for long. I burn.

I would miss the foghorns' nightly dirges, and the many bewitching nooks and crannies of Martha's Vineyard—Beetlebung Corner, and the wild Squibnocket shore, and Menemsha, with its tangled heaps of lobster traps and tethered boats nudging in the harbor, this morning's catch of bluefish, and the snow on the driftwood, and summertimes with Ruth, Gar, Thornton, Carly, and the Styrons, dear friends through the decades, and my beloved Wooden House on Lake Tashmoo, as close to heaven as anywhere on earth.

But there is a New England village with white clapboard houses, circa 1800. It has two churches with steeples, a school, a library, a general store, a bank, and a post office; there are cornfields and cows on hills beyond hills, and horses and silos and tumbledown barns. Nestled on the outskirts of this town is Frog Hollow.

Woodland encircles the white farmhouse and the lake it intimately faces. There is a knobby field at the back, hemmed carelessly by a colonial stone wall; a mossy creek holds back the dense woods and winds along the right of the field toward its upper, northeast corner, where a plain wooden bridge crosses the stream and leads past a greenish secret pond into the deep woods.

The lake in front of the house is a good five or six acres in size, with an island in the middle big enough for the spruce tree that angles over the water, two sizable rocks you can sit on, a profusion of blueberry and alder bushes, and, in the spring, a goose nest. On the narrow ring of a beach, early in May, a goose couple launches its progeny; it is also where the blue crane wades and watches the beavers ceaselessly trafficking the lake. There are almost no mosquitoes, which seemed a minor miracle after the Vineyard. My school friend Casey has a home nearby, and the Styrons winter here.

During the filming of *A Midsummer Night's Sex Comedy* we packed up the encyclopedias, the red canoe, my grandfather's crucifix, and the music box Frank gave me, and we moved everything into the new house. That it was a little run-down didn't matter; but the house had no showers, and since Woody wouldn't touch a bath, I had a fine tile shower built just for him and I hoped he would be comfortable and grow fond of the house and be there as much as possible.

There was no doubt in my mind that the gleaming shower would please him; on the evening of his second visit I watched him take a white rubber shower mat (for germs) out of his bag and carry it into the bathroom. But seconds later he emerged with the mat still rolled under his arm. "What happened?" I asked. "What's wrong?"

"The drain is in the middle," he said, shaking his head dismissively, as if I should have known. No further explanation ever came.

This was an instance when a shower was more than just a shower; it was the reason, he said, that he could not stay at Frog Hollow for longer than a brief overnight visit. So I was determined to get things right. According to his specifications, in another part of the house, I had a whole new bathroom built with a shower that had a drain in the corner. It was called "Woody's bathroom."

We were still shooting *A Midsummer Night's Sex Comedy* and settling into Frog Hollow when out of nowhere, *he* began to look for a house. He showed me brochures of fabulous beach houses, but he didn't ask what I thought about them, and when he went to see them, he took Jean, not me. It was as disturbing and mysterious as the drain.

In a short time he bought a beach house in the Hamptons for millions of dollars. Through the winter of 1981–82 he and his decorator conferred, and renovated, landscaped, painted, and furnished, and every once in a while Woody was driven out to check the progress. Sometimes he brought seven-year-old Fletcher along. Finally, one windy afternoon in early spring, he took the kids and me out to East Hampton for an overnight visit in the newly completed house.

It was impressive, bigger even than I had imagined. A mansion facing the waves, with many cavernous rooms impeccably furnished with pale-pine antiques, all in shades of white except for the Laura Ashley curtains in the bathrooms and a brand-new restaurant-style kitchen. Every appliance, towel, plate, pillow, and billiard ball was in place.

While the children flew excitedly in all directions, Woody and I walked down the beach. The sun was setting. It was a lovely evening. But he was troubled, there was something about the house, some indefinable thing he didn't like. He wasn't sure he would even be able to spend the night there. I tried to be positive: the place seemed imposing now but it was only our first visit, it was a big house, it would become familiar, and it would be great to be able to come out on winter weekends, build a fire, and watch storms over the sea. Frog Hollow, I thought to myself, would still be there for summers, when the beaches got hot and crowded. It would all work out. It would be great. And we would get out of the city during the winter months —as things stood we weren't going to Frog Hollow more than once every five or six weeks, because even with the new bathroom he didn't want to go.

He paced and worried through the evening. The next morning we left and he sold the house and everything in it.

Then Woody hired a woman whose only job was to check out the best available places on the shores of the Hamptons, Montauk, Maine, Nantucket, Martha's Vineyard, Block Island, Fisher Island, Rhode Island, and Cape Cod. He was nervous about flying in small planes, so whenever we went to look at a house, he chartered the biggest aircraft that the seaside airport could handle.

Meanwhile I fixed up Frog Hollow and tended my garden. I carried stones out of the field and I mowed it with my tractor. The children learned to swim, fish, and canoe. They made friends with neighbor kids and they brought their New York friends to visit. They played badminton, softball, tennis, and basketball. They made snowmen and ice-skated, they rode bikes and horses. Peering into a crate of squirming mutt puppies at the town fair, the kids clamored for the yellow one, and so Mary joined the family, then another kitten. We celebrated each season, but our Christmases and Easters were the high points of the year. I watched my children grow, and I collected the memories.

When Woody took me to see these other, much grander houses, it was hard to ignore a gnawing little knot of anxiety—if he ever found what he was looking for, if it existed, one way or another it would eventually replace Frog Hollow. We would move in, and put our stuff in the drawers and closets and on the shelves but not (he was clear about this) on the walls, and the children would make the new house their own and grow to love it, and probably I would too. But I would always be reminding myself that if something happened, if anything went wrong, we would have to take our things out of the drawers and closets and off the shelves, and we would leave. Because it wouldn't *really* be our house.

It wasn't simple for Woody either. Even with the best and biggest airplanes it seemed in the end that no house was worth the flight. His search ended with less than a whimper on a Sunday morning; we were at the airport going to see another coastal property that sounded perfect. The plane was chartered and waiting on the runway. But Woody was still in the terminal, staring at the space between his shoes, or walking up and down the hallway with his hat on and little Fletcher trotting respectfully by his side. Nobody said a word for maybe two hours, then finally Woody turned to my son and said, "Fletch, do we really want to do this?"

Fletcher looked up and softly replied, "I don't think so."

"Me neither," Woody said. "Let's go home."

For a time Fletcher was the child who worshipped Woody the most. He was an openhearted, persistent little boy who by midweek always found the courage to ask Woody, Do you think we could have a play date this weekend? Although this enthusiasm was decidedly one-sided, Woody tried to accommodate my son's requests. On Saturday mornings he took him, sometimes with one of the other children, to the arcades on Broadway; in Grand Central station he showed them how you can whisper from one corner of the great station and be heard in the oppposite corner; he purchased elaborate "effects" at the magic shop that they would perform for the rest of us; and he took Fletcher up on his terrace to shoot pigeon eggs with his BB gun—Woody waged war on pigeons because they messed up his terrace.

After a visit to the model shop, my small son would lug home hundreds of dollars worth of motorized model-airplane kits, when that same week I might have denied him a ten-dollar box of Lego. In Woody's world of expensive restaurants, fine wines, chartered airplanes, enough caviar for even the littlest kid, and chauffeur-driven stretch limos complete with VCR, I struggled to keep things in perspective for my kids. We still lived in the rented apartment with my mother on Central Park West, on my salary, which was $150,000 per movie, increasing, over a dozen years and thirteen films, to $375,000. My goal was to put enough aside for each child's education. André and I split the tuition for the six children we shared.

On workdays Woody frequently brought Fletcher along to his editing room or, if we were shooting, to the set. There he was given a walkie-talkie and a "job" as a production assistant. In 1986, when Fletcher was twelve, Woody cast him in *Radio Days* (he's the blond kid: there's a great close-up of him on the rooftop watching the teacher undress).

For the first years of our relationship, I never stopped

hoping he would finally find my kids irresistible. Everyone who ever met them said how wonderful they were. They were special. But although he saw them just about every day, and although they tried, some more obviously than others, to win his heart, he barely acknowleged them, and one by one, they gave up. One of my greatest regrets is that I permitted this to continue through twelve irreplaceable years of their childhoods.

But then he was king in our midst: the one who knew everything, whose concerns were greater than most, a *superior* person. His opinions were the final word. And he could cut you quicker than you could open your mouth. We admired him and we were afraid of him, each in our own way.

André still traveled most of the time, but he loved his children and they loved being with him. It was a treat for us all when he came to visit. The piano resounded throughout the house and the children couldn't wait to bring him up-to-date on all their activities and accomplishments. There were many times when André and Woody were there together, making small talk. How very Noël Coward of us, someone remarked.

Only Moses did not have a father, and although André was particularly kind to him and always included him in whatever was going on, as Moses grew from babyhood into childhood, he wished for a father of his own. During his toddler years, not surprisingly, he viewed my boyfriend as an interloper, especially since Woody's infrequent attempts to interact with him were jarringly out of tune with this fragile little boy, and roughly aggressive. Because Woody said Misha was "a wimp's name," we changed it to Moses after the basketball star Moses Malone. I hoped the fact that we had named my son together might arouse some paternal feelings in him. But "feelings" in Woody were subtle, and could easily escape detection.

By the time Moses was seven Woody had been my partner for five years—for as long as Moses could remember.
One evening while Woody and I were lounging on my bed
watching *60 Minutes*, Moses, who had been quietly standing
there for some time, whispered to him, "Are you my father?"

"Sure, kid," Woody replied lightly, and he seemed
amused by the awkwardness of the request, or the predica-
ment he unexpectedly found himself in.

After that, when Woody came to Frog Hollow, he sometimes played chess with Moses, or basketball, or catch, but
never for longer than five or ten minutes. Fifteen tops. He
didn't want to break a sweat, he said. Nobody cares about
that, I told him. But he did, and he still wouldn't take a
shower at our house, not even with the new bathroom, and
his own shower mat, and his special shower shoes.

The whole family was playing chess by then. Woody
hired a grand master to come to his apartment once a week
and give us lessons. As a gift to those of my children that
were interested, Woody had him give them lessons too, over
at my apartment.

Since 1977 Woody had made a picture in New York City
every year, with more or less the same crew. By the time I
came along, everyone knew one another and the way
Woody liked to work. Each film was budgeted to include
reshoots, which he considered an essential part of the cre-
ative process. We reshot most films scene by scene as we
went along, the following day; then we reshot again after
the film had been edited. Fully half of *Purple Rose* was rewritten and reshot after editing; so was a substantial portion of *Hannah and Her Sisters*, and about a third of *Crimes and
Misdemeanors*. *September* was entirely rewritten, and then reshot
with a different cast.

WAFP—"Woody Allen Fall Project"—was the perennial

working title for his films. He seldom decided upon a title before shooting, and in any case he insisted that everything about the film, including its title, be kept secret until its release. At any given moment he had at least two ideas for the next movie. Since his personal life was not separate from his professional life, a great portion of our time was spent discussing whatever we were working on, or, even more, the future project. An ideal time to talk was during our long walks around his neighborhood, the East Side. He would say, "You mind if I bounce some ideas off you?" And I was happy that my reactions meant something to him.

On one early tour of the East Side Woody pointed out William Buckley's house. This was a point of interest for him since the Buckleys, their family, and their friends are in essence what drew him to the East Side. But the precise location of the Buckley house failed to lodge in my mind, and some months later, when again we were walking in that vicinity, I asked in passing whether a familiar-looking house might be William Buckley's. To this day I don't know what prompted the attack that followed, which was more stunningly awful than I had ever weathered in my life, and it did not cease until I was sobbing on the sidewalk, vaporized in front of a house that presumably was not William Buckley's.

The WAFP was an unquestioned fact of life for the many men and women who were employed year after year. As sure as the swallows return to Capistrano, Woody Allen would come up with a screenplay to shoot each fall. He led a disciplined life. While we were making a movie, he edited on the weekends, and was all the while making decisions about the next project. He thrashed out plots while pacing back and forth on his terrace, and he wrote his scripts in longhand on a yellow legal pad, while lying on his side, on

the bed in the back bedroom, where the kids slept on weekends. He then typed out his pages on the same typewriter
he had used for twenty years. It was always a great day
when we walked over to studio duplicating to deliver the
completed screenplay, so that they could print out the first
neat stack of copies. Even when he was writing we tried to
meet at some point during the day for a walk, and of course
for dinner. Without fail, no matter what else was happening, he called me four or five times a day, minimum.

As shooting schedules go, our working hours were unusually civilized. We never started before eight in the morning, and rarely worked past six in the evening. At that point
Woody would go to his editing room to see dailies, while I
hurried home for dinner with the children. It was an ideal
job for a mom. Whichever kids were not in school came
with me to work. I turned dressing rooms and campers into
playrooms with colorful posters on the walls, a little table
and chairs, pots of clay, stacks of paper, glue, blocks, pens,
scissors, puzzles, books, and cassettes. During the breaks I
played with the children, read, or knit. I made elaborate
samplers and cross-stitched the names of each child, and
Woody. Sometimes he and I played chess. But mostly he
made phone calls. Lots of phone calls. He had a California
lawyer on retainer and it seemed that he was always trying
to sue somebody. I once told him he was "suit-happy" but
he corrected me—it's called "litigious."

In 1983, when my mother moved out of the apartment to
marry James Cushing, I gained a wonderful stepfather and
an extra bedroom, which, for a large family in New York
City, is nothing to scoff at. That was the year of *Zelig*, our
second film together. In contrast to *A Midsummer Night's Sex
Comedy*, *Zelig* was a happy experience for me: I had few lines
to speak, and the character came easily. Of all the films we
made, the atmosphere on this set was the most relaxed.

The next year, 1984, was the year of the *Roses*. *Broadway Danny Rose* and *Purple Rose of Cairo* were artistic triumphs for Woody and for me. The very disparate characters of Tina in *Danny Rose* and Cecilia in *Purple Rose* were two of the best and most rewarding roles I had ever been given. Of the movies I have been in, *Purple Rose* remains one of my favorites.

After *Danny Rose*, our producer, Jack Rollins, told me he had initially protested Woody's casting me in the role of Tina, a tough Brooklyn-Italian "broad." That I was not Mr. Rollins's first (or fiftieth) choice was understandable. In order to play Tina, I had to change everything about myself. I took the look and attitude from two women: "Honey," the former wife of Frank Sinatra's buddy Jilly Rizzo, and Mrs. Rao, owner of Rao's restaurant. I drank milk shakes all day to gain ten pounds, and I worked to lower my voice. I taped hours of conversations with Brooklyn women, and listened to them day and night. I watched Martin Scorsese's *Raging Bull* on video countless times.

Rehearsals, apart from a couple of perfunctory, disjointed camera run-throughs during which Woody paid little or no attention to the actors, were nonexistent. I knew I wouldn't have the chance to try out *being* Tina, so I had to be well prepared. I found a "Tina voice" and attitude, and my new weight was assisted by large (removable) breasts, tight sexy clothes, stiletto heels, and big hair. But my eyes kept giving me away. We discovered that even with a ton of makeup they undermined the toughness I needed (unless I squinted, which I couldn't do for the whole movie). So I wore sunglasses throughout, except for one scene that lasted only a few seconds, without dialogue—just a glimpse of my head in a bathroom mirror. That moment was jarring when I saw the movie: as if, in spite of me, a different character had suddenly intruded, or an unintended dimension of the same character.

In our real lives, Woody and I had settled into a steady, secure, and satisfying relationship. I got used to his triumvirate incarnations as partner, director, and actor, and he had, I think, become used to me. In *Danny Rose* we played opposite each other for the third time (after *Midsummer Night's* and *Zelig*). Woody the actor had long ago invented his screen persona: a lovable nebbish, endlessly and hilariously whining and quacking, questioning moral and philosophical issues great and small. He was a guy with his heart and his conscience on his sleeve, whose talk was peppered with quotes of Kierkegaard and Kant: an insightful and unthreatening mascot of the intelligentsia. A guy who is nothing like the real Woody Allen.

With the two of us connected in so many complex ways to each other and to the everyday life we shared, it was difficult for me as an actor to build another, separate reality and to feel free within it. Furthermore, whenever Woody the actor and I were doing a scene, Woody the director would be standing outside it, appraising the performances. Especially at first, working this way took every ounce of my concentration and resolve.

Following the year of the *Roses*, although outright compliments were rare, I felt Woody was pleased with my work and that he trusted me. "Mia is an extraordinary actress," he told his biographer. "She shows up and can always do it. If you ask her to play that shrinking character in *The Purple Rose of Cairo*, or the silly cigarette girl in *Radio Days*, she does it. If you ask her to play nasty, she does it. If you ask her to play something sexy, she does it . . . And she's real sweet. She'll come to the set and quietly do her needlepoint, and then put on her wig and dark glasses, or whatever, and just scream out the lines and stick a knife in your nose—and then go back to sewing with her little orphan children around her."

Most directors shoot a scene from many angles: at a minimum there is the master shot, providing "coverage" of the whole scene, then the "over-the-shoulder" shots onto each actor, and finally all the close-ups. When an actor moves within the scene, the camera follows, and then the other actors are "covered" from the new perspective. It can be a tedious process. Woody worked very differently. He always found a way to shoot a scene in one or at most two setups. Commonly, we filmed six- and seven-minute scenes; the longest (in *Husbands and Wives*) was nine and a half minutes, when we shot until we ran out of film. By skillfully moving both actors and the camera, he eliminated the need for coverage. Over thirteen movies I can count my close-ups on the fingers of one hand. For the actors and the camera crew this approach was both terrifying and exhilarating, like opening in a play without rehearsals. Walking onto the soundstage, that first glimpse of the set with the lights pouring down on it, knowing as you approached that everything was ready to go—that moment was electrifying.

The way most films are shot, if a scene doesn't work, there are plenty of options in the editing room: it can be tightened; lines can be dropped or lifted from different takes; when an actor is weak, the scene can be played on another actor—there are alternatives. But Woody's method of working left no margin for error. That is one reason that so many reshoots were necessary. The other reason is because, as we shot scenes, problems with the script were revealed, or Woody simply saw ways to rewrite and improve it.

Whenever I had a scene with actors I hadn't met, I would find them in the makeup room or I'd knock on their dressing-room door to say hello. People were always nervous, not knowing what to expect. Nobody ever told them anything. Most often they had only read the pages of the scene they were in, not the whole script, so they didn't know what the story was about. I'd ask them if they wanted to run lines or anything. They almost always did. I did too, because it was all the rehearsal we were likely to get. We knew that if they didn't get it right they'd get fired, like Michael Keaton, Christopher Walken, Sam Shepard, and my own mother.

Whether it was a comedy or a drama, the atmosphere on the set was intense, hushed. Woody never raised his voice. Actors knew not to expect discussions, explanations, encouragement, enthusiasm, or compliments. Criticism was quiet, quick, and cutting. I told people that if he said "okay" or "fine" after a scene, that meant it went really well. As long as he didn't interrupt the scene, or say anything negative, it meant that he was pleased.

Since there was no coverage, the editing went quickly. Once the movie was assembled, he put in music, usually from his own record collection. Then he screened the film for more or less the same group of eight or ten people. When the lights came on he asked questions and from the reactions he got a sense of the problems and strengths of the film. He then rewrote for a few weeks, and recalled everyone for reshoots. Scenes were often reshot four or five times—throughout the year. We were doing reshots on *Danny Rose* for more than a year, right up until the month it was released.

We didn't have much of a social life. I can recall our going to three parties in a dozen years. I introduced him to all my brothers and sisters, and I tried to share my friends—Leonard Gershe, Maria Roach, Tom Stoppard, Stephen Sondheim, Betty Comden, Nancy Sinatra, Liza, John Williams, Casey, John Tavener, the Styrons, and Yul, Eileen, and the Kanins—but really he wasn't comfortable with them. He enjoyed the Kanins, but although Ruth thought well of his work, she didn't like him. "It was the cause of one of our few quarrels in over forty years," Garson told me. "We had had dinner, the four of us, and walking home Ruth said, 'He may be brilliantly talented, but he's no good. I wouldn't trust him from here to the end of the block.' "

Apart from the ever present Jean Doumanian and her boyfriend whom I liked very much, Woody was most comfortable with his chilly but eager-to-please assistant, Jane, and his costume designer, Jeffrey. I never knew anybody, man or woman, who cared so much about clothes as Woody Allen. He pored over *Vogue* magazine each month. His own "casual, rumpled look" was in fact carefully assembled: the linen suits and tweed jackets were tailor-made, his shirts were the finest Sea Island cotton, his sweaters were cashmere, in grays and browns. He never failed to notice and comment on what people were wearing, and he was intensely contemptuous of a poor choice in style, color, or fabric. That my sister Steffi could wear a pink T-shirt left him confounded and dismayed.

When we went out to dinner, it was Woody who decided which restaurant, and what time, and who would join us, and the topics of discussion, and when to leave. Invariably he paid the check.

We almost never saw his sister. We had dinner with her, or maybe it was lunch, only once in a dozen years. His parents were there too. It was somebody's birthday, an awkward, awful affair, as was every encounter with his parents. I grew up in Beverly Hills. I went to convent schools. I have moved in circles where people are polite to one another. I never saw anyone treat another person the way he behaved with his parents.

Of course with the Horowitzes it was a different story. Vladimir and Wanda Horowitz were the only friends we made as a couple. When we were introduced, Wanda said, "Mr. Woody Allen, you look the same as you do in the movies. No worse, no better."

No matter what restaurant we went to, Horowitz ate the same thing: Woody's assistant had to call ahead to make sure his sole, boiled potato, asparagus, and crème caramel were available. While we ate, Woody's chauffeur went to Times Square to pick up the next morning's *New York Times*, which Vladimir had to have every night or he couldn't sleep. From the start of the meal he fretted about getting it.

When we went to their brownstone to pick them up, Horowitz would immediately ask us about the weather. "How is it outside?" he would say. And we would tell him it was warm or coldish. Then while we chatted over a drink, he would phone the weather at ten- or fifteen-minute intervals until we left.

He had a television in his living room, and a VCR with the control panel covered with black tape, so that he couldn't push any wrong buttons. It was somehow comforting that the world's greatest pianist couldn't figure out his VCR. He watched two movies every night. I asked what kind of movies he liked. "I don't care what I watch," he shrugged. "The store just sends them to me."

Before we went out, no matter what the climate, he took time to carefully pull on his black leather gloves, working them meticulously over each famous finger. Once, while we were in the car heading for the restaurant, he pointed out the window, exclaiming, "Wanda look! A *bicycle!*" And then he laughed for a good long time. Woody said the reason he liked Vladimir was because "he's crazier than I am." Wanda, who herself was a riot, was always grumbling about how she had spent her whole life taking care of two men— her father, Arturo Toscanini, and then Horowitz.

Woody and I were watching the news when we learned of Vladimir's death in 1989. Of that moment, Woody said in his biography, we were "not exactly stunned, but Mia and I were saddened. Within a minute we agreed to call Wanda. Then one of the kids ran into the room. The cat had jumped up on the kitchen table. We hurried to get the

cat off while the other kids came marching in demanding
dinner. Suddenly the enormity of the passing of a human
life was becoming history. The more pressing trivialities of
life interfered. Mia was immediately the hard-pressed
mother, grabbing the cat and ladling out the pasta. 'See
how life goes on?' she said to me. It's a concept that causes
me great trouble when I stop to think about it, which is
often. That is, just how fragile and fleeting life is in the
relentless flow of minor necessities that make up day-to-day
existence."

The success or failure of our movies had little impact on
our, or at least my, consciousness, except of course for the
New York Times review, which Woody usually had some inside word on, and which he read the minute it hit the
stands. The relationships he cultivated on the *Times* were
important too. We had dinner with the major critics of
Time and *Newsweek.* But Woody reserved special contempt
for film critics on television. "The Chicago morons" was his
label for one high-profile pair. We were always at work on
the next project when a film came out, and everyone around
us knew not to mention reviews in our presence. Woody
advised me not to read them. "Just keep your head down
and do good work," he said.

Other films were offered to me during those years, even
some good ones. But with our schedule, and reshoots all
through the year, it would have been difficult to take on a
separate project. My availability enabled Woody to rewrite
and reshoot our scenes whenever he wanted. And truthfully
I didn't have much ambition beyond what we were doing. I
just wanted to be with him and my kids, not interrupt our
routine, and to do good work. I must have been the envy of
every actor in the land. If there was a drawback, I didn't see
it.

Most of the films we made together were artistic and

critical successes. A couple were even commercial successes. One of these was *Hannah and Her Sisters*, which Woody described as "middlebrow." Although the reshoots on *Hannah* were extensive, he never came up with an ending that satisfied him. Its success confirmed his feelings about its essential mediocrity. "If one of my films is widely accepted," he said, "I am immediately suspicious of it."

His Oscar and other prizes were kept at his parents' house. "The whole concept of awards and being honored is silly," he said. "It's a popularity contest." The fact that Gordon Willis was not even nominated for his superb work on *The Godfather* and *Manhattan* was the example Woody always fumed about. So awards had no significance in our lives. I only found out on the day of the broadcast that I had been nominated for a Golden Globe for best actress (for one of the *Roses*, I forget which), and then only because Woody asked me which photograph they should use on television when they read my name. We didn't watch the show: by dinnertime that night we'd forgotten all about it.

"What would you think about us having a baby?" I asked when we had completed *Zelig*.

After the little cough he gave when he was uncomfortable, he said without looking at me, "Well, I don't know. I would have to think about it." Which meant he would discuss it with his therapist. There were three of us in the relationship: Woody, his shrink, and me. No decisions were ever made without her. He didn't even buy sheets without talking to her. I know that part of several sessions went into his switch from polyester-satin to cotton.

Eventually, with the understanding that I would be responsible for the baby in every way, he (they) agreed.

That Woody had been in psychoanalysis two or three times a week for about thirty years was astonishing to me. I myself had never been to any kind of psychiatrist, and I was highly skeptical. Woody had no problem admitting that for him therapy was "a crutch," and he credited it with enabling him to work as productively as he had. I couldn't argue with that.

The subject of marriage came up a few times over the years. "It's just a piece of paper," he would say. And intellectually I could see that. His was the more evolved position. Our relationship had to be truer, purer, more responsible, more committed, *better*, because it stood solely on the quality of its own trust and love. Ours, surely, was the highest form of marriage. He was never kinder or more reassuring than in those moments of my insecurity. "Do I not behave as if we are married?" he would ask, and I would answer that he did. The "piece of paper" was irrelevant. Of course. And the dark thoughts would scamper away.

In 1985 Eileen got sick. She sent me a picture of herself taken in the hospital: there was a tube coming out of her nose, a shower cap on her head, and she had sores all over her mouth with yellowish cream on them. She didn't have her teeth in and she was laughing into the mirror. That same week someone called to tell me that she had died.

I went to the funeral parlor to say good-bye. I worried that they might have fixed her face funny, put makeup on her, or given her a strange smile or something. She looked all right; dead, but all right. She was wearing her good, shiny blue dress, the one she'd worn the night she came to see me on Broadway, and I wondered how they got it on her. Someone once told me that undertakers cut clothes right up the back so they can put them on you after you're stiff. Eileen wouldn't have liked her best blue dress being cut. And she wouldn't have liked the idea of lying around with her eyes closed in front of her friends either. I put my hand on her hand, which was room temperature, and I

thought, Good-bye Eileen, I have loved you all my life, and
I will love you until my last thought.

WAFP 1984–85 began like all the other WAFPs: weighing
one idea against another. After endless talk over many
months, he finally settled on a subject that had long intrigued him—sisters. He had been close to Janet Margolin,
his leading lady in *Take the Money and Run*, and her two sisters; then with Diane Keaton and her two sisters; and now
there was me and my three sisters. My youngest sister Tisa
had even played a role in his film *Manhattan*. While we
walked, worked, ate, slept, and lived our lives, the story of
Hannah was fleshed out, detail by familiar detail.

Finally he placed a fresh script in my hands with instructions that I could play whichever sister I wanted, but he felt
I should be Hannah, the more complex and enigmatic of
the sisters, he said, whose stillness and internal strength he
likened to the quality Al Pacino projected in *The Godfather*.

It was the first time I criticized one of his scripts. To me,
the characters seemed self-indulgent and dissolute in predictable ways. The script was wordy but it said nothing.
Woody didn't disagree, and tried to switch over to the alter-
native idea (which might have been a murder mystery, I
forget), but preproduction was already in progress and we
had to proceed. It was my mother's stunned, chill reaction
to the script that enabled me to see how he had taken many
of the personal circumstances and themes of our lives, and,
it seemed, had distorted them into cartoonish characteriza-
tions.

At the same time he was my partner. I loved him. I could
trust him with my life. And he was a writer: this is what
writers do. All is grist for the mill. Relatives have always
grumbled. He had taken the ordinary stuff of our lives and
lifted it into art. We were honored and outraged.

And a small sick feeling stirred deep inside me. What I

shared with nobody was my fear that *Hannah and Her Sisters* had openly and clearly spelled out his feelings for my sister. But this was *fiction*, I told myself, or at most a *fantasy* inspired by passing thoughts. Even President Carter had fantasies. And Woody was a morally superior person. Besides, my sister was now happily married with a newborn baby, my godson. So I put those thoughts out of my mind. My mother and I played our mother-daughter roles, and she was fabulous. My old friend Michael Caine, who five years earlier had introduced Woody and me, played my husband.

Much of *Hannah* was filmed in my own apartment, which we were also living in—the children and I, Mary the dog, a cat, three chinchillas, two hamsters, six mice, assorted fish, a canary, and Edna the parrot. The place was pandemonium. The rooms were clogged with equipment, forty people arrived at dawn crowding into any available space, our personal treasures were spirited away to who-knew-where. The kitchen was an active set for weeks (we ordered out). Some nights I literally couldn't find my bed. In its own way it was a little Zen lesson—a shove toward acceptance and letting go, finding serenity in the center of chaos.

It was strange to be shooting scenes in my own rooms— my kitchen, my pots, my own kids saying lines, Michael Caine in my bathroom, wearing a robe, rummaging through my medicine cabinet. Or me lying in my own bed kissing Michael, with Woody watching.

Years later, I was in bed late at night flicking through the channels, and just at that moment I happened to catch my bedroom on television, and the same bed I was actually lying on, and me. Even my television was on television. I think I screamed.

The commotion, and not being able to find anything, sometimes got me a little crazy. But the kids loved it. All of them appear in the movie. Moses, Fletcher, and Daisy played my screen children, so they got to stay home from school (they were tutored). The cat has never been the same.

Two years had passed and still we had not conceived a child. I was nearly forty. The notion of adoption was not appealing to Woody, but finally, after I assured him once again that the child would be entirely my responsibility, and he told me it would not end our relationship, I applied to adopt a child.

But it was not a topic we could discuss. During the waiting period, as we walked in Central Park, in a swell of excitement and against my better judgment, I began babbling about the baby, and he cut me off. "Look, I don't care about the baby. What I care about is my work."

Given everything he had said, and the awful, undeniable fact that he had "zero interest" in my seven children, who were as dear as any on earth and who one by one had given up trying to win his heart; given all this, I don't know how I still hoped that he would love this child, that she would be the one to open his heart, and that through her, he would learn to love without suspicion; that through her, he would see that a person other than himself, with needs and interests distinct from his, can exist not as a threat, but as one worthy of respect and love. And discovering this, he would surely acknowledge all my children, he would see who they are as human souls, and in knowing them, how could he not love them? And then he would know all they mean to me, and finally he would understand who I am; and knowing my heart, he would feel safe and love me back with certainty. In loving this child, he would place her needs before his own—he would begin to hope on her behalf, and in doing that he would have access to a purer, deeper connection to life; and we would all be there together, a family. That is what I hoped.

Chapter Nine

In the summer of 1985, newborn baby Dylan came home. It was no accident that she was a little blond girl—the kind of child, he said, he would be most inclined to view positively; although, he was careful to add, it was certainly no guarantee. Soon-Yi and I traveled to a state in the Midwest, and together we brought baby Dylan home to Frog Hollow.

Since Moses was already two years old when he arrived, there had not been an infant in our family for eleven years. Eight wondrous faces crowded around the wicker basket, we watched her in her dreams, and we watched her study the birch leaves moving against the summer sky. Moses and Fletcher, proud and careful, pulled her about the garden in their red wagon, padded now with the patchwork quilt I'd made for the twins, sixteen years earlier. I named her after Dylan Thomas, and Casey became her god-mother.

In the fall, when Woody and I went on our walks and discussed the upcoming WAFP, *Radio*

Days, baby Dylan nestled snugly in the pouch on my chest, so quiet and small he barely noticed her. In preparation for my role of Sally the cigarette girl, I took daily singing lessons with my new daughter in my arms. My teacher even remarked on her perfect pitch.

By the time we began *Radio Days* that winter at Astoria Studios, Dylan was a serene and purposeful little girl with the beginnings of blond curls and a surprisingly raucous laugh. Even Woody was beginning to find her irresistible. It seemed to be the miracle I had hoped for. We shared our delight in the baby, and even discussed adopting a sister for her the following year.

"It might make sense to find a place big enough for all of us," he said to me one day. "I could have my own floor or wing away from everybody, so I can work. The kids would love living in a house. It could be like in *Meet Me in St. Louis.*"

I proposed sharing my apartment, which was larger than his. But it wasn't nearly big enough, he said, and it wasn't on the East Side. I pointed out that if we got a place on the West Side, it would cost much less, and over the years I'd be able to pay him back for my half. I told him I'd feel better if I could do that, because if for some reason our living together didn't work out, I didn't want to have to pack up my eight children and move out. I didn't want to do that again, and I didn't want the kids to have to go through it either, because wherever we lived should be their *home*. So, if we ever decided to go back to living separately, I would do my best to pay him for the whole house. But places on the East Side, in the neighborhood he was talking about, cost many millions of dollars.

"Keep your apartment as a backup," he said. I could see he was losing interest.

"But that's just it: I wouldn't be able to keep it, it's 'rent stabilized,' " I heard myself yammering, a little too brightly. "If we're not living in it, if it's not our primary residence, the landlords can up the rent as high as they want. Our apartment's been in the family for twenty-something years, it's a big deal to lose it. I'd never find another place big enough for all of us that's this affordable."

"Well, you'll have to work that out," said Woody. Which I never managed to do.

We had another talk about marriage, our second; eight or nine sentences was all, repeating what had been said before. Then I brought up the thing that worried me most: the thing that happened in front of the house that wasn't William Buckley's; and another time, when I didn't know the name of a certain kind of pasta; and again, when I was off in my estimate of the weather by only four degrees; and when I asked about a dream he'd had the previous night, when he had mumbled the words "Dolly Parton." Each of these times he had become so enraged, and his attacks were devastating. He always apologized afterward, but still, I was afraid it might happen again. If we were living together, it might happen more frequently, and maybe even worse. What if it got worse? And how can you avoid making someone angry when you don't have any idea what happened or why? And most important, what if he ever turned that anger on one of the kids?

He promised me it would never happen again. Ever. And I could tell he meant it this time. So we began, cautiously, to look at big houses and double penthouse apartments on the East Side. We found the house of our dreams on Seventy-third Street: every room was filled with sunlight, and it had been built on two lots, so the garden was extra large—the kids would be able to go outside whenever they felt like it. They could make snowmen, we could plant flowers and vegetables, strawberries, and jasmine. What a different New York life it would be! Moses would collect bugs after school; he and Matthew would play chess under the apple tree; we would build a tree house; Lark would do her cartwheels on the grass; baby Dylan would have her very own swings and sandbox right here in Manhattan. I pictured the kids and their friends playing badminton, reading in the hammock, shooting basketball. Soon-Yi would find more four-leaf clovers, and my mom would come to visit. We'd all have lunch outside and then she'd play old songs on the grand piano while I made tea. Woody would have his private space for work, and his special bathroom, and a poolroom and a Ping-Pong table. We will be the *Meet Me in St. Louis* family. We will watch the children grow. From our places by the fire we'll talk and laugh and wonder and love until we are worn-out.

Woody put in a bid to buy the house. Then, while we were dreaming, the owner changed his mind. We went on looking and working and living our lives in all the same ways with one small but growing difference, baby Dylan.

Winter had set in when we began *Radio Days* in late 1985. My feet were blocks of ice, while in snappy, forties high heels I painfully clomped the streets near Shubert Alley. Winds below zero froze my nylon stockings and silk dresses. With bright red lips and chattering teeth, I kissed a soldier in Grand Central Station. But mostly we were in Queens, at Astoria Studios. Fletcher, then eleven, was given a role that required him to be at work more than me, but on different days. Woody offered to bring him to and from the studio and assured me he would look after him there.

I loved playing Sally, the airheaded cigarette girl, and it suited me fine that it wasn't a long part. I brought Dylan with me to work, but I preferred being at home with her. Times were good. When occasionally a small cloud covered the sun, the powerful winds of our good fortune blew it quickly past; but it was strange, for that moment, how dark the clouds seemed in a perfect, clear sky.

Fletcher was pale and quiet when Woody brought him home one evening. His ear ached, he said. He couldn't get warm and he was beyond hunger. They had been shooting outside all day on a rooftop. The forties-period costume Fletcher had to wear was scarcely effective against the wind and cold, and the scene had taken almost all day to shoot. Instead of breaking for lunch, cups of hot soup had been handed out to the crew, but nobody gave anything to Fletcher.

It was the first time in our five and a half years together that I confronted Woody in real anger. It was unthinkable to me that he could have been there in his Eddie Bauer arctic gear, drinking hot soup, without any thought or feeling or sense of responsibility for Fletcher.

Not two weeks later we had a similar conversation when he brought Fletcher home deeply upset after shooting. Woody had taken him to see dailies, a scene in which, as Sally the cigarette girl, I came on to this guy, and he was all over me. There were two or three complicated shots, so a number of takes were printed, and it took a long time to view them all—an eternity, apparently, to my eleven-year-old son. And I knew just how he felt, having, as a child, watched my own mother in the arms of Joseph Cotten.

Some days after that, with a face full of worry, Fletcher told me about an actress at work who was being affectionate in the extreme with Woody, which, come to think of it, had not escaped my attention when we were making *Hannah*. There was just a moment—a greeting she might have done differently if she'd seen me in the doorway. Except, of course, it was out of the question: she was so nice and he loved me more than ever, and he was top-drawer in every significant way, so I certainly didn't need to worry about her hanging around the editing room. It was understandable: she was trying to learn the trade, he said, so she could direct a movie herself someday. Besides, I do not rush to judgment. I block it out.

Still, Fletcher was hoping Woody would come to his sixth-grade graduation that June, and Woody had told him he'd see if he could make it. But as the weeks passed with no further word, Fletcher prodded me to ask him.

"I don't want you to feel pressured," I said, as we were crossing West Seventy-second Street, "but it would mean a lot to Fletcher if you would come to his graduation."

"I'll have to think about whether you have any right to ask me that," he said, cold as ice. Better he had slammed a fist in my face. Then he was talking nonstop like always about the next movie, so he didn't notice how, right there on Seventy-second Street, a part of the dream began to die.

Of course I didn't bring it up again. He didn't come to the graduation. And he didn't seem to notice as Fletcher quietly withdrew.

In the summer of 1986 Casey and I took our kids in my big red Suburban to visit my mother and stepfather in up-state New York, then on to a grand adventure exploring the Howe Caverns, while Woody in New York was busy writing the next WAFP, *September*.

Initially he planned to make the film at Frog Hollow; ever since he first saw the place he'd been saying how perfect it would be to shoot a movie there, the way the rooms flowed into one another, the relationship of the house to the lake and the guest cabin, the woods, and the field, his favorite place to walk. But we were locked into a winter shooting schedule, and he wanted a sun-drenched Chekovian summer, so we ended up back at Astoria Studios.

September had been structured as a play, but shot as a film on a single set of adjoining rooms. It explored the relationships of six characters in an isolated summer house, and the long-term traumatic effects of an incident that had long intrigued Woody: the killing of Lana Turner's lover by her teenage daughter. Strains of Chekhov's *The Cherry Orchard* can be traced throughout.

The wedding party: Patrick and Susan Farrow, me,
Frank, and Prudence.

Steffi, Mom, Dolly Sinatra, Johnny, Martin Sinatra, and Tisa Farrow.

The presentation of an English cab to Frank—Yul has the papers and George Jacobs is at attention.

The day I cut my hair.
(Courtesy of 20th Century–Fox)

With Neile Adams and her husband, Steve McQueen, my friend Leonard Gershe, and Liza Minnelli at Andy Warhol's Factory in Manhattan, 1967.
(Courtesy of Archive Photos)

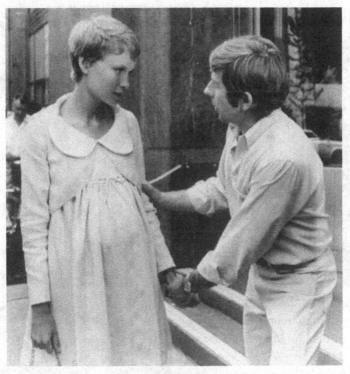

With Roman Polanski
shooting *Rosemary's Baby*
on a New York street.
(Rosemary's Baby © *1968 by*
Paramount Pictures)

My friend and
assistant Barbara Daitch
in her orange hat.
(*Photo by Raymond Kissack*)

Spring of 1968 in India: Patty Jamison, John Lennon, Mike Love, the Maharishi, George Harrison, me, Donovan, Paul McCartney, Jane Asher, and Cynthia.

(Courtesy of Rex USA Ltd.)

Johnny, me, and John Lennon.

Johnny and me in our hut of palms in Goa.

Joseph Losey on location in Holland shooting *Secret Ceremony.*

With Elizabeth Taylor in *Secret Ceremony,* 1968.
(Courtesy of Universal Studios)

With Dustin Hoffman in *John and Mary,* 1969.
(Courtesy of 20th Century–Fox)

The Haven, in
Reigate, Surrey,
where André and
I lived with the
children.

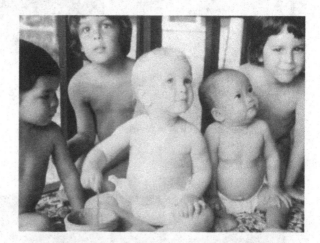

Lark, Sascha,
Fletcher, Daisy,
Matthew—the
first five, 1975.

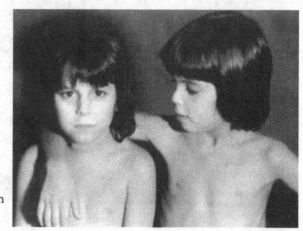

The twins:
Matthew (left)
and Sascha, born
in 1970.

Three Sisters on the London stage: Joy Parker, me, and Gwen Watford.
(*Courtesy of the Hulton Getty Picture Collection*)

Lark and me.

Bette Davis in *Death on the Nile*, 1978.

Moses joins the family in 1980; here he is napping with Fletcher.

Fletcher and Daisy, the second set of "twins."

In front of our house on Lake Tashmoo. *(Photo by Steve Schapiro)*

Lark, Soon-Yi, and Daisy on Martha's Vineyard.

André, Fletcher, Sascha,
Matthew, and
Daisy at the piano.

My friend Casey Pascal holding
her godchild, Dylan.

Lark, Sascha, Daisy, me, Fletcher, Matthew, and Soon-Yi in our
apartment on Central Park West in New York.

Lighting candles for peace on New Year's Eve at the Cathedral of Saint John the Divine in New York.

Dino De Laurentiis, Sven Nykvist, and me on Bora Bora for *Hurricane*, in 1978.

At Frog Hollow: Isaiah seated on the wall.

Moses Amadeus Farrow.

OPPOSITE TOP: Satchel
O'Sullivan Farrow.

OPPOSITE BOTTOM:
Thaddeus W. Farrow and
Isaiah Justus Farrow.

Dylan O'Sullivan Farrow.

In Ireland for *Widow's Peak* with Tam, Isaiah, and Moses.

The boys—Satchel, Thaddeus, and Isaiah—get ready for bed.

My mother holding Kaeli-Shea, with Dylan on the left, Tam behind, and Satchel on the right.

Tam and Frankie-Minh Farrow.

The next generation: Lark and Daisy and my first two grand-children, Sara and Patrick.

Matthew, Lark, Satchel, Daisy, and Tam at Sascha's wedding.

The screenplay of *September* was ambitious and problematic. We reshot every single scene as we went along, sometimes four or five times. Woody rewrote major scenes overnight or during lunch, while the cast scrambled to learn the rewrites and to make the long speeches and sometimes ponderous dialogue sound credible and fresh. Fine actors fell by the wayside, including my mother. Parts were recast. There was a shaky feeling in the air. I was relieved when my mother went back with her husband, to the safety of their lives upstate.

When finally the main shoot was over, Woody assembled the footage, looked at it, and threw out the entire thing. Within five weeks he had rewritten the script and we were back at Astoria reshooting the film with a different cast.

As usual I brought Dylan to work, and her crib and toys filled my dressing room. She was now an active toddler who made full use of the long studio hallways. At eighteen months she could sing a dozen songs and speak her mind clearly; she loved being read to and she could identify all the letters of the alphabet. At home and at work she was doted on. And to everyone's astonishment, no one was more doting than Woody Allen.

Woody's parents, the senior Konigsbergs, wintered in Florida, but when they were in New York we dropped by to see them with some of the children every few weeks or so in a ritual that did not vary. Woody would ring their doorbell and then cover the peephole. They always opened it anyway. From the time we walked in until we left a half hour later, he did not address them directly, or sit down or stop moving.

His father was usually watching television when we arrived. Both parents were hard of hearing, as is their son, so the volume was way up.

"You could change the channel and he wouldn't know the difference," said Woody loudly.

"What'd he say?" his mother would ask.

"I don't know," I would answer.

"Can you believe I came from these people?" he said. Of course I could, because he looked exactly like his mother. They seemed like lovely people, but early on things had gone wrong, and Mrs. Konigsberg was always eager to talk about it.

"I don't know," she used to say. "Maybe I was too hard on him when he was young."

"She hit me every day of my life," Woody would call out from wherever he was in the room.

"He was difficult," his mother went on. "Running, jumping, and pulling off his clothes, he was never still. I didn't know how to handle that type of child, he was too active. I was strict with him. Maybe if I hadn't been so strict he would have been different—softer, maybe. Warmer. With his sister it was different, she was an easy child. You could put her down and she would stay there. I was much sweeter with her. Maybe I was too hard on him." Her voice would trail off. She always asked me about my mother, and about each of the children by name. Mr. Konigsberg didn't talk much.

Mrs. Konigsberg passed out chocolate-chip cookies, and with amazement tinged with disapproval, she watched her fifty-two-year-old son romping, cuddling, crawling, and clambering after Dylan.

"It's too much," she'd say to the kids and me as we sat on the sofa eating our cookies, waiting for the half hour to pass. "It's not good for her."

"Twist her nose off," Woody would order Dylan. "She's the wicked witch. Go on, twist it off."

"What'd he say?" his mother would ask.

"Nothing." I'd shake my head. "Dylan, why don't you

come over here and have one of these good cookies? Everybody, careful, don't get chocolate on this white couch."

Woody's response to Dylan was more than I ever imagined. In truth it was much more than I had seen in any father toward a child in my whole life. And I'd been married to an Italian, a passionate, emotional guy who was nuts about his daughters; and to André, who, when he was there, was an affectionate and demonstrative father. But the most effusive description of Woody Allen could not truthfully include the words passionate, emotional, affectionate, or demonstrative. His reaction to Dylan was a radical departure from his usual behavior. I told myself he'd never really played with a child before, he just didn't know how. Surely he would relax in time.

I had to believe that the participation of the man I loved in the parenting of my child, a situation I had long hoped for, was an answered prayer, a door opening, a new shared, sacred dimension of our lives. And though work remained far and away his priority, by 1987 Dylan was becoming a central consideration in his life. I still hoped his feelings for her would lead to a deeper commitment to the entire family. But not all of the signs were pointing that way.

He asked me for the key to my apartment. On days we didn't work, he would arrive at about dinnertime. The kids were either in their rooms doing homework or still at the long kitchen table, where the events of the day were related and opinions aired in the liveliest fashion. Our adored housekeeper, Mavis Smith, who had been with the family since 1979, always cooked a terrific meal, and made fresh brownies or chocolate-chip cookies before she left for the evening. Even if Woody and I were planning to go out to dinner later, I served the food and sat with the children.

We'd hear the doorbell's short, loud burst, then the turn of the lock, the heavy slam of the glass-and-wrought-iron front door, and he was in our kitchen. With barely a nod to me or the other kids, he headed for Dylan. With his mouth wide open, bigger than a grin, his eyebrows high over the black frames of his glasses, it was a face unaccustomed to its own expression—an expression so asymmetrical, large, unguarded, hungry, and foreign, that I would blink to make the strangeness pass, as he scooped Dylan out of her high chair and carried her off into another room.

Woody had been in favor of me adopting another baby when we had talked about it months ago. "The other kids are so much older, it would be good for her to have a playmate, a little sister," he had said, and now I found myself thinking, Surely another baby will dilute this intensity.

All of the children I had adopted before Dylan had been classified as "difficult to place." With my fingers crossed, I showed Woody pictures of little girls in the United States and other parts of the world who were no longer babies, or who had disabilities. When my mother asked why, I told her that I had learned from Moses, firsthand, that meeting special needs is a special privilege, which brings a parent special rewards. It seemed that on the deepest level the other children understood this. Matthew, at seventeen and Yale-bound, had written in his college application essay, "Only now do I fully understand that my mother's way of making life meaningful was to give a home to orphaned children. As a result she has saved four lives and enriched her own. If I can do so much, my life will have been a success."

Woody hadn't been open to the idea before, but now he didn't rule out the possibility, so long as it was a girl. We would see. Dylan wasn't yet two. We were still slogging away on *September* when I learned I was pregnant.

Woody's response was unemotional, almost formal. *September* was in its seventh month, I reasoned, and had taken its toll on all of us. It was understandable. Having a baby was the last thing on his mind.

I can only suppose it had never occurred to my children that their mother would ever do anything that could result in pregnancy. It was an adjustment for all of them, and they seemed a little stunned at first, particularly Soon-Yi, whose dislike for Woody had always been palpable. Because she had arrived in our family just as André was leaving it, I worried that she had lacked a positive male role model in her life. So when she was little, I asked Woody several times if he would take her for a walk, buy her an ice cream or something, but he had declined. Now, when I told her I was pregnant, she burst into angry, uncomprehending tears. She didn't like Woody, she said, he was nasty and ugly, and the baby would be ugly like him. I held her and tried to reassure her.

My own reaction was more surprising. I'd given up thinking it was possible for Woody and me to have a child. My first elation turned to worry: Woody's lack of enthusiasm was depressing, I felt shut out. I began to wonder where I stood and to take stock, to clarify the way I *wished* things were for this coming child, and for all my children, and for me. I had begun to feel that his behavior with Dylan was strange. And it was not easing off, it was growing more extreme. But when I tried to talk to him about it, he got so angry. He had grown remote since our first years together, and cruel; not all the time, but so often he made me feel stupid and worthless. We were in each other's company constantly, but I no longer felt needed or loved. I did love him, but for the first time I admitted I was afraid of him.

I felt I should end the relationship, but I didn't know if I would be able to do that. Emotionally I was dependent on him, and the possibility that he would not want to work with me anymore was frightening. I seemed to have lost whatever definition I had once had of myself as an independent working woman, and in the process I had also lost confidence in my ability to survive without him.

Perhaps the new life inside me gave me the strength to tell him that the relationship, as it existed, was unacceptable. The conversation took place first thing in the morning. Standing face-to-face in his dressing room at Astoria Studios, I told him everything I felt. He was surprised and angry. Finally I said that I couldn't continue, and that I needed some distance from him.

But he didn't go away. He would not go. It was so strange. *September* ended, and he kept right on coming over to my apartment every single day. He started showing up at five-thirty and six in the morning. He'd be sitting in my kitchen hours before anybody was up. He came to Frog Hollow too, even overnight. I didn't know what to do. We politely ignored each other while he followed Dylan around. And then, after some weeks of this, I lost my resolve, the line blurred, and we were together again. I needed him and I loved him.

We went on a trip together that same summer of 1987. It was the first time we had brought all the children to Europe. I was no longer throwing up, and I felt fine. It was the celebration of our new beginning. Woody is a restless traveler so we kept moving—Paris, Stockholm, Helsinki, Venice, London, Luxembourg—we were averaging almost a country a day. We drove, in a van and a limo, six or seven hours at a stretch. We were driven from Paris to Mont-Saint-Michel, which has probably been a tourist trap since the Middle Ages, only nobody told us. Woody took one look, checked the rooms, ate an omelette, and we drove *all the way back*. We would have stayed overnight, but there was something wrong with the bathroom.

Parisians are a lot nicer if you're with Woody Allen. His efficient assistant Jane was there, ensuring things went without a hitch. During the day, while the kids and I goofed around in the hotel suite or went sight-seeing, Woody would write in the separate room he kept, for that purpose and for the bathroom.

One night in Paris, after Dylan's second birthday, I'd just given her a bath and put her to bed when, for the first time, I gathered all my courage and told him what I'd been thinking for many months and could no longer remain silent about: that I was worried about his behavior with Dylan. I had been hoping it would change, but it hadn't. It was getting worse. I told him that he'd been looking at the little girl in a sexual way. He stared at her whenever she was naked, and he was all over her, all the time, fondling her, not giving her any breathing room.

All that happened was that he got very angry.

When we returned from the trip I learned that the baby, due in December, would be a boy. A more perceptive person might have noticed Woody's interest slip from zero to minus. His focus was on the next movie. And Dylan. He wanted to adopt her, to be her legal father, but his lawyers didn't know if it would be possible since we weren't married. They were trying to figure out a way. I just listened. And privately, I worried.

The next WAFP, in 1987, was *Another Woman*, a film for which I had inadvertently provided the pivotal device. A year or so earlier, Woody and I had been sitting in my living room. I was staring at the fireplace, thinking about how fascinating apartment buildings are, with people living their separate lives inches apart from one another. In fact, just on the other side of my own living-room wall, a renowned therapist conducted her sessions; some of her patients were acquaintances of ours, including Woody's agent. We used to see them in the hallway coming and going.

"Wouldn't it be so cool to get one of those spy listening devices?" I said to Woody. "We could hear what they're saying through the wall."

"Would you want to define yourself as a person who would do that?" he asked disapprovingly.

"God no, absolutely not, just joking." I felt like a worm. My unworthy thought was somewhat redeemed when the script of *Another Woman* was built around just such a situation.

I was seven months pregnant when we began shooting *Another Woman*, and I worked right up until a week before the baby arrived. Gena Rowlands played the lead. Sadly, her husband, John Cassavetes, could not join her in New York for the filming; he was in California seriously ill with a liver disease. Woody persuaded my old friend Sven Nykvist to shoot the film; he had been Ingmar Bergman's cinematographer on so many of Woody's favorite films.

As my body expanded I felt fat, undesirable, and exhausted. Woody seemed put off by my condition; he never touched my stomach, or felt the baby kick, or tried to hear his heartbeat. In fact he scarcely mentioned the baby. So I wasn't surprised when he declined to be my Lamaze coach. Casey took the classes with me.

On December 19, 1987, the baby was delivered by cesarean section. To my great surprise, Woody agreed to be in the operating room with the provision that if it got too disgusting, he wouldn't stay. I wouldn't have blamed him, but I think I hung on to his hand so tight he probably couldn't leave. He was by my side even when the epidural wore off while they were cutting me open.

We called our not-so-tiny (nine pounds, four ounces) baby Satchel, after Satchel Paige the ballplayer. The name was Woody's suggestion. I wasn't sure about it, but it was better than Ingmar, which was his first choice.

On the second day of my stay in the hospital I was given a form, the umpteenth, which I filled out and gave back. The next morning my doctor came into the room looking slightly embarrassed to say that unfortunately I couldn't legally fill out the box marked "Father" because I wasn't *married.* If I wanted a father listed on the certificate, I would have to give the form to that person, and he could have his name put on it. If he wished. The doctor, a nice man, gave me back the original form along with a new, blank one, and he apologized again. I said, Oh I see, I'm sorry, no problem.

I didn't know whether Woody would want his name on the form or not. I decided I would pick a moment to give him the form and just tell him it was an option. No big deal. Whatever. I hated the form.

Later that week I gave it to him. He said he'd have his lawyer deal with it.

I had never spent even one night away from Dylan and I was eager to get back home. Christmas is a Very Big Deal in our family and there were only a few days left. Because of the fall work schedule, I always began shopping and organizing in August. So the lists were already checked off, the tree was trimmed, the stockings were hung, and presents were in giant labeled bags hidden in my closet. Mavis would make her stuffing, and there was nothing left to do until Christmas Eve.

During the operation I had lost more blood than was usual; I felt as if I'd spent a week with vampires. The doctor told me I could go home on the morning of the third day, provided I had a hospital nurse around-the-clock for a week.

"What's that for?" Woody asked the nurse with the wheelchair when the day arrived for me to go home.

"It's to take her downstairs," she replied.

"We don't need it," he said. I was all stooped over, and I couldn't straighten up, my stomach hurt so much. Step by tiny step we made it to the car, settled ourselves into the back, and started home.

"Please," I begged the driver, "go slow." And I cried all the way up First Avenue.

One of my eight children was entering Yale and another was about to begin nursery school. I had been picking up pieces of Lego for almost two decades.

So when I had entered the hospital, it was with confidence that I'd bounce back from the cesarean in no time. I would pouch my baby and take him everywhere. This baby I would nurse as long as he wanted, like mothers do all over the world. The other kids would accept and adore him just as they had Dylan, who for months now had been laughing at the thumps from my stomach. "*My* baby," said Dylan as she folded the tiny clothes and put them into freshly lined drawers. She could hardly wait to help me dress and bathe the new baby. We taked about how she would curl up beside me while I read to her like always, and "her" baby would sleep peacefully in her arms along with her teddy, Flo-Bear.

But the baby screamed day and night. When sleep overtook him for scant minutes at a stretch, he jumped himself awake in full cry. It was colic, said Dr. Stone, he was a "high-needs baby," he had an "immature nervous system." He was exhausting.

"Take him outside for a walk," the doctor finally suggested.

"Throw him away," wailed Dylan, fed up with so much howling. I would put on his woolly hat, pop him into the pouch, strap him onto any willing brother or sister, zip a goose-down jacket over the two, and send them out the door. As the elevator descended and the screams faded, I fell back in bed. Never had I been so tired.

At night I put Dylan's favorite part of Vivaldi's *Four Seasons* on the stereo, and I lay on her bed with my arms around her, and told her how I loved her, and that I was eating my spinach, so soon I'd be as strong as Popeye, and we would ride on the merry-go-round, and ice-skate in

Central Park, and visit the elephants at the museum. Then just when the flowers are opening, we will go to Frog Hollow, and a beautiful giant butterfly will be waiting in the field. We'll climb on its back and fly up into the sky where we can bounce on pink clouds with baby angels and slide on the pieces of rainbow they keep up there. And our own baby will stop his crying: he'll look around, and when his tears are dry, he will smile, he'll be so happy to see us all, especially Dylan.

Dylan and I had planned for this to be our special shared time, but now I could barely stand up, and Woody kept taking her off to other rooms. He rarely came in to see me and he hardly glanced at the new baby. He never held or touched him, and he didn't seem to like me nursing him. He seemed stern—or was it angry? It made me cry.

The doctor told me to eat meat for anemia, so Woody brought me steaks. "Thank you," I said, "and thank you for offering to pay for five days of a private nurse. You've done these nice things for me, but you're so cold."

This was a mistake, because he shouted, *"That's a lie, that's an out-and-out lie!"*

Scared in my bed, I said, "I'm sorry, I just meant I need you to be kinder. I feel you don't love me anymore."

But he was on his way out of the room. "Please leave Dylan with me," I called after him. "Every time you come over, you take her away from my room. No, don't go. I'm sorry. It's the hormones, or the operation, or it's that I haven't slept in weeks, the baby cries all the time. I don't know what it is, but I'm sorry."

Less than a month after the birth I was back in the camper with Dylan and Satchel, for reshoots—now with a pillow to replicate my pregnant stomach. My costumes were adjusted to accommodate nursing the baby. At that moment I would have given almost anything not to have had to work, but at least my part wasn't huge. I never saw the movie, or *New York Stories*, which followed immediately. All I remember about making them is wanting to go home.

The baby finally stopped crying, and eventually I was *almost* as strong as Popeye.

In the summer of 1988 the whole family went on another trip. We visited Grieg's birthplace in Norway, and the Munch museum, and we wandered aimlessly around Helsinki. The centerpiece of the trip, our visit to the Soviet Union, lasted less than twenty-four hours. Woody was so unnerved by the way of things there—the lines for tour buses and terrible food, the fact that he was just another tourist in Leningrad. So he told his assistant to get us out on the *next flight*, he didn't care where to.

Two weeks later we were in London, heading home. The breast pocket of his rumpled, black linen jacket was bulging with stationery from hotels in Norway, Helsinki, Stockholm, Salzburg, Copenhagen, Rome, Venice, Lake Como, and London on which Woody had written the first draft of *Crimes and Misdemeanors*.

In the fall of 1988 we began *Crimes and Misdemeanors* (or, as Moses would pronounce it, "Crimes and Mister Meaners"), a chilling but brilliant movie about getting away with murder, conscience-free. There were the usual problems with the script, especially the section involving Woody and me. He rewrote and reshot all of our scenes and at least a third of the rest of the movie.

Salvador Dalí died early in 1989. I hadn't seen him since I visited him and Gala at the St. Regis Hotel in 1980, when he lowered himself to his knees and kissed my hand, and then had trouble rising to his feet. But on Palm Sunday, every year since 1966, I had received a telegram from him: each one said "Palm Sunday," and some said it many times.

I had not slept through the night in more than a year.

But Satchel, though nocturnal, was a blessing: an affectionate, thoroughly rewarding little boy, and a silver-haired,
blue-eyed replica of my brother Mike. He began to speak at
seven months and was astoundingly articulate well before
his first birthday. Even so, Woody remained indifferent, at
best. Not entirely in jest, he referred to him as "the little
bastard," or "the completely superfluous little bastard." to
which the child responded with equal measures of indifference and hostility.

In the summer of 1989 we all went to Europe again—
Venice, Vienna, Rome, Switzerland, Belgium, and Paris, I
think. To avoid the unpleasantness of airports, this year
Woody chartered a private jet for the entire trip. Fresh gua-
camole and chips were out on the table when we boarded
the plane at Teterboro Airport in New Jersey. The seats
were huge and cushiony, the enchiladas (our food of choice
for the flight) were tops; there were dozens of movies to
choose from. You couldn't help feeling guilty at the luxury
of it, but it sure was an easy way to travel. You come and go
whenever you want (the crew stays in a hotel). Customs
people come right on board to stamp passports.

One major benefit of our summer travels *en famille* was
that they seemed to have brought Woody closer to the older
kids. Indeed, in 1990 he would suggest that I amend my
will so that in the event of my death, the care and custody
of all my minor children would be left to him. I thought it
was a beautiful and brave and generous gesture for which I
was immeasurably grateful. Immediately I redrafted my will,
and delighted in the new relationships that were forming. I
noticed Woody in conversations with Daisy, and even
Soon-Yi seemed to be warming toward him. When he finally became more considerate with her, it was wonderful.
There was no doubt in my mind that it would be good for
her.

Without complaint he attended Soon-Yi's sweet-sixteen
party. And that year he began stopping by her desk as she

did her homework in the evenings, before we went out to dinner. Now, whenever he came over, Soon-Yi would appear in the room. When he sat in the library watching baseball, basketball, and football on television, Soon-Yi sat quietly beside him as he explained the games to her. Her brothers and sisters began to tease her, saying she had a crush on him.

For her next birthday Woody and I took her and a few of her friends to dinner at the Russian Tea Room, then we dropped them at *Phantom of the Opera*. Woody and I didn't go to the play, but he sent his limo to pick up the girls afterward. Soon-Yi's braces were off, and she was a lovely seventeen-year-old beginning her junior year at Marymount, an all-girls Catholic school on Fifth Avenue. An autographed picture of Fred Astaire hung by her bed. Her friends were already dating, but Soon-Yi showed little interest in that. She had never had a single date or even a phone call from a boy. She was a diligent worker in school and I was proud of her accomplishments, but privately I was beginning to wonder whether a coeducational school might not have been better for her.

For years Woody had had four season tickets to the Knicks basketball games. Since I didn't much enjoy attending them, he usually went with other friends, or, if the season was unexciting, he gave his seats to guys on the crew. Lark, Matthew, Daisy, and Moses were passionate basketball buffs, and over the years I had tactfully and unsuccessfully tried to get Woody to bring them to a game. So I was delighted when that year he asked if he could bring Soon-Yi to a Knicks game. After the third game, though, I suggested he invite Moses or Lark. They were dying to go, and it was only fair. So the next time, he took Lark and Moses to their very first game, along with Soon-Yi.

It was around then that Soon-Yi developed another new interest; she began talking about modeling and auditioning for acting parts. But she had wanted to be a psychologist, and had never shown the slightest interest in acting, or even been in a school play. Acting is a tough business with lots of rejection built-in; I would have tried to dissuade any of my children from entering it. I hoped they would find professions that were relatively solid. Soon-Yi was still in high school, with college ahead. I didn't want her trying to model—the values in that world are all screwed-up. I asked Woody to please not encourage her. But his casting director was already sending her on auditions.

That fall, and through the winter of 1990, we shot *Alice*, my first major role since Satchel's birth. He still awoke during the night, and there were days when I came to work exhausted, but I was eager to be back on the job, excited about the movie and thrilled with my part, and I was going to be working with Joe Mantegna, Alec Baldwin, and Bernadette Peters. Again we reshot at least half of the movie as we went along, and, predictably, after the rough cut there were more reshoots. The ending was a problem.

In the meantime Woody's lawyers weren't getting anywhere in their efforts to arrange for Woody to co-adopt Dylan. From time to time over the years he would bring a lawyer to the set or my apartment with papers for my signature. Before I signed anything, I always asked the same question: "I wouldn't be giving up any of my rights, would I?" And in chorus Woody and his lawyers would say, "No, of course not."

But the fact that we weren't married seemed to be an insurmountable obstacle for the court—quietly I was relieved and hoped the issue would disappear. My concern about his behavior with Dylan, now five years old, his insistence that there was nothing unusual about it, and the unpleasantness my objections caused had created specific tensions between us. But I supposed that no relationship of ten years' duration was without its problems, and those tensions aside, our life was moving forward in all the same ways. The commitment of a decade together, I felt, had provided us with a permanent, solid base. If the pattern of our lives was in some respects less than ideal, it worked in other respects.

"It's sort of like just enough," Woody told his biographer. "Perhaps if we were to live together or if we met at different times in our lives, it wouldn't work. But it seems to be just right. I have all the free time I want and it's quiet over here, and yet I get plenty of action over there. I think it's because we don't live together and that she has her own life completely and that I have mine, that we're able to maintain this relationship with a certain proper tension. If we got married years ago and lived together maybe now we'd be screaming, 'What have we gotten into?' These things are so exquisitely tuned. It's just luck . . . Mia's been a completely different kind of experience for me, because the predominant thing has been family . . . She's brought a completely different, meaningful dimension to my life. Yet the two of us have so little in common that it always amazes us.

"I could go on about our differences forever: She doesn't like the city and I adore it. She loves the country and I don't like it. She doesn't like sports at all and I love sports. She loves to eat in, early—five-thirty, six—and I love to eat out, late. She likes simple, unpretentious restaurants, I like fancy places. She can't sleep with an air conditioner on, I can only sleep with an air conditioner on. She loves pets and animals, I hate pets and animals. She likes to spend tons of time with kids, I like to spend my time with work and only a limited time with kids. She would love to take a boat down the Amazon or go up Mount Kilimanjaro, I never want to go near those places. She has an optimistic, yea-saying feeling toward life itself, and I have a totally pessimistic, negative feeling. She likes the West Side of New York, I like the East Side of New York. She has raised nine children now with no trauma and has never owned a thermometer. I take my temperature every two hours in the course of the day . . .

"I can only think that what made us throw in our lot together is that the two of us met slightly later in life and that we both have our own developed lives—her with a major family and me with a career—and we don't share the same house. I'm able to live with it when she goes to the country for the summer. She's able to live with it that I don't. We both have our own lives and just enough intersection so that it's fun but not smothering."

His biographer, Eric Lax, who hung around through five films over nearly four years, observed that "few married couples seem more married, however. They are in almost constant communication and there is what can only be called a sweetness about them; at the few parties they attend they usually shyly stand off in a corner, holding hands."

During the summer of 1990 we all went to California and stayed at the Bel-Air Hotel while Woody shot *Scenes from a Mall* with Bette Midler. Maria Roach, my childhood neighbor and friend, and I took Woody on a tour of Beverly Hills. He was completely entranced, exploring our old haunts, and said over and over what a great movie the story of my life would make.

Back in New York he finished filming *Scenes from a Mall* at Astoria Studios. The 1990 season of Knicks games began with Soon-Yi eagerly attending. Woody even got her a job as an extra on the movie, and as he had with Fletcher, he offered to take her to and from work.

On the job she met a new friend, a woman she described only as "older," and "in her late twenties." On weekend mornings Soon-Yi left the apartment to visit her new friend, not in her customary jeans, sneakers, and flannel shirt, but wearing miniskirts, makeup, and cute hats.

Soon-Yi had always been completely reliable and responsible, so at first I wasn't worried. But as the weeks went by I began to be concerned: she was young and trusting, who was this older woman, and why did she never come to our home like all the other friends of the children? When I asked to meet the woman, Soon-Yi resented my intrusion and angrily declared she would not see her again. Still, she continued to leave the house early on weekend mornings, to shop at Bloomingdale's or to visit school friends, dressed in the new way.

But it was more than Soon-Yi's clothes that were changing. My eldest daughter seemed to be going through a "difficult phase." She had become uncommunicative, which is not unusual for a teenager, but now she was cold, and so openly contemptuous of me and of my opinions that I remember saying to Woody (and this for me was an unimaginable thought) that I was beginning to actually welcome the time when she would go away to college. "Maybe it will be good for both of us," I said.

It was wonderful for me that Casey lived, as I did, in New York and in Connecticut. She had three small children the same ages as Dylan and Satchel. One afternoon when Casey and I were minding our kids in a playground in Central Park, Woody appeared unexpectedly and out of breath. With barely a nod to us and without a glance at Satchel or Moses, he spotted Dylan and ran after her. In his hat and glasses and army jacket, he ran up and down the hill, chasing Dylan through swarms of tiny kids, crawling after her through tunnels and jungle gyms, along the walkways, up and down the slides.

Casey turned to me and said, "I hope this is a great thing."

·   ·   ·

We didn't spend our weekends at Woody's apartment at this time: the teenagers in the family refused to go there, and Satchel was still nocturnal. So it was difficult. But we went out to dinner most evenings, and Woody spent about an hour with us at my apartment in the mornings and evenings. When we went to Frog Hollow for the weekends, he came to stay overnight. Otherwise any moments of intimacy had to be stolen from our busy schedules.

His behavior with Dylan was getting worse. "Obsessed" was the word most frequently used by my family and friends. He whispered her awake, he caressed her, and entwined his body around her as she watched television, as she played on the floor, as she ate, as she slept. He brought her into bed when he was wearing only his underpants. Twice I made him take his thumb out of her mouth.

But more even than any of these specifics, there was a wooing quality to his approaches: a neediness, an aggressive intensity that was relentless and overpowering. Now, at the sound of the doorbell and the slam of the front door, Dylan fled from the kitchen to closets, bathrooms, under beds and desks. "Hide me . . . *Hide me!*" she would scream to her older brothers and sisters. It was not a game.

Please don't hunt her down like that, I said for the umpteenth time. If you'd just let her come to you she wouldn't be so scared, *it's too much.* But he wouldn't listen.

Most of the time Dylan was a bright, chatty little girl, brimming with opinions and observations. But in his presence she withdrew, her talk became sketchy and hard to follow, and instead of answering his questions, she looked around the room. When he became more insistent, she hummed, talked like a baby, barked like a dog, sang, did anything to deflect his attentions; and this only made him more insistent. When she wouldn't say good night, when she wouldn't even look at him, he pinned her shoulders to the bed and demanded a response while her head thrashed back and forth.

"C'mon, just kiss her good night and leave it at that," I begged, tugging him off her. I found myself policing his behavior, which made him angry.

If there was a problem he insisted that it lay with me, in my misinterpretations of his very normal paternal affection. I was accustomed to thinking he was right about everything; he had to be right about this. I couldn't accept any other explanation.

"*Spoilsport,*" he exploded angrily when I pulled Dylan out of the bed where he had been wrapped around her like a python in Jockey underpants.

"*What* sport?" I asked him. "Just what *sport* am I spoiling?"

A psychologist who was already helping another child in the family (Woody believed everyone would benefit from therapy) witnessed only one brief greeting between Woody and Dylan, but it was enough for her to mention it to me, and express her concern that Woody's attitude was "inappropriately intense, because it excluded everybody else; and it placed a demand on a child for a kind of acknowledgment that I felt should not be placed on a child."

"That was *nothing!*" I told the therapist, and the years of fear, disbelief, silence, and denial welled into words. I told her all of it, and I prayed she would be able to help.

To my great relief, the therapist began to work with Woody, to help him to understand that his behavior with Dylan was "inappropriate" and had to be modified. Now many of the things that had so disturbed me seemed to improve. She made him stop putting his hands under Dylan's covers, stop putting his face in her lap, stop the constant caressing, stop hunting Dylan down, stop having her suck on his thumb.

Although the therapist addressed the specifics, she was unable to modify the overall wooing quality of Woody's

approaches, his own neediness expressing itself to Dylan.
And if I left a room with Woody and Dylan in it, when I
returned, I was still likely to find him doing those same
things again.

At least now, when he got mad at me, he was more likely
to come around later and say, "Look, I'm really sorry.
You're right to tell me when this kind of thing happens.
Just tell me. It's okay."

So we had come a long way, I had articulated my concerns, he had acknowleged there was a problem, and a therapist was in place addressing the issue with him. He was
making an effort. I had to believe that everything would be
all right. I had to.

My mother and my youngest sister, Tisa, who is a nurse
working and living with her family in Vermont, came to
Frog Hollow with her daughter Bridget during Dylan's fifth
summer. "It was a typical Edward Albee family get-
together," Tisa recalled. "Mom and I were sitting down by
the water's edge. Bridget was about two. Both our little girls
were naked. It was buggy and sunny. Woody started rub-
bing some sunscreen on Dylan's shoulders. Then he got to
her bottom, and there he took his time. It was a momen-
tary thing, but it was so *glaringly* inappropriate. Just not
something a grown man does to a child. If someone did
something like that to my child I'd haul off and whack him.
You know how you teach your child about 'good touching'
and 'bad touching'? This was such a classic example of 'bad
touching.' I didn't know anything about him and Dylan
then. Mom and I talked about it later. She had noticed it
and she was disturbed too."

We needed help.

Chapter Ten

Why did I stay with Woody Allen when so much was wrong? How can I explain it to my children, when even to me it is incomprehensible and unforgivable? Was he only an illusion I loved all along? What was missing in me that compelled me to hold it all in place? When did the illusion become a lie? Why did I expose my children to his disregard for so long, and place them at risk? Why did I allow therapists to override my maternal instincts and doubt my own eyes? Wasn't it my own appalling denial of the facts that permitted him to inflict his damage on those I love most?

I could protest that I didn't know—how could I have known—what he was capable of. How could I believe it. I could argue that the world I had occupied with him for a quarter of my life was so utterly removed from any other that it was impossible for me to envision a life for myself beyond it. Every aspect of my existence was interwoven with his.

I could tell my children all this, but no explanation seems adequate. In the end all I can do is accept my share of responsibility, and hope they can find it in their hearts to forgive me.

"What's this movie about?" asked John Cusack good-naturedly.

The entire soundstage at Astoria, the huge one where a gleaming mall had bustled for *Scenes from a Mall,* was now a drab Kafkaesque town with twisting cobbled streets and crumbling buildings with slanty roofs. Inside one of these houses, the other actors and I sat around a brightly lit table waiting for last-minute camera adjustments before we plunged into a long scene. Around the table Jodie Foster, Lily Tomlin, and Kathy Bates, all dressed as prostitutes, were smiling at the audacity of John's question: they had no idea what *Shadows and Fog* was about because of course they hadn't been given the script.

"Well, it's, I guess it's sort of . . . an existential comedy." I squirmed apologetically. They all laughed and were too gracious to pursue it.

It was the fall of 1990. Since that summer Woody had been without energy, exhausted all the time. Throughout the workday, at every opportunity, he lay down. His doctors thought he might have Lyme disease, or chronic fatigue syndrome; there was talk about Epstein-Barr. Unless he was in front of the camera as an actor, he went days without shaving or washing his hair.

Most of my scenes were with John Malkovich. Some weeks into the movie Woody said, "You can laugh and flirt with John Malkovich all you want, but just don't tell him anything about the movie."

I stared at him, too shocked and horrified to respond with more than a weak nod. John was delightful company and a wonderful actor, but there had been no flirting between us. I hadn't flirted with another man in more than eleven years. On the other hand, if I *had* been flirting, why would it be okay?

One morning, after awakening Dylan, who slept in the bed next to Satchel's, Woody stood staring at his three-year-old son. As usual Satchel yelled at him to go away, but on this morning Woody grabbed him by the leg and started twisting it. "I'm going to break your fucking leg," he said, and I really thought he would. Satchel screamed in pain. Dylan screamed. I flew over to the bed and pulled Woody off him.

In vain I had tried to promote a better relationship between Woody and Satchel. When Woody took Dylan off into other rooms, I would mime, "Take Satchel too." When he brought Dylan a present, I asked that he bring one for Satchel, and for Moses too. I pointed out Satchel's many accomplishments and interests, and I suggested ways that Woody might become involved with him. But eventually I realized that he was not withholding his affection: it simply did not exist for Satchel, or Moses, or any of the other children. Lightning would not strike twice in our family: Woody would love one child only, and his love for her was an unusual kind.

In the spring of 1991 I was told about an orphaned six-year-old boy in Vietnam. He was unable to walk because of polio, they said, and had been in an orphanage all his life. It seemed an omen to me: a post-polio child who needed a home. Woody was far less opposed to the idea of adopting this child than he had been to the adoption of Dylan. In fact, when pictures of the boy arrived that May, we looked at them together and noted that in four of the five snapshots a girl was standing next to the boy, a girl of about ten or twelve who was obviously blind. Woody commented on how pretty she was and said, "If it's not a big deal, why don't you see if you can get the girl too?"

You could have knocked me down with a feather. I hugged him tight. "Really?" was all I could say. "Really?"

"You might as well," he said, hugging me back. "I'm not a bad guy."

It turned out that the little girl had been in the Vietnamese orphanage for six years. Her name was Tam. I began the paperwork for both children.

That June, Lark and Soon-Yi graduated from their high schools. Woody surprised all of us by showing up at Soon-Yi's graduation. Both young women had been accepted at the colleges of their choice, Lark at New York University and Soon-Yi at Drew University. They were beautiful, and polar opposites. Lark, all passion, generosity, love, and laughter, had always been in so many ways the heart of the family. Even the parrot Edna would call, "Lark, Lark." I doubt if in her life she has gone through a single waking hour of any day without trying to do something for somebody else.

Soon-Yi was quiet, reserved, and cautious. Dr. Audrey Sieger, whose doctorate is in learning and reading disabilities, had tutored her from the sixth grade through the twelfth. "She's a very typical learning-disabled kid, very socially inappropriate, very, very naive," said Dr. Sieger. "She has trouble understanding language on an inferential level. She's very literal and flat in how she interprets what she sees and how she interprets things socially. She misinterprets situations . . . During those last six months of high school there was a definite change."

In the summer of 1991, Woody and I took the whole family—minus Matthew, Sascha, and Soon-Yi, who had jobs in New York—and we drove around the west of Ireland for a couple of weeks. I'd always told Woody he'd like it there, and he did. After the trip the kids and I returned to Frog Hollow while, in the city, Woody prepared *Husbands and Wives* for the WAFP 1991.

The younger children and I missed the older kids, who

were home less and less, but everybody came up to Frog Hollow with Woody on the weekends. I was proud of the young adults they had become and I loved their company. The twins were twenty-one, and had both been doing well at top colleges; that summer Sascha was managing a city store, while Matthew was working for the ACLU. Both boys had wonderful partners of long-standing who by then were practically family members, and they were looking out for Soon-Yi, who had a job at Bergdorf Goodman.

In August Woody again brought up the subject of adopting Dylan. He and his lawyers had a new idea, one they hoped would be effective: if he were to adopt Moses, the only other child in the family who had no father, his petition would be much stronger. At thirteen, Moses could be articulate in his wish for a father. Moses would "piggyback Dylan's adoption," Woody said.

He had now been trying to adopt Dylan for about three years. I doubted it would ever happen, but ever since Moses had been a tiny child, he had wished for Woody to be his father. It was his dream. Even if it never got to court, it would mean the world to him that Woody had tried.

We called Moses into the living room and asked if he would like Woody to be his father. Moses just lit up. He smiled and smiled for days.

Later that same September I traveled to Vietnam to bring home the two new children. My friend Casey, her husband Jack Pascal, and three-and-a-half-year-old Satchel accompanied me on the eleven-day journey. Woody was adamant that Dylan, now six, should not be taken out of school. But he was very supportive about the trip and about the new kids. He even tried to coax a film studio to provide a jet for the trip, and when that fell through, he offered to help me pay for it. I worried about leaving Dylan, but Lark and Sascha would be staying at the apartment to baby-sit, along

with Fletcher and Daisy, who were seventeen. Soon-Yi
promised to come from college in nearby New Jersey every
weekend. I also had a baby-sitter I trusted, the therapist was
in place, and over and over Woody promised he would
remember not to let things get "too much."

In the rice paddies near Ba Vi, the midday heat pressed
heavily on the countryside. An old woman looked up from
her work to stare at the time travelers as we streaked rudely
past.

I lifted the little boy out of a crib, which he shared with
another child of roughly the same size, whose wrist was tied
with a knotted rag to the rusted bars. There was no mattress; the children sat on sagging wooden slats without
blankets or sheets. The walls were pitted and stained, and
the windows had no glass.

I opened a suitcase full of toys from the Danbury Mall
and passed out the little cars, rocket ships and airplanes,
Power Rangers, crayons, pads of colored paper, bubbles,
and dolls to the thin, ragged children, their eyes alight.
Almost immediately a woman moved quietly behind them
taking their toys, putting them into her upturned straw hat.
Forget it, I was told: she will take the toys home to her own
kids.

I asked for the little girl, Nguyen Thi Tam, but was told
that she had been moved to an institution for the blind.
Her papers were not complete, so she wouldn't be able to
leave with me after all.

It seemed that people there, three hours outside of Hanoi, had not seen too many blue-eyed, white-haired three-
year-olds. Satchel was an attraction and everybody wanted
to touch his hair.

Later, in Hanoi, a ragged boy of about nine ran along
the sidewalk bare-legged with a small child wearing a newspaper hat tied to his chest, asleep against his shoulder. The

streets were a wild jumble of bicycles, pedal-rickshaws, and people on their haunches in clusters cooking, eating, and talking. A mirror nailed to a tree served as a barbershop, houses left by the French crumbled elegantly in bleached colors under the hot sun, and laundry hung from windows. A sheet of canvas or plastic supported by poles was roof enough for a shop, a restaurant, or a home. These ticky-tacky appendages added a lively look.

I was taken to see Nguyen Thi Tam, who recoiled from the stuffed bear I had brought for her. The workers explained that she thought the bear was real. When she was taken away after less than ten minutes, I wondered if I would ever see her again.

By chance Mother Teresa was also having breakfast one morning in the dining room of the Hanoi Government Guest House, unruffled by the giant rats that zigzagged across the room and under the tables. I all but genuflected when she said, "God bless you," just as she had in New York in the early eighties, when I had brought the kids to the United Nations to see a documentary on her life, and to meet her. She was the embodiment of everything I had tried to teach them about true success and what one person with conviction and courage can accomplish. As we spoke in Hanoi, I recalled how Matthew, Sascha, Soon-Yi, Lark, Fletcher, Daisy, and I had stood in line for our chance to meet her, and then I had run around to the end of the line to do it again. Michael Douglas and his lovely wife were standing next to Mother Teresa, so I met them twice too.

My initial policy in Hanoi was to eat whatever was served if it didn't have a fly on it at the moment I saw it, and if I could identify it generically; but I loosened up on both points. I gave Satchel only the food we had brought with us in cans, jars, bottles, and packages, because who knew, and because he had his own rigid food policies. We kept his stuff in the little refrigerator in our room. Once I left the grape jelly out, and within twenty minutes insects were marching in an organized line from the window across the floor up the refrigerator and swarming the sealed jelly jar. Bathroom bugs came in three varieties: little black hurriers, laid-back centipedes, and huge, disgusting, fleshy ones, possibly of the water bug family. Whenever I went into the bathroom, I would first make a lot of noise, clapping hands, stamping feet, or singing loudly to send them scurrying. There weren't enough analysts in the world to have gotten Woody through this trip. But Satchel could not have been more thrilled; I'd go so far as to say that the bugs *made* the whole adventure for him, and I thought of how Moses would have loved it there.

As I shampooed lice off the little boy's head, I saw that his back was humped, and his limbs were quite shriveled; he could not move his legs. Although I had been told that he'd had polio, I'd seen enough of that disease to doubt it. Nor did it seem to be cerebral palsy, since his muscles were flaccid, not contracted. And even given the incalculable deprivations of his circumstances, this six-year-old boy did not appear to be functioning normally. I brought my concerns to the head of the Hanoi-based American adoption agency, and told her we needed to have the child evaluated before I went further.

On the forms she'd originally sent to me there were lists with boxes to check: acceptable, not acceptable, and willing to discuss. In the not acceptable category, I had made only two checks: profound retardation and degenerative illnesses. While considering the adoption of a child with special needs, I had concluded, out of fairness to my existing family, that any child who joined us should one day be able to live independently. It didn't seem right that a decision of mine should knowingly present a burden to the other children.

In Hanoi, the head of the agency admitted that the boy had never been examined by any medical person, and said that I wouldn't find competent doctors there. She recommended I take him to Bangkok. We did that, and in the hospital, English-speaking doctors confirmed that it was not polio, but some other thing that had caused his condition; the possibilities included degenerative muscular diseases. Further diagnosis would take weeks.

Worried, exhausted, and in a quandary, Casey and I called Woody from the hotel in Bangkok to explain the situation. He advised us to bring the boy back and have him thoroughly tested in the United States. The agency agreed. They said that if the problems turned out to be more complex than I felt we could handle, they already knew of an excellent family in the United States who couldn't afford to travel or to pay the fees, but who were looking for just such a child.

When we got him home, testing revealed that the boy was afflicted with a rare type of cerebral palsy, and that he was functioning at the level of a sixteen-month-old. He screamed through much of the day and night. In family conversations that included Woody, we decided that the boy's retardation would present overwhelming and ongoing problems for the younger children particularly. So after only five traumatic, heartbreaking days in our home, he left to join his forever-family.

In the quiet, after his departure, the children and I talked about how he would be with good people where his needs would be well met: things don't always turn out the way we hope, God has His own plans, but our role in the boy's life had been an important one: we had helped him along the journey to his permanent home.

Meanwhile, we were told that Tam would join us at Christmastime.

． ． ．

I had scarcely recovered from that experience when we began shooting *Husbands and Wives*, WAFP 1991, my thir-
teenth film with Woody. He was already busy firing a young
actress when I began to focus on the film and learn my
lines. He sent me to a noon showing of *Cape Fear* to see
whether I thought Juliette Lewis could play his college-girl
flirtation. I returned raving about Ms. Lewis and she got
the job. Sydney Pollack and Judy Davis were also in the
movie, and Liam Neeson, who became my friend.

Woody now seemed preoccupied and cold, and he was
still tired all the time. When I tried to discuss what could
be wrong, he talked about Lyme disease, and chronic fatigue
syndrome, and how he had to get tested for HIV.

"How could you possibly have that?" I asked. "We've
been together for nearly a dozen years." He answered that
there was a long incubation period for HIV.

"Then get the test," I urged. "You've spent a whole year
worrying. This is no way to live. You *don't* have it. You'll be
so relieved when you get that news it'll be like a new life.
Please do it." He was tested around the time of his fifty-
sixth birthday, and the results came back negative.

Then news of another kind increased his happiness: the
surrogate's court had agreed to let him adopt my children
Dylan and Moses.

Although Woody's behavior with Dylan was not yet on
course, I believed he would continue to work on it in good
faith. In addition to the therapist we had originally con-
sulted, there was now a second psychologist for Dylan
whom Woody had employed at the urging of the first, to
address Dylan's fearfulness and inability to communicate
with him—and of course presumably there was his own
psychiatrist. I felt the matter was in responsible hands and
indeed I had observed positive changes. I wanted to trust
that all would be well.

Still, on that day of December 17, 1991, I was concerned enough that before I would agree to accompany Woody to court for Dylan's and Moses's adoption, I made him promise that he would never try to take Dylan for overnight visits without me, and that if, God forbid, our relationship should ever falter, that he would never seek custody. This he promised me. He gave me his word. We were sitting in the camper and he put his arm around me and said, "I would not even *want* the kids to live with me. I don't want kids around all the time, you know that. C'mon now, what kind of thoughts are you having?"

I expected to spend the rest of my life with Woody Allen and was willing to do whatever was necessary for our relationship to continue in a good way. I had never refused him anything. Now I feared that if I denied him the adoptions, it would end our relationship. He had already suggested that I might find it difficult in the real world to work and support the children.

How many times have I wished that I could go back to that day in the chambers of Judge Roth. Dylan, whom I held in my lap, was whispering in my ear, "I want to go home." Moses sat across the table, radiant, next to his soon-to-be "dad."

The judge was radiant too, when suddenly she blurted to Moses, "Do you know who I am?"

"No . . . ," Moses said.

"You don't know who I am?" she went on.

"No," Moses repeated uncomfortably.

The judge looked slightly crestfallen. Then she jumped up, ran over to the closet, and whisked out her long black robe; holding it up to her chin, she sashayed toward him and asked again, "*Now* do you know?"

In a tiny, miserable voice, Moses said no. He was mystified—he thought she wanted him to say her actual name. Now he wanted the floor to open up and swallow him.

It was a relief when finally the judge returned her robe to

the closet and her attention to Woody. Once I interrupted
to say, "I'm not giving anything up, am I?" Which must
have seemed such a non sequitur that she looked at me for
the first and only time that day. "No, of course not," she
answered. Then I signed the papers.

Afterward we returned to the set of *Husbands and Wives*,
and the kids went back to their schools, and things went on
the same as always, except that Moses was walking on air.

Two days later, on December 19, we celebrated Satchel's
fourth birthday, and then it was Christmas. Because we
were scheduled to work right through the holidays, I had to
be in the city, but the kids and I went to Frog Hollow for
the weekend. Soon-Yi, however, asked to stay in New York
to shop. When she arrived at Frog Hollow just days before
Christmas without having bought any presents, I took her
shopping. "Do you think Woody would like this?" she
asked, examining a small, delicately engraved antique letter-
opener. "Sure he would," I said. "It's beautiful."

On Christmas morning, in the city, after opening the
presents, the nine kids and I filled a pew at Mass and then
returned to a veritable feast. Our table was decorated with a
tiny Christmas tree and holly and a Swedish centerpiece
with candles and carved angels, and there were two turkeys
(many kids want a leg). Mavis had made her special stuffing; and there were mashed potatoes, gravy, orange squash,
cranberry sauce, and bowls of fresh-fruit punch and eggnog.

We were in the middle of our meal when Woody walked
in. He disliked Christmas and did not celebrate it himself
(except for one year, when he put up a bare tree for us in
his apartment with a black bat at the top). Nonetheless, he
showed up just like every other day. He presented the older
kids each with an envelope containing a check for fifty dollars. There was an extra chair but he chose to stand, behind
Dylan. I told him how beautiful the carols had been and

what a fine voice Matthew has, and he said, "Pardon me while I puke." Then he went over and turned on the juicer, which to my knowledge he had never noticed before. It was deafening, so we all stopped talking and waited for him to finish. He shouted out, "Anybody want juice?"

We shook our heads because it was the middle of Christmas dinner and besides, as anyone could see, we had these two enormous bowls of eggnog and punch right on the table. But he went on, "Somebody get me some apples." Lark jumped up and got apples out of the refrigerator. "Would you cut them up?" he shouted over the noise. Lark cut them up and returned to her seat. We all sat and waited, it was useless to talk. Finally he turned off the machine and held up a large glass of apple juice. "Nobody wants this?" he asked us. Again we shook our heads, and he poured the juice into the sink. Then he took Dylan out of her chair and went to another room.

We continued filming *Husbands and Wives*, waiting eagerly for Tam's delayed arrival in New York. All the kids were home from school. I brought the youngest ones to work with me, and I tried to spend time with the older ones. On New Year's Eve Woody and I got dressed up to have dinner at an expensive restaurant. Another night we took Fletcher, Moses, Daisy, and Dylan to the Russian Tea Room. We took Soon-Yi out to Sparks, a steak house we'd told her about.

On the evening of January 12 the whole family had Chinese take-out in the kitchen, the same as every Sunday. While I cleaned the kitchen Woody drifted into the living room with Dylan. When I joined them, Fletcher and Soon-Yi were there too. Woody brought up the idea of us all moving to Paris. That was always fun to talk about. As usual we got carried away: Woody told Fletcher about the French film industry, because Fletcher was showing an in-

terest in making films, and now that Soon-Yi was switching
her major from psychology to art, I said it would be great
for her to spend time in Paris.

I wasn't working the next day, so I accompanied one of
the children to a therapy session at Woody's apartment. I
let us in with the key Woody kept under the umbrella stand
and sat down with Isaiah Berlin's *The Crooked Timber of Humanity* in the corner room where I usually waited. Knowing
I'd be there, Woody phoned from work. We chatted lightly
as we always did several times during the day, then I hung
up the phone, and as I turned toward the center of the
room, on the mantel, there was a stack of pornographic
Polaroid pictures: a naked woman with her legs spread wide
apart. It took me a moment to realize it was Soon-Yi.

I couldn't stop shaking. I called his office and said it was an
emergency. Minutes later he called me back.

"I found the pictures," I said. "Get away from us."

I hung up the phone. I put the pictures in my bag. I put
a coat on the child and we went home. I passed Mavis and
the baby-sitter in the kitchen.

Sascha was in the hallway. I said, "Woody's been fucking
Soon-Yi. Call André." I went into Soon-Yi's room and
showed her the pictures. *"What have you done?"* I shouted.

I went into my bedroom and closed the door and tried
to call André with no success. It was hard to breathe. I
wanted to take a bath.

Suddenly Woody was opening my door. Sobbing, I tried
with all my strength to push him out.

"I'm in love with Soon-Yi," he said. "I would marry
her."

It took me a moment to respond. "Then take her," I
finally said, "and get out."

"No, no," he recanted immediately. "That's just something I thought of to say in the car coming over here. It's not what I feel. I don't want that."

"Get out," I said, crying hard. "What am I supposed to tell the kids? That their father wants to marry their sister?" But he wouldn't leave. I washed my face. I wanted a bath.

For the next four hours he was in my room talking, talking.

"What have you done to her?" I said.

"I think it was good for Soon-Yi. I think it gave her a little confidence."

"*Confidence in what?*" I exploded. "You made her betray everything she had, and everyone. And you say it's *good* for her?"

"I love you," he kept saying. "Let's use this as a springboard into a deeper relationship."

"What about Soon-Yi and me? What happens to *our* relationship? What happens to our whole family?"

"We have to try to put all of it behind us," he said soothingly.

"How do we do that? She's my daughter. She's the sister of your children."

"I'm sorry," he said, "I lost control. It will never happen again. I can only say I'm sorry."

"How long?" I asked. "How long has this been going on?"

"I don't know," he said, "several months."

"How long is several?"

"I don't know," he repeated. "Look, it was just a tepid little affair that probably wouldn't have lasted more than a few weeks longer anyway. I told Soon-Yi she shouldn't expect anything. I encouraged her to go ahead and sleep with other guys."

"Go away."

"Let's turn this thing around right now. It was nothing. Just an aberration."

I was crying the whole time. "I trusted you, we all

trusted you. You're supposed to do the right thing. *You're not supposed to fuck the kids.*"

Just then Sascha knocked at the door. "I've got André on the phone," he called.

"No, *no!*" Woody pleaded desperately, doubling over. "Don't tell André. Don't tell André. Don't tell him."

I picked up the phone and told André. "Woody's been fucking Soon-Yi."

"Oh, this is so humiliating." Woody was on the floor, groaning. "Oh, my stomach. Ohh, ohhh."

"What's that?" André asked.

"That's Woody, rolling on the floor," I said.

"Get him out of there right now!" ordered André, from California.

"I'm trying, but he won't go. What do I do? What do I do with Soon-Yi? Will you take her till the holidays are over? Till she can go back to school? She's your daughter too. I need help, André."

But André didn't know what to do. He was shocked and furious, horrified and disgusted. He wouldn't talk to Soon-Yi and he sure as hell didn't want her at his house in New York.

However I begged him, Woody wouldn't go. He talked in circles. He talked nonstop. He said everything I had ever wanted to hear during our dozen years. "It's conceivable that somewhere down the line we might even get married," he said to me. But I just kept saying, "I don't know, I don't know."

"I feel terrible," he said, "but we have to move on from here. I love you. I'm asking you to trust me. You can trust me. I will prove it to you over time. As horrible as this has been, it has shown me something, and right now you couldn't find a more trustworthy man on this planet."

"I don't know," I kept saying. "I have to take a bath."

When I went into my bathroom, I discovered little

Satchel crouching under the sink; he must have heard everything. I took him out to the baby-sitter.

Woody went in to talk to Soon-Yi: to tell her, he said, that he was wrong to have started a relationship with her and that it would not continue. My bath was drawn when he came back into my room.

"Please go away now," I said. "I'm going to take a bath. Please just go."

But he talked and talked and wouldn't stop talking until I gave up. I lay down on my bed exhausted. All those hours in that room—it was an existence unto itself. There were times when I expressed my rage and disbelief and horror, and there were times when he became again the man I loved and wanted and needed with all my being. At one point he kissed me and I, still crying hard, kissed him back. "Trust me," he said, "I love you." He was rocking me as if I were a little baby. "I know I did a bad thing," he said. "Shhhh. I can only promise you nothing like this will ever happen again. I will devote myself to making you happy. You'll see."

Finally I got him to go by leaving the room myself. He followed me, still talking, to the front door and out into the hallway, and he was talking when I pushed the button for the elevator, and while we waited, and even as the elevator doors closed.

I had a bath. I telephoned Matthew at Yale and told him there'd been a catastrophe.

Less than an hour later the kids were sitting at the dinner table. Sascha had told the older ones what had happened—but not Dylan, of course. Satchel knew what he knew. It was a stunned, silent meal. Woody walked right in and sat down next to Dylan at the table as if nothing had happened. He said hi to everybody and started chatting to the two little ones. One by one Lark, Daisy, Fletcher, Sascha, and Moses took their plates and went to their rooms, closing their doors.

I didn't know what to do. I went out, following them a little. Then, standing in the hallway, I said to Woody, "You can't just come in here and sit down at the table as if nothing happened. People have feelings, and very strong feelings." He told me to come into the living room, and there followed another hour of him talking and talking and me crying. I don't even remember what he said, and the whole time I was begging him to leave. Finally he went.

Nights were the worst.

"Please come over and talk to Soon-Yi," I asked Casey the following day. "Make sure she knows I still love her, she needs to know that. But I'm too angry to do it."

For the first time in my life I sought professional help. I saw to it that those of my children who needed it, including Soon-Yi, also received counseling to deal with the trauma. Woody encouraged this and paid for it. All the while I tried to see to it that life continued as normally as possible for all of us. I got the children up at seven and fed them, teeth were brushed, they were dressed and taken to school at eight, when the baby-sitter arrived. The two youngest children saw and heard Soon-Yi crying, and although I tried, it was not possible to entirely conceal my own distress.

It took two weeks for me to reach a point when I could send the baby-sitter to Woody's screening room to take away his key. Until then he kept on coming to our apartment and he went on talking; each time he came over, and every time he called me on the phone, I came undone all over again.

We went to Frog Hollow that weekend: all the children, including Soon-Yi. In the lobby of our building I hugged her and told her I loved her.

"You're incredible, Mom," she said.

As a family we were in the habit of discussing everything, but the trauma of these last days and my own implosion had prevented me from forming a coherent picture of what had happened. Still, I felt it was important that we find a way to talk, so I scribbled a note and used it to open a dialogue in our kitchen.

January 18

My children,

An atrocity has been committed against our family and it is impossible to make sense of it. You know that I share your pain and bewilderment and anger. But I feel the need to talk and think further with you. It is essential that none of us permit ourselves to be in any way diminished by these events—we must struggle to find a way to learn and perhaps even grow stronger through them. We have seen firsthand that there are terrible consequences to terrible acts, and therefore how crucial it is that we proceed through our lives with respect for others, and be guided by a sense of responsibility. You have seen the full measure of my love for Soon-Yi, and therefore for each of you—my love for you is unshakable, and that is no small thing. Here, in this moment, in the bright light of pain, we have been able to define ourselves, to ourselves and to each other. We have been granted a perspective that only a trauma such as this could lend. Let us hold it close, never allow it to fade, and let us use it to enrich and enlighten our present, and to build our future.

Finally, know how grateful I am to each of you. You have brought depth and joy and meaning to my life. I love you beyond all words. Because of you, even my darkest days have not been without light.

Soon-Yi left the room. In the talk that followed, Daisy, who was seventeen, told us that over the last three years Woody had tried to initiate four intimate conversations with her. He had asked her how old her friends were when they began doing things with boys, and how old she was when she started fooling around, and what sorts of things she'd done. Daisy told us he'd said, "Tell me everything you've done that you wouldn't tell your mother. I promise I won't tell her." Woody had never talked to Daisy privately before, and she was uncomfortable with his line of questioning. She didn't have anything to tell him anyway, and she didn't stick around.

Lark said, "He probably didn't try with me because Jesse"—her football-star boyfriend, who was also present— "would have thrown him through the window." Then Jesse recalled a trip back to New York the previous summer in the limousine with Lark, Soon-Yi, and Woody. He'd been dozing in the back; opening his eyes, he saw Woody place his hand on Soon-Yi's thigh and caress it. He had told Lark, and she had refused to believe it. Fletcher remembered a moment the year before when he had walked into the laundry room and Woody had spun away from Soon-Yi. Sascha, Lark, and Daisy remembered that during the previous summer Soon-Yi had questioned them about birth control. Moses recalled coming into our study when Woody and Soon-Yi were sitting on the sofa watching a ball game. They both moved over so that Moses could sit down. Soon-Yi was wearing a miniskirt. As Woody moved, he dipped his head for a very long second and looked between Soon-Yi's bare legs.

Now I viewed his behavior with Dylan in a completely different light. I no longer believed he could control himself. I no longer believed he was dealing with his problems responsibly, I was no longer sure that his "inappropriate" and "intense" behavior with Dylan was not sexual. At exactly what point does it become child abuse? What kind of person puts his thumb in a little girl's mouth for her to suck on? And when he was told by the therapist that it was not appropriate and *no good* for Dylan, what made him persist? The last time I caught him doing that had been when I came back from Vietnam. Dylan was six. Satchel was asleep when I walked into the kids' bedroom. Woody was standing next to Dylan's bed. He had his thumb in her mouth, and the nursery night-light was reflected in his glasses. "Please," I said, and he quickly pulled his thumb out of her mouth.

I redrafted my will. In the event of my death the children were to remain together in the care and custody of their adult brothers, Matthew and Sascha. I then remembered that only three weeks earlier I had signed papers that made Woody the adoptive father of Moses and Dylan. In horror, I called the lawyer, Mr. Weltz, who had set up the adoptions for Woody. I told him there had been a terrible mistake—I had not known the facts. Woody Allen had deceived me, deceived him, deceived the judge, and deceived the children. For months, maybe years for all I knew, he had been screwing one of my kids. He had taken pornographic pictures of her. He was completely untrustworthy. He was without morals or self-control. He was not at all the man I supposed I knew. He was not an appropriate father for my children. He was dangerous. We needed to go back to the judge and tell her. She would have to undo the adoptions, because *we were tricked.*

Mr. Weltz was outraged and said he would do everything he could to ensure the protection of my children, but he did not see how we could overturn the adoptions. A second legal opinion was far more promising; there was precedent in the state of New York for undoing adoptions on the basis of "fraud against the court."

I insisted that since I had been deceived into consenting to the adoption, Woody should agree to waive his custodial rights if I predeceased him. On February 3 we both signed a document to that effect. I attached a statement, which I showed only to Woody, articulating my concerns about his behavior and my reasons for believing he would be an inappropriate custodial parent; and as proof I included photocopies of the Polaroids he'd taken of Soon-Yi. We sealed the documents and gave them to Woody's business manager to be kept in a vault, and opened only in the event of my death.

On the same day, unbeknownst to me at the time, Woody signed a second document in which he stated that he had no intention of abiding by the agreement we had just signed.

The few scenes I had yet to shoot for *Husbands and Wives* were put off for ten days. I don't know how I went back and filmed them. Woody's behavior to me on the set was gentle, apologetic, and caring.

But as the days went on and I reran the events in my mind over and over, I could not believe that the Polaroids were left out accidentally, as Woody claimed. He was not an incautious man. He was meticulous, he had a cleaning woman and a housekeeper; in twelve years, nothing in his apartment was ever moved or out of place. And he knew I would be in that room. It was his phone call that brought me within inches of the pictures. Why?

Perhaps, as my son Moses believes, deep inside Woody there was an unfathomable and uncontrollable need to destroy everything good and positive in his life, and so he tried to destroy our family. For him to have sex with one of my children, a child he had known as my daughter since she was eight years old, was not enough: he had to make me see, graphically, what he was doing. What rage did he feel against me, against women, against mothers, against sisters, against daughters, against an entire family? The pictures were a grenade he threw into our home, and no one was unharmed.

• • •

After January 13, I didn't leave him alone with any of my kids.

At one point, toward the end of that first week, I went to talk to Soon-Yi. She was sitting on the floor with the phone in her lap. I asked her when this had begun. "Senior year in high school," she said. Unbearable details emerged. I pounced on her. I hit her on the side of her face and shoulders. I went into the kitchen, crying. In her room I heard Soon-Yi sobbing, "I'm a bad girl. I'm a bad girl."

What were we supposed to do?

I went back into her room and told her I loved her. "He shouldn't have done this to us," I said. "We shouldn't *be* in this position."

She was my child, but I could not help her. I could scarcely look at her. We had become something else to each other. We had to go through this separately. In anger she threatened to kill herself. In anger I told her I hated her. It was a relief when she went back to college. I loved her, I missed her, and I worried for her, but it was hard for me to be near her. She gave me her word that she would not have any contact with Woody and promised that if he tried to call her, she would hang up the phone.

Panic attacks are visitations of undiluted terror. I have had four in my life, all between January and March 1992. Those were weeks of sleepless nights filled with rage and tears when I phoned Woody and expressed my fury at what he had done to us. Some nights he called me ten or twenty times or more and I'd hang up. Other nights I called him to say, Please don't leave me now, I'm so afraid. I couldn't let him go from my life, yet I could not even look at him. In my worst anguish, he was the one I needed most. But there had been so much damage. Now when I looked back over the years, I saw that they had been paved with lies and deceptions.

For my birthday Woody gave me three lovely leather-bound volumes of Emily Dickinson's poems, and he took me to dinner at Rao's.

At that time I wrote a note to Maria Roach, my childhood friend in California.

Dear Maria,

I have come perilously close to a genuine meltdown of my very core. I know now that my vision has been unclear and I have spent more than a dozen years with a man who would destroy me and lead my daughter into a betrayal of her mother, her family, and her principles, leaving her morally bankrupt, with the bond between us demolished. I can think of no crueler way to lose a child, or a lover, and with them, a treasured part of my life. I have spent long years with a man who had no respect for everything I hold sacred—not for my family, not for my soul, not for my God or my purest goals. But in the end I must pity him. He has spoiled and mutilated that part of himself which is improved by right conduct and destroyed by wrong: is there any part of us that is more precious? Today I stand, with washed eyes, gazing clearly into an unknown future. I will travel lightly there, carrying only the essentials, trusting that a new life will create itself.

Chapter Eleven

This is the Hour of Lead—
Remembered, if outlived,
As Freezing persons recollect the Snow:
First Chill—then Stupor—then the letting go—
— EMILY DICKINSON

The fact that Woody had slept with my daughter had to be kept secret from the outside world. He was terrified that the public would find out, and desperate to get the Polaroids back. But I kept them hidden in my room until February, when I took them to a lawyer, who put them in a vault. I asked the older children not to tell anybody. In our isolation, we grappled with shock, grief, and anger. At this point, I had three objectives: to protect the children from further harm, to get through this trauma intact, and to separate from Woody Allen.

Concerning Woody's forty years of psychoanalysis, my friend Lenny Gershe said, "You can't say his therapy was a failure. Who knows, without it he might have been a serial killer." But I had never been more skeptical about psychiatrists and the benefits of long-term analysis. Looking at the place psychoanalysis had occupied in Woody Allen's life, it seemed that it had helped to isolate him from people and the systems we live by, and placed him at the center of a different reality—one that exists only after he has bounced his views off his therapist. Woody lived and made his decisions while suspended in a zone constructed and controlled almost entirely by himself—a world that he used his therapists to validate. He did not acknowledge other beings except as features in his own landscape, valued according to their contribution to his own existence. He was therefore unable to empathize and felt no moral responsibility to anyone or anything. When I turned to his psychiatrist to ask for his help in protecting my family, he told me that "it's not a therapist's job to moralize." I had to wonder what decades of such thinking had contributed to Woody's perspective.

In February I received a call from an adoption agency that had for some time been trying, unsuccessfully, to find a home for a baby boy. He was about to be placed in permanent foster care, and they wondered if I would take him. He was African-American, from an inner city, with the possibility of medical problems. A decision was needed immediately. I discussed it with the children, and in the midst of all the pain, we said yes. Again I placed the bassinet with the patchwork lining beside my bed.

I named my sixth beautiful son Isaiah Justus Farrow, after Isaiah Berlin, and that first Isaiah, the most interesting of the prophets.

Later that same February, Tam, the little girl I'd spent ten minutes with in Vietnam, finally arrived. We guessed that she was about ten or eleven years old. She was malnourished, frightened, angry, depressed, and covered with lice. I was as busy as I'd ever been, looking after the children, seeing social workers, and setting up elaborate braille and special-educational programs for Tam, who had never been to school.

Now I only saw Woody when he came to visit Dylan

and Satchel, for one supervised hour most weekdays. Occasionally he persuaded me to go out to dinner with him, but invariably I left the table in tears. Sascha's wife, Carrie, recalled that "when Woody came to the apartment he was all over you. He brought flowers and kept saying, 'I love you.' We didn't know whether to hit him, or how to protect you. Sascha and I asked you what you wanted, and you looked so confused, you said you didn't know."

"What would have happened if I hadn't found the pictures of Soon-Yi?" I asked Woody one day.

"Nothing," he replied. "I thought this would be just a pleasant little footnote in Soon-Yi's history."

But her analyst told me, "Unfortunately Mr. Allen has crushed the fragile relationship you had built with Soon-Yi." Now I understood the reason for the dramatic change in her attitude the previous year, the new little laugh of superiority, the smugness, and the coldness to the other kids. I didn't know how we would ever repair things, and this thought broke my heart.

A counselor for one of the teenage kids advised me that even Woody's brief appearances in our apartment were having a disturbing effect; that both Woody and Soon-Yi had been "sexualized" in the minds of, probably, all the children. "The home has to be viewed as a safe place," she said, and the child she was counseling felt "unsafe" when Woody was present. I was advised that if I wanted to see him, I should do it outside the apartment, without telling the kids.

By early spring Woody was no longer saying how sorry he was, or that he couldn't live without me, or that he was the most trustworthy person on earth. Now he was saying, "If we don't get back together, then I'm free to date Soon-Yi, or anybody I want."

"How are the kids supposed to live with that?" I asked

him. I pointed out that, psychologically, this was incest. "What are they going to do at PTA meetings, introduce Soon-Yi as their sister and stepmother? How do you think, practically speaking, everybody would handle it? This is crazy! I can't be your mother-in-law!"

Despite everything that had happened, all the agony, and all his years of therapy, the moral dimensions of the situation still utterly eluded him. We had been over it and over it, and still he didn't get it, even though he was now seeing two therapists and sometimes had appointments twice a day, including Sunday.

When Woody's psychiatrist was unhelpful, I went to Dr. Willard Gayland, a noted ethicist, who was sympathetic, but didn't have time to take Woody on as a full-time patient. Then I went to a brilliant Jesuit priest who agreed to talk to him, but Woody refused.

By late spring, when Woody called or came to see the children, he was tough and entirely unrepentant; if I got angry or cried, he threatened to put me in a mental hospital and have the children taken away.

In the foyer of our apartment one day, I was trying to push him out, saying, "Get out. Please, please go," as some of the kids gathered around—Fletcher, Moses, Dylan, Tam, and Satchel.

"I'm going to take these kids out of here," Woody was saying loudly, over and over.

Suddenly Fletcher was coming at him, saying, *"Get out now. Get out and leave Mom alone."* Woody fled.

About that time Moses handed a letter to Woody.

> . . . You can't force me to live with you . . .
> All you want is the trust and relationships you
> had in the beginning of the time. You can't have
> those worthy things because you have done a

horrible, unforgivable, needy, ugly, stupid thing,
which I hope you will not forgive yourself for
doing . . . I hope you get so humiliated that
you commit suicide . . . You brought these
things to yourself, we didn't do anything wrong.
Everyone knows you're not supposed to have an
affair with your son's sister including that sister,
but you have a special way to get that sister to
think that it's OK. Unfortunately, Soon-Yi
hadn't had a serious relationship before and
probably thought "OK, this is a great chance to
see what a serious relationship is like." That's
probably why she did it . . . I just want you to
know that I don't consider you my father anymore. It was a great feeling having a father, but
you smashed that feeling and dream with a single act.

I HOPE YOU ARE PROUD TO CRUSH YOUR
SON'S DREAM.

Although Moses had refused to see him after January 13,
Woody continued to visit with Dylan and Satchel, supervised. I did not allow him to take them to his apartment.

In April Dylan's therapist, Dr. Schultz, informed me
that Dylan had to be told what was going on—that the
little girl, now nearly seven years old, had seen me crying,
and overheard me on the phone with Woody, and heard
Soon-Yi saying she wanted to die, and Woody endlessly
arguing with me, and although I'd asked the older children
not to discuss the matter within earshot of the younger
ones, obviously they too were upset and needed to talk.
When the little kids were supposed to be asleep, we had
found them listening outside closed doors.

Dr. Schultz said she had been trying to convince Mr.
Allen for some time that it was necessary to tell Dylan, but
he had opposed it vehemently. He wanted the little girl to

be told that somehow I had misinterpreted a joke between him and Soon-Yi. But the therapist was adamant that that would not suffice, given the very real distress in the family. So I was instructed to explain it to Dylan in the doctor's presence, and told precisely what words to use. I would have preferred to cut off my legs.

Dr. Schultz and I were both looking at Dylan as she played on the floor near the fireplace. I took a deep breath. "Dylan, I know you've noticed that sometimes Mommy has been crying. Mommy has been sad; and Soon-Yi was crying and now she hasn't been coming home, and Mommy seems upset with Daddy, and Daddy gets upset, and now I guess you need to know what's been going on. Well, Daddy became sort of like a boyfriend to Soon-Yi. And that was wrong because daddies are supposed to be daddies. But he is sorry, and he's getting help, and we promise you it will never happen again."

Dylan was moving two little dolls around on the floor. She never looked up. I hugged her. After a few minutes of nobody saying anything, Dr. Schultz asked me to leave them alone together.

Soon-Yi didn't come home anymore, and she didn't phone me. To be perfectly honest, I wasn't ready to have her back. When, in early May, I asked her for reassurance that she would have no contact with Woody, she said, "Stop asking me for things," and hung up the phone. Her brothers and sisters, every single one of them from Moses on up, got on the phone: and although they were angry and disgusted, we all said we missed her, and we loved her. We needed to hear her say, Look, I've made a terrible mistake. I'm sorry for the pain I've caused, and it isn't going to happen anymore. We needed that, but we couldn't get it.

•   •   •

Summer arrived and the children and I went to Frog Hollow. When Woody came to visit Dylan and Satchel once a week, the older kids left the house to stay with friends. It was hard for us to have him there. Woody and I had already agreed to a legal settlement, scheduled to be signed on August 6, defining our rights and responsibilities with regard to the children. Most important, it ensured that his contact with the children would be supervised. And it did not entitle him to spend the night at our home. I was eager for that date to arrive because, despite the obvious distress his visits were causing to my family and my repeated requests that he sleep elsewhere, he insisted on staying at Frog Hollow. Just then I didn't press the point further because I feared he would try to have that privilege written into the settlement contract.

That summer I taught Tam and Dylan to swim, and Satchel to read. Baby Isaiah, a sweet-natured and beautiful little boy, was already smiling and growing so fast I had to move him from his bassinet to the antique crib beside my bed. As usual, I videotaped all the children's accomplishments. Throughout this time, Tam was an inspiration. Although she had lost everything—her parents, home, country, language, friends, and her sight—still, with doubts and difficulties, she was able to open up to each member of the family, one by one. I have never respected anyone more than Tam. She helped to restore my perspective, and taught me about surviving with grace and without bitterness.

I reconnected with my old friends and slowly, piece by piece, I began to reclaim my *self*, the identity that had somehow, over the years, slipped almost out of existence. That same essential self who emerged from the polio wards, strong and determined, awakened from a long, deep slumber.

.   .   .

Now, when Woody came to Frog Hollow for visitations, Dylan would get headaches and stomachaches. She curled up in the hammock, or lay in her bed under her quilt with the door closed. On three occasions during his visits, she locked herself in the bathroom, once for four hours.

When he arrived for his visits I usually took Tam, Moses, and Isaiah out, often with Casey. I had a trustworthy baby-sitter, Kristie, and that summer we also had Sophie, a French tutor for the children; I told them both never to leave Woody alone with Dylan. He promised me that under no circumstances would he ever be alone with either Satchel or Dylan.

But in the dark of the early mornings, even though I forbade it, he would creep upstairs from the guest room to lie on the floor beside Dylan's bed. A couple of times when Tam, who shared the room with Dylan, got up to go to the bathroom, she stepped on Woody, and woke up the whole house with her screams.

Tam hated Woody. Undoubtedly she had overheard negative comments from the older kids, and through my letters that had been read to her she knew vaguely that an older sister, a sister she had met only once (but who had been described to her at length in my letters) had disappeared under ominous circumstances related to Woody. And perhaps she had heard me crying in my room at night, or whenever Woody phoned. But primarily she disliked him because he never ever spoke to her, and since she couldn't see, it frightened her the way he would suddenly be in the room, near her, telling Satchel to pull her hair, and always with bags full of presents for Dylan and Satchel, and nothing, not a word, for Tam.

With an escalating intensity, Woody tried to persuade me to give him the Polaroids of Soon-Yi. "Let's burn them together," he said. But I told him they would stay in the vault for the rest of my life. I would never take them out, but I wouldn't destroy them either: I was sure that if I did, he would deny they ever existed.

I had persuaded Soon-Yi to take a job I found for her as a counselor at a summer camp in Maine. In July I received a letter from the camp's director, saying Soon-Yi had been fired because the scores of phone calls from a "Mr. Simon" had prevented her from becoming involved with the activities. She had left the camp, but I didn't know where she was. Woody finally admitted that he was Mr. Simon, but denied knowing where Soon-Yi was, or even her phone number. "André and I wanted to get her away from all this; we hoped she'd make connections with kids her own age," I told him. "Now you've ruined that."

"Leave her alone," I implored. "Out of respect for our twelve years together, or for me as the mother of your child, or for those of my children you claim to love; out of respect for Soon-Yi, and her relationship with me, her mother—I am begging you. Leave her be. Let her come home to her family. Let her have a life she can be proud of."

"Well, I'd like to do this for you," he said. "I will promise to leave Soon-Yi alone, if you will give me the pictures. Or we can burn them together if you like." But I did not, would not, give them to him.

By the end of July, Woody's people were trying to dispel the persistent rumbles in the press that we were splitting up, and that it had something to do with one of my daughters. He asked me to issue a joint press release saying there was nothing to the rumors, that everything was fine, and that we were looking forward to beginning our fourteenth film in September.

"We have to stand together on this," he told me. I said I wouldn't say anything, period, but I wasn't going to lie about it.

"Then I'm going to defend myself," he said. "I'm not

just going to stand there and let myself get crucified." I told him his position was indefensible—he'd had sex with one of my kids and taken pornographic pictures of her, that was the truth and what else could he say?

"You'll find out. And you're not going to like it," he warned. "I'll say that Soon-Yi and I love each other," he said. "If it gets out, my analyst says I have to defend myself. So, be prepared. Now, if you want to join me in a joint statement where we deny it, that's another thing."

"I never talk to the press," I said. "They know that. I'll just keep quiet."

"But I'm telling you the thing is now looming in the newspapers. If you can't see your way to helping me out of this, then I'm going to defend myself. I think we should issue some kind of statement saying that this is ridiculous, and we're doing a movie together in a few weeks. Then we do the movie, and we put this thing behind us. If that can be done, there's no limit to what we can have together . . ."

"I don't feel very safe with you."

On August 4, when Woody came to Frog Hollow for his specified visit, I was out shopping with Casey, Tam, and Isaiah. Kristie, Sophie, Casey's three children and her baby-sitter, Alison, were at the house with Dylan and Satchel. Moses was off by himself taking a walk.

After a couple of hours, Casey and I returned, and the children rushed to greet us. It was momentarily jarring when Sophie pointed out that Dylan had no underpants on under her sundress since, at seven, she was extremely modest. I asked Kristie to please put some underpants on Dylan.

At dinner that evening at a local restaurant, Woody talked nonstop about *Manhattan Murder Mystery*, which, despite everything, we were planning to begin in a few weeks.

When we got back to the house he went upstairs, sat on Dylan's bed, and began a bedtime story for her and Satchel. Tam, realizing who was in the room, started screaming, while Woody angrily and determinedly proceeded with his story. I tried to calm Tam. After a while I asked Woody if he'd please hurry the story a little, but he glared at me and continued. Dylan and Satchel were staring worriedly at Tam and nobody could hear anything but screams. When finally he finished and went out, Tam brightened up. I kissed all the kids, turned on their night-light, and left the room.

Woody was waiting in the hall, livid. "Just look what you've done," he said. "You'd better shape up, or there's no way you're going to be in this movie."

I started crying again. "Why is everything always my fault?" I said to his back, as he went down the stairs. "Does it never occur to you that you might be in some part responsible for any of this?"

The next morning, after Woody left for the city, Casey phoned to say that her baby-sitter, Alison, had seen something at my house that had bothered her. While Casey and I had been out shopping, Alison had gone to the television room, looking for one of the Pascal children. She saw Dylan "sitting on the couch, staring straight ahead with a blank expression." Woody was kneeling in front of her with his face in her lap. Alison told Casey she was "shocked," because it seemed "intimate, something you'd say, Oops, excuse me, if both had been adults." I remembered that Dylan had not been wearing underpants.

I hung up the phone and asked Dylan, who was sitting at the foot of my bed, "Did Woody have his face in your lap yesterday?" He had been told by the therapist not to do precisely that thing.

"Yes," she said.

I had just been videotaping the baby, so I grabbed the camera. Dylan went on to say that he was breathing into her, into her legs. She told me he was holding her around the waist and that when she tried to get up he "secretly put one hand here"—she pointed—"and touched my privates, and I do not like that one bit."

She told me that Woody had taken her upstairs into the attic, and that he had touched her private parts with his finger. "Don't move," he had said to her. "I have to do this. If you stay still, we can go to Paris. Don't tell."

"He was kissing me," Dylan said. "I got soaked all over the whole body . . . I had to do what he said. I'm a kid, I have to do whatever the grown-ups say . . . It hurt, it hurt when he pushed his finger in . . . he said the only way for me to be in the movie is to do this. I don't want to be in his movie. Do I have to be in his movie? He just kept poking it in . . ."

I immediately telephoned my lawyer, who instructed me to take her to the doctor. Barely audibly, Dylan told our pediatrician that Woody had put his face in her lap and had touched her. But when she was asked where, she wouldn't talk anymore. The doctor told me to bring her back the next day. When we got into the car, she said, "I just don't like talking to strangers about my private parts."

Over the next twenty-four hours, whenever she brought it up, in fits and starts, I switched on the camera. We returned to the doctor's office the next day, and Dylan repeated what she had told me. The doctor called later to tell me that he was required by law to notify the authorities, and he was going to do so although the physical exam of Dylan showed no sign of sexual abuse.

I phoned the therapist who'd been working with Woody for almost two years about his behavior with Dylan. As soon as I told her what Alison had seen him doing, she interrupted. "He's not supposed to do that."

I told her all of it, and she said that if the Connecticut doctor was going to report it, then she would have to report it as well to the New York authorities. But first she was going to tell Woody.

"Don't tell him," I said. "I'm scared of what he'll do. Can't *you* just deal with it? Don't report it to the authorities. That will destroy everything. It's too big. Terrible things are going to happen!"

I was standing outside near the lake, holding the cordless phone. It was a hot August afternoon. The kids were playing on the beach. A robin hopped across the grass. Everything looked so normal. Except that Dylan was lying in the hammock wrapped in a quilt. I stood, frozen in horror, and thought, Jesus Christ, Jesus Christ, what's going to happen now?

The full force of what had happened hit me. In that instant, the pain and confusion of the past seven months fell away. My mind was clear. My only objective now was to protect my child.

When Kristie, the baby-sitter, returned from her regular days off, I asked her what had happened that day. She told me that Dylan and Woody had disappeared that afternoon. She had looked for them in all the rooms of the house, upstairs and down. She had called out Dylan's name. Sophie, who was outside, said they weren't there. She hadn't wanted to tell me, but for about twenty minutes, they were missing.

The Connecticut state police instructed me to bring Dylan in to meet with child-welfare authorities. The interviewing caseworker determined that there was cause to believe that sexual abuse might have occurred. With that, the police opened an investigation. Later, the Child Welfare Services caseworker in New York, Paul Williams, spoke to Dylan's psychologist, who belatedly reported Dylan's statement to her that Mr. Allen had put a finger in her vagina.

Now Dylan seemed withdrawn. Sophie said, "Countless times I would look for her in the middle of the day, and then I'd find her in her bed, under the blankets, all alone, awake, when it was a beautiful day and everybody else was outside playing. I would ask her to join us, but she wouldn't." Dylan wet her bed several times after August 4, something she hadn't done since she was three years old.

Over the next weeks, every time she brought up the experience, I tried to comfort her. "I don't want him to do it again, Mommy. I don't want him to do it again."

I was terrified of all that was ahead of us. Once I said to her, "Dylan, it's important that you tell the truth. This is a very big deal. Woody says nothing happened in the attic."

"He's lying," she said.

In one of our last conversations Woody had asked me, "Is there any way out? I just want to be friends."

I said, "You're crazy, Woody. I really think you're crazy." I was still hoping that this hadn't happened to my child. "Where were you when everybody looked all over the house? If you weren't in the attic, where were you?" He stumbled and stuttered, but he wouldn't answer my question. I asked him and I asked him. I asked him every which way, maybe twenty times: "Woody, just tell me where you were." But he would not answer me.

On August 13, 1992, seven days after Woody learned of Dylan's accusation, papers were served to me ("the Respondent") in Connecticut. Woody Allen ("the Petitioner") was initiating a suit in the New York State Supreme Court for custody of Dylan, Satchel, and Moses. In this suit, Woody stated that:

• The Petitioner is the father of the following children:

(i) SATCHEL FARROW, born on September 19, 1987 [wrong: he was born in December], the natural child of Petitioner, and

(ii) MOSES AMADEUS FARROW, born on January 27, 1978, adopted by Petitioner December 17, 1991. Moses was previously adopted by Respondent, in the State of Massachusetts pursuant to an Order of the Probate of the Court of Dukes County, entered on January 9, 1981; and

(iii) DYLAN O'SULLIVAN FARROW, born on July 11, 1985, adopted by Petitioner December 17, 1991. Dylan was previously adopted by Respondent.

Moses, Satchel, and Dylan are hereafter collectively referred to as "The Children." The Children from birth or from the dates of their adoption have been physically resident and domiciled with Respondent at 135 Central Park West, in the City, County, and State of New York ("New York Residence"). There are no other children to which this application applies.

• Petitioner is presently 56 years of age and Respondent is 46 years of age. Although Petitioner and Respondent have had an ephemeral relationship for the past twelve (12) years, they have never cohabited with one another and have always maintained separate residences.

• Until January, 1992, Petitioner visited with The Children on a sustained basis at Respondent's New York Apartment and elsewhere, for daily breakfast and dinner and other activities. In or about January, 1992, Respondent commenced preventing Petitioner from having regular visitation with The Children. Since August 5, 1992, Respondent has prevented Petitioner from any visitation or contact with The Children.

• Respondent has been, and presently is, emotionally disturbed and is under constant heavy medication.

• Upon information and belief, Respondent has physically abused one or more of her children.

• I believe that The Children are in great fear of the Respondent by reason of her emotional instability and abusive conduct.

• Respondent's past and present actions have created great emotional distress for The Children, which has necessitated psychiatric intervention.

• Respondent has falsely accused the Petitioner of sexually abusing Dylan and Satchel and continues to falsely claim that Petitioner is guilty of sexually abusing them.*

• Respondent is brainwashing The Children with respect to false allegations of sexual misconduct on the part of Petitioner.

• Respondent, who is unable to manage the rearing of nine (9) children, recently adopted Tam Farrow and Isaiah Farrow. Tam is twelve years old and blind. Isaiah is a seven-month-old crack baby. Petitioner has been informed that the Respondent has made application to adopt two additional children, both of whom are blind.** Respondent is incapable of raising any additional children.

• The presence and condition of Respondent's additional eight (8) children are inimical to the

---

* Satchel had never been sexually abused, and no one ever asserted that he had been.
** At that time I had not made any further applications to adopt children.

health, welfare, and best interests of The Children.

• It is in the best interests of Satchel, Moses, and Dylan, that physical and jural custody be awarded to their father, the Petitioner herein.

• The Petitioner respectfully requests that the court direct the Respondent to physically produce the three (3) children on the return date hereof.

• Petitioner is a capable and fit parent to assume sole custody of The Children, and possesses the ability to provide them with a happy, healthy and stable home and environment.

Within moments of these papers being filed, even before I knew of their existence, the news was leaked to the media. Incredibly, in a frantic effort to distract the public from the facts and salvage the mythology of his reputation, Woody was seeking to make me the issue. It was a preemptive legal action initiated when it became apparent to him that a criminal investigation of his conduct was about to become public. If he was believed, then *all* my minor children would surely be taken away. The ones he didn't want—Isaiah and Tam—would be put into foster care.

Four days later the Connecticut state police publicly confirmed that they were conducting an investigation that involved Woody Allen.

The following day, Woody gave a press conference on national television. He denied that he had sexually abused Dylan and claimed the allegations were nothing but "a currently popular though heinous card played in all too many custody fights . . . Regarding my love for Soon-Yi," he went on, "it's real and happily all true. She's a lovely, intelligent, sensitive woman who has and continues to turn around my life in a wonderfully positive way."

At Frog Hollow, several of the older kids and I watched

this press conference in horror and stunned disbelief. My lawyer responded, stating only that Mr. Allen had filed his custody suit to deflect attention from child-abuse investigations that had been ongoing for the past two weeks in Connecticut and New York City. He also pointed out that the investigations were not instigated by me, as Woody Allen was claiming, but by the child's doctor, who had notified the authorities.

But Woody was louder and far more relentless. He began a campaign of damage control that reshuffled the chronology of events. In late August he gave lengthy interviews to *Time* and *Newsweek* magazines. *Time's* Walter Isaacson asked him: "But wasn't it breaking many bonds of trust to become involved with your lover's daughter?"

"There's no downside to it," replied Woody. "The only thing unusual is that she's Mia's daughter. But she's an *adopted* daughter and a grown woman. I could have met her at a party or something."

"Were you still involved with Mia when you became interested in Soon-Yi?" Isaacson asked.

"My relationship with Mia was simply a cordial one in the past four years, a dinner maybe once a week together. Our romantic relationship tapered off after the birth of Satchel, tapered off quickly."

"What was your relationship with Soon-Yi when you first started going over there to visit your children?"

"I never had an extended conversation with her," Woody admitted. "As a matter of fact, I don't think she liked me too much. The last thing I was interested in was the whole parcel of Mia's children . . . I spent absolutely zero time with any of them. This was not some type of family unit in any remote way." He went on to say, "I didn't find any moral dilemmas whatsoever. I didn't feel that just because she was Mia's daughter, there was any great moral dilemma. It was a fact, but not one with any great import . . . These people are a collection of kids, they are not blood sisters or anything . . . It wasn't like she was my daughter."

When asked if he considered his relationship with Soon-Yi a healthy, equal one, he answered, "Who knows? . . . The heart wants what it wants."

Regarding Dylan's claims, Woody said he had not been alone with her that day. "Nothing at all happened," he said. "In light years I wouldn't go into an attic. I wouldn't even know how to find Mia's attic."

"This is so laughable," he went on in *Newsweek*. "I have never been in an attic. I'm a famous claustrophobic . . . wild horses couldn't get me into an attic." (But after the police found hair samples in the attic that were microscopically similar to Woody's, he changed his story. He later testified that "Mia showed me the crawl space up there. I'm not saying I didn't pop in and say it's a very nice place and search it. By the way, I may have reached in.")

As untruthful and hurtful as those interviews were to me, seeing his words, his thoughts, in print gave me some of the objectivity I had lost.

André quickly came to my defense. "If Mia is not a good mother, then Jascha Heifetz didn't know how to play the violin. I am terribly shocked and saddened that he would choose to have a relationship with Soon-Yi. As a father I don't think I have a colorful enough vocabulary to tell you what I think. It is an unspeakable breach of trust which has caused a great deal of anguish in the family. This is a first-time experience for her. She only just got out of high school last year. Accusing Mia of being a bad mother is bizarre and irresponsible. She's a remarkable mother: our six kids together are happy, healthy, well-educated, and secure, and the other children in the family are in exemplary shape as well."

The Sinatras also gave me their support. Frank even offered to break Woody's legs.

It was mayhem at Frog Hollow: we were besieged by hordes of reporters. A satellite dish was set up in the tiny village. We couldn't leave the property without being followed by packs of cars. I stopped reading the papers and I couldn't turn on the television. There were so many crazed letters that I finally threw away my mail unopened. When it got dark, and the press began to filter down the driveway, I called the police. I was alone in the house at night with the little kids. We didn't have any curtains, so we couldn't be sure there was no one outside the windows, looking in.

Trucks labeled CRIME SQUAD pulled up in front of the house. The attic and everything in it were dusted for fingerprints and searched for hair samples. The press called incessantly. I changed my phone number for the second time in a week, and when it rang within the hour, I picked it up warily; it was Fox Five News. I screamed.

Our New York apartment was also besieged by the press. The older kids, who were spending their summer in the city, had jobs and college classes. In order to come and go, they had to fight through tangles of reporters, who pushed microphones in their faces and hurled questions at them. When the kids came to my defense, Woody publicly criticized me for it, but I couldn't have stopped them if I'd tried. My brothers and sisters rallied around me. My mother, who had stood by me all my life, was now strong, furious, and anguished. She and my stepfather did everything they could to help and protect us, calling every day and sometimes twice when she sensed I needed the extra support.

While we waited, I did my best to preserve some semblance of normalcy for the younger kids. Casey and her children came over, and everybody played and swam as usual until, overhead, helicopters drove us inside. When my lawyer learned that Woody had hired private investigators, he warned us, even the kids, to be wary of new friends. The house might be bugged, he said, and the car; the phone could be tapped, and there might be a transmitter near the house. "Oh, and don't accept any flowers." Flowers?

Woody's private detectives contacted the baby-sitters and Sophie, who hung up on them. Someone in Woody's film crew called, warning me that his investigators were interviewing people at work, asking for any damaging information about my family. Detectives even showed up in a small town in Vermont, where my brother told them to go back to New York. A man's raspy voice on the phone warned, "I hear there could be an accident. Watch out for yourself on the road." On three consecutive Sundays a gray car came down the driveway and took away our garbage. Moses, in his leg brace, ran after it, shouting, "Give it back! Give us back that garbage!"

The last time we spoke, I told Woody I thought that something in him must have ruptured. I don't know why I bothered saying again how much he'd taken from all the kids, and maybe from Soon-Yi even more than from Dylan. When I begged him for the children's sake to stop the publicity circus, he told me he hadn't even begun; that I was already "the laughing stock of the country" and that "by the time I'm finished with you, there will be nothing left." When I howled to him that in court he wouldn't be able to say things that weren't true, he replied, "It doesn't matter what's true; all that matters is what's believed."

New York Times, August 26, 1992. In the eye of an extraordinary media storm, Woody Allen and Mia Farrow and their lawyers met last night in the chambers of Judge Phyllis Gangel-Jacob. Mr.

Allen and Ms. Farrow arrived separately for the meeting last night at the sealed-off court building at 111 Centre Street and left the same way, without speaking a word to the press. Indeed no one expected grand revelations, but that did not deter scores of reporters, photographers, and spectators from clogging the street in anticipation of both the arrival and departure of the two celebrities. Mr. Allen somehow managed to get inside without being seen. Ms. Farrow was not so lucky. Arriving about fifteen minutes before the 6 P.M. meeting, her chauffeur-driven car was set upon as if by locusts, with photographers rushing the car and adhering to the windows before the car was able to shed them and disappear into a basement garage. "This is incredible," said Gerry Migliore, who stood on the corner of White and Centre Streets at about 6 P.M., during the height of the media crush. He said it was the biggest media onslaught in the court neighborhood in his memory. "In eleven years I've never seen anything like this. Not even for Bernhard Goetz," he said, recalling the famous subway-shooting case.

I had never seen anything remotely like it either, not even during my years with Frank Sinatra. It was as if something had landed from outer space. In disbelief and horror I could see the entire area awash in an unearthly white light from countless floodlights. The street outside the courthouse was lined with camera trucks, satellite dishes, and press people. I wonder how my heart didn't stop. For only a moment I went undetected inside the radio cab as it drew near the Supreme Court of New York State. The traffic moved slowly through white, waiting stillness. I didn't move or say a word. The lawyer beside me was quiet too. I could scarcely breathe. Then all at once someone shouted, and barricades broke, and photographers rushed at my cab, covering it. I heard yelling, and the sickening thud of countless lenses hitting against the windows. I don't know how everything didn't break.

Inside the courthouse, the judge denied Woody's request to see Dylan, but said he could see Satchel, supervised, to which I had no objection. Woody refused, saying that if he couldn't see both children, he didn't want to see either. The judge said she would have thought, in this family, that Woody would be most interested in the little boy who was his biological son. But Woody was adamant: he didn't want to see Satchel without Dylan.

"I find that bizarre," said the judge.

In New York, Paul Williams, the Child Welfare caseworker, reported that "based on Dylan's demeanor and her responses to my questions, and my conversations with the caseworker in Connecticut, and my experience from interviewing hundreds of children who had been abused, I concluded that abuse did occur and that there was a prima facie cause to commence family-court proceedings against Woody Allen. Then the barriers came down. There came a litany of reasons why we should not go forward. My superior said that Woody Allen is 'an influential person,' she talked about his films, and his 'position.' As more evidence came through interviews, I insisted that the case should have been filed. Managers at the Child Welfare Agency responded that 'pressure [to drop the case] is coming all the way from the mayor's office.' " The New York investigation was abruptly called off. The mayor's office denied the allegations.

I didn't know what to believe. What was Woody capable of? Where would it stop? Who would draw the line? As I stood at the kitchen sink peeling potatoes, I thought that maybe if I just kept on peeling, and didn't do anything else, no more bad things would happen.

In September we moved back to the city and the kids returned to their schools. In order to get Dylan out of the apartment building without exposing her to the photographers, I carried her out of the basement door wrapped in blankets. Nonetheless, despite all the chaos, Dylan began to blossom. She no longer locked herself in bathrooms, or fled from room to room screaming, Hide me, hide me! Gone were the days in bed under her quilt, the evasive looks, and the unconnected, unfinished thoughts. Gone too were her stomachaches and headaches. Her haunted little face opened into sunshine as we sat around the table each evening, reporting the events of the day. Outside, Dylan was still shy, but she was growing more confident in her friendships, as if seeing the world as a safer place. It was wonderful. There had been two changes in her life: she didn't have to see the therapist she disliked, and she didn't have to see Woody Allen. Indeed, she adamantly refused to see him and became fearful once more at the mention of his name.

The older children seemed to be handling things with equanimity, but they had been profoundly affected. I found myself experiencing the same creeping fear I'd had as a child, after the polio: that I had unknowingly brought danger into my family and that I might have contaminated those I loved the most.

Woody's custody trial was held in abeyance, pending word from the criminal investigation in Connecticut. In December, when Dylan was interviewed by a representative of the Connecticut police, she again went through the details of August 4, just as she had before, to the police, the doctor, social workers in New Haven, child-welfare agencies in New York and Connecticut, and to my lawyer, Eleanor Alter. In December Dylan told the police about another occasion, when she was climbing up the ladder of a bunk bed in the playroom. She said that Woody had slipped his hand inside her shorts and touched her there, and she was illustrating graphically where, in the genital area. She told them about the time Woody had angrily pushed her face into a plateful of hot spaghetti, and then whispered he was going to do it again. She described how she had seen Woody "trying to bend Satchel's leg the wrong way," and she took the anatomically correct doll and showed them, twisting the doll's leg backward, and she told the police that "Mommy stopped him."

She also recounted a time, more than a year earlier, when the weather was warm, and she was at Woody's apartment with Satchel and Soon-Yi. She said that she and her little brother were left in front of the television while Soon-Yi and Woody disappeared. After a while Dylan went upstairs to look for them. She saw them out on the terrace with their arms around each other. She called to them and they told her to "go away," they wanted "a little private time." Dylan said she pretended to go away, but she hid on the staircase next to the bedroom door, facing the glass doors to the terrace. She saw them walk into the bedroom, and the door was left partially open. Dylan crept up and watched. She saw Woody and Soon-Yi on the bed, on top of the covers, and "they were doing compliments and making snoring noises." That is what she said. And that "he was putting his penis into Soon-Yi's vagina."

For a moment, in cold December, a familiar, long-ago self breathed beside me. This other self of mine had embraced all the Christmases of her life with a delight usually reserved for children. I had knit nine beloved names into the long red and gold and green and white stockings, and hung them before the fireplace, acknowledging that my finest dreams had come true.

From days of youth and travel, I had gathered handsome ornaments, and each December, together with my children, we placed them among fragrant pine branches and rejoiced at miracles, and we sang the Christmas songs, strung fat cranberries, draped the lights of gold, and bowed with shepherds and kings before the solemn crèche. And when we gazed straight into the eyes of baby Jesus, we were grateful, and certain our Christmas was as glorious as any on earth.

But this Christmas, demons danced in the place of peace. Bolts of terror split the moments, shattered the nights, froze me at my tasks. I slipped into still, dangerous darkness. We had howled our terror, our outrage, and our pain. We had wept ourselves empty. We had tried, alone and together, to understand, but we could make no sense of it. Later we would speak again of people torn away and all the ways we loved them. But now, this Christmas, we were straining impossibly for the sound of a single sleigh bell.

That was the landscape of my mind. But I was in fact before the fireplace in our warm farmhouse in Connecticut. It seemed as after a death, unchanged, unreasonably so, yet altogether different. The light was harsher, sounds were louder, the edges sharper. I could see the world and my place in it from the top of a pin.

The stockings were hung, all but one. The children were merry and eager, playing beside the tree. Hope leaped and flickered with the flames.

The Connecticut state police continued their investigation, interviewing baby-sitters, all the children, our neighbors, doctors, and schoolteachers. To determine whether a criminal prosecution should be pursued, state's attorney Frank Maco referred Dylan to a team of two social workers and a pediatrician at Yale-New Haven Hospital. He asked them to "assess whether there were any impediments affecting the child's ability to accurately recall events related to the abuse claims, and whether a trial would put her at risk of further traumatization." While the Yale-New Haven report concluded that there had been no sexual abuse, the pediatrician who wrote the report never even met Dylan. The report was widely criticized, and state's attorney Maco publicly announced that he gave it "little weight" and that the criminal investigation of Woody Allen would continue.

On March 19, 1993, with only two hours' notice, Woody's custody trial began before Justice Elliott Wilk in New York State Supreme Court. He was represented by six different law firms, led by a criminal attorney.

In attempting to make the case that the children should be taken away from me, Woody took the stand as his own first witness. Early on, he and his attorneys tried to dismiss the issue of his affair with Soon-Yi. "I didn't envision that I would maintain necessarily a long relationship" with her, he testified, and "I felt nobody in the world would have any idea about it except Soon-Yi and myself." At which point the judge asked dryly, "Wasn't that enough? . . . That *you* would know that you were sleeping with your children's sister?"

"No, I didn't see it that way," Woody replied. "She was an adopted child and Dylan was an adopted child." He testified that my family was more like a "foster home" with kids from different parts of the world; that he "did not conceive of this as a sister relationship between the kids" because "a lot of kids were adopted and Soon-Yi was older."

Woody talked about Satchel's negative attitude toward him and claimed that I was responsible for it. To demonstrate his point he submitted a drawing that he swore under oath was made by Satchel. It was a drawing of a heart with five faces inside and names beneath them: Satchel, Dylan, Moses, Mommy, and Daddy, drawn with glasses.

But under intense and wily cross-examination, Woody grew increasingly flustered; then, in one of the most peculiar moments of the trial, he confessed that in fact he had drawn the entire picture himself.

"You drew the heart?" asked my attorney, Eleanor Alter.

"Yes," said Woody, "and put the faces of the family in it." Justice Wilk rose out of his chair to peer at the drawing Woody held.

"You drew the faces of the family?" she asked again.

"That's correct. And Satchel blackened my face out and he drew a heart and drew a line through it and wrote the word *no*, and crossed out my name."

"So it wasn't accurate yesterday when you said it was a drawing by Satchel?"

"Well, some of it is," Woody insisted stubbornly. "I just drew it and he crossed my face out."

"But it was actually your drawing?"

"This? Yes."

In his redirect testimony the next morning he returned to the subject of the drawing. "Satchel blackened out the face," he said. "I drew the heart and inside the heart I put Satchel, Dylan, Moses, Mommy, and Daddy, because my practice was always to promulgate for Satchel some kind of warmth and respect for his mother and for his, for you know, Dylan and for Moses. And Satchel looked at the heart and then blackened my face out, eliminated it, blackened out the word *Daddy*, eliminated it, drew his own heart with a line through it, a 'forbidden' line, and wrote the word *no*."

He acknowledged that he had called the children "little bastards," but never "in the pejorative sense." I listened to him deny pushing Dylan's face into a plate of hot spaghetti —an incident witnessed by most of our family. He denied twisting Satchel's leg. He denied that he'd had sex with

Soon-Yi while Dylan was in the apartment, or at any time before the adoptions of Dylan and Moses.

Asked whether he considered Moses, Dylan, and Satchel to be brothers and sister, he replied, "I think in a certain way they are brothers and sisters. It's not an easy question, not in the traditional sense, not in the way I am with my sister, no. They are not brothers and sisters. There is a difference between a biological brother and sister and adopted brothers and sisters." Then he conceded that Moses did consider Matthew his brother, and Satchel his brother, and Daisy, Lark, and Soon-Yi his sisters. He reluctantly admitted that Dylan's favorite person in the world, next to her mom, was her sister Lark. Further questioning revealed that he knew next to nothing about the lives of the children he sought custody of: he did not know their friends, their teachers, their doctors, or even the names of their pets. He had testified that there was a "special arrangement" for Moses's tuition; under cross-examination he admitted that "the arrangement was that Miss Farrow pay for it."

Over his days on the stand, Woody became increasingly inarticulate. The *New York Times* observed that "on his first day of testimony, he seemed relaxed, one arm draped over the back of his chair giving answers that were lengthy, conversational, even funny. But yesterday he spoke quietly, sometimes mumbling, often asked that questions be repeated, and at times searched in vain for a way to phrase his answers." On the last day of his three days of testimony, the *Times* noted that "Mr. Allen sat on the stand with the hunched-over posture of someone who half-hoped to disappear by scrunching up into a small ball. He found it difficult to remember details and had to refer to printed transcripts, taking off his glasses and bringing his nose in contact with the paper, looking remarkably like a befuddled old man."

Without respect for truth, he took the intimate moments of my pain and shock and horror and spun them into grotesque anecdotes for strangers. While I watched him talking, talking on the witness stand, I thought I saw a strange thing: like Clark Kent pulling apart his shirt, Woody opened his chest with his two hands and inside, where a heart and soul and conscience ought to be, were entrails, and dark things burrowing, unaccustomed to the light.

Then his attorneys called me to the stand. According to the *New York Times*, "Elkin Abramowitz, representing Mr. Allen in his custody suit against Mia Farrow, tried to portray her as a woman so wounded by Mr. Allen's affair with her adopted daughter that she would stop at nothing to strike back: a devious, manipulative woman whose thirst for vengeance had turned her into a howling fury. But someone slipped a different Ms. Farrow into the witness box. The woman who calmly answered Mr. Abramowitz's questions throughout a long, often tedious day looked like a Roman Catholic schoolgirl . . . The stricken look with which she recounted the demise of her relationship imposed a kind of respectful silence on the courtroom . . . Even the din of the construction work outside the building seemed to halt when Ms. Farrow described the cooling of Mr. Allen's affection."

Woody brought forth his witnesses: a handful of employees, followed by shrink upon shrink upon shrink. Secure in their Freudian castles in a gray Jungian jungle, they streamed their jargon like television cult leaders who know their scriptures too well. While the press dozed, I wandered my own bleak terrain, and all the shrinks blurred into one fuzzy Babylonian ball.

During the six weeks of testimony, not one of his witnesses testified that Woody Allen should be granted custody. None of the mental-health professionals had ever dealt with a situation in which the children were forced to confront an ongoing sexual relationship between their father

and their sister. One volunteered that in these circumstances, "We're flying by the seat of our pants."

The judge informed us that the decision would be handed
down in several weeks—one morning before eleven o'clock
—so we shouldn't sit by the phone all day. Throughout the
trial my lawyer reassured me continually that Woody had
no chance of obtaining custody, that he had not remotely
succeeded in proving me an unfit mother, and that no judge
would take three children away from their siblings to live
with a father who was living with their sister. Editorials and
countless letters of support from all over the country reinforced her assurances. Still, I never stopped worrying. If he
were awarded custody, what would I do? I knew that if
Moses, Dylan, and Satchel were forced to live with Woody
Allen, it would destroy them. And what would happen to
Tam and Isaiah? And what would then become of the other
kids? Beyond that I couldn't think. My lawyer said that
Woody's suit was so outrageous that he would surely be
ordered to pay my legal fees, estimated at well over a million dollars that I didn't have. But what if she was wrong?

The younger kids had only the vaguest notion of why I
had been going to court. I didn't want to worry them. As
they went about their days, I got myself an agent, and luck
came through with a movie to be filmed in Ireland that
coming summer; I even started learning my lines. When I
couldn't sleep, I went into the nursery to watch the children
safe in slumber.

Malignant specters of the dark nights move into familiar
positions. Hounds tug on taut leather lines, howling horrible. While the children sleep I dream of Ireland awakening
in gentle light; gray stone walls hemming the damp fields,
sheep across the stretch of the Wicklow Mountains and the

glowering hills of Connemara; apples in the branches near Inistioge; oars dip the sea at Ballyhack; the blue-eyed daughters of Ballyknocken trudge to school.

A shy new moon slips into a starless sky. A cough stirs the dozy parrot—his beaky profile gives a one-eyed stare. My silver-haired son comes wordlessly in small steps to lie beside me; blue veins beneath marble.

I rise to rock the baby Isaiah, his eyes are drowsy, opal seas. I cup the metal curls and rock him till his breath evens and the small fist falls from my shoulder. Then I lay him back in his crib and return to my big bed to gather the white child in my arms. Him too I place in the cot, beside his brother, and both are asleep in the nursery light.

These several things I do and then I lie down to push back the scorched imprints of the long day.

On the weekends we drove to Frog Hollow, and before two weeks had passed, I found myself watching the telephone in the mornings from ten until eleven. The older kids called me from their schools to see if there had been any word. Every day I reassured them that all would be well, that nothing would tear us apart. Our last shred of trust hung in the space between Justice Elliott Wilk and my family.

On the morning of June 7 the phone rang. I picked it up. My lawyer, Eleanor Alter, was in a phone booth at the courthouse. "We won," she said. "We won!"

I rushed over to her office and there I sat down to read the lengthy judgment, which addressed the many complicated issues that the custody trial had unearthed. In his state supreme court decision,* Justice Wilk determined that:

---

* See Appendix for the entire decision.

WOODY ALLEN

• Mr. Allen has demonstrated no parenting skills that would qualify him as an adequate custodian for Moses, Dylan, and Satchel.

• He showed no understanding that the bonds developed between adoptive brothers and sisters are no less worthy of respect and protection than those between biological siblings.

• Mr. Allen's deficiencies as a custodial parent are magnified by his affair with Soon-Yi . . . Having isolated Soon-Yi from her family, he left her with no visible support system. He had no consideration for the consequences to her, to Ms. Farrow, to the Previn children for whom he cared little, or to his own children for whom he professes love.

• Mr. Allen's response to Dylan's claim of sexual abuse was an attack upon Ms. Farrow, whose parenting ability and emotional stability he impugned without the support of any credible evidence. His trial strategy has been to separate his children from their brothers and sisters; to turn the children against their mother; to divide adopted children from biological children.

• His self-absorption, his lack of judgment and his commitment to his divisive assault, thereby impeding the healing of the injuries he has already caused, warrant a careful monitoring of his future contact with the children.

MIA FARROW

• Few relationships and fewer families can easily bear the microscopic examination to which Ms. Farrow and her children have been subjected. It is evident that she loves children and has devoted a significant portion of her emotional and material wealth to their upbringing . . . She is sensitive to the needs of her children, respectful of their opinions, honest with them and quick to address their problems.

• There is no credible evidence to support Mr. Allen's contention that Ms. Farrow coached Dylan or that Ms. Farrow acted upon a desire for revenge against him for seducing Soon-Yi. Mr. Allen's resort to the stereotypical "woman scorned" defense is an injudicious attempt to divert attention from his failure to act as a responsible parent and adult.

• Ms. Farrow's refusal to permit Mr. Allen to visit with Dylan after August 4, 1992 was prudent. Her willingness to allow Satchel to have regular supervised visitation with Mr. Allen reflects her understanding of the propriety of balancing Satchel's need for contact with his father against the danger of Mr. Allen's lack of parental judgment.

• In a society where children are too often betrayed by adults who ignore or disbelieve their complaints of abuse, Ms. Farrow's determination to protect Dylan is commendable.

• Ironically, Ms. Farrow's principal shortcoming with respect to responsible parenting appears to have been her continued relationship with Mr. Allen.

DYLAN FARROW

• The credible testimony of Ms. Farrow, Dr. Coates, Dr. Leventhal and Mr. Allen does prove that Mr. Allen's behavior toward Dylan was grossly inappropriate and that measures must be taken to protect her.

CUSTODY

• None of the witnesses who testified on Mr. Allen's behalf provided credible evidence that he is an appropriate custodial parent. Indeed, none would venture an opinion that he should be granted custody. When asked, even Mr. Allen could not provide an acceptable reason for a change in custody.

• After considering Ms. Farrow's position as the sole caretaker of the children, the satisfactory fashion in which she has fulfilled that function, the parties' pre-litigation acceptance that she continue in that capacity, and Mr. Allen's serious parental inadequacies, it is clear that the best interests of the children will be served by their continued custody with Ms. Farrow.

VISITATION

• The common theme of the testimony by the mental health witnesses is that Mr. Allen has inflicted serious damage on the children and that healing is necessary. Because, as Dr. Brodzinsky and Dr. Herman observed, this family is in an uncharted therapeutic area, where the course is uncertain and the benefits unknown, the visitation structure that will best promote the healing process and safeguard the children is elusive. What is clear is that Mr. Allen's lack of judgment, insight, and impulse control make normal noncustodial visitation with Dylan and Satchel too risky to the children's well-being to be permitted at this time.

• It is unclear whether Mr. Allen will ever develop the insight and judgment necessary for him to relate to Dylan appropriately. My caution is the product of Mr. Allen's demonstrated inability to understand the impact that his words and deeds have upon the emotional well being of his children.

• I believe that Mr. Allen will use Satchel in an attempt to gain information about Dylan and to insinuate himself into her good graces. I believe that Mr. Allen will, if unsupervised, attempt to turn Satchel against the other members of his family. I believe Mr. Allen to be desirous of introducing Soon-Yi into the visitation arrangement without concern for the effect on Satchel, Soon-Yi, or the other members of the Farrow family. In short, I believe Mr. Allen to be so self-absorbed, untrustworthy, and insensitive, that he should not be permitted to see Satchel without appropriate professional supervision until Mr. Allen demonstrates that supervision is no longer necessary.

• Because Mr. Allen's position has no merit, he will bear the entire financial burden of this litigation.

After so many months of fear and horror it would take time before I could believe we were really safe. I telephoned the older kids at their schools and returned to the apartment where the younger ones were just coming home. I held them tightly. They didn't know what this day meant or how much had been at stake. I never told them that they could have been taken away from me, and from their brothers and sisters. All those mornings when I had left them to go to court, I said only that there were "problems" that had to be dealt with; that Woody Allen was not happy about certain things, but that all would be well.

That night Sascha and his wife Carrie, Matthew,

Fletcher, Daisy, Lark, Moses, and I gathered around the table after the little kids went to sleep. The atmosphere was subdued as we shared our emotional exhaustion and immense relief. It had been so long since we had awakened to an ordinary day.

Chapter Twelve

A month after the court's decision, Moses, Tam, Dylan, Satchel, Isaiah, and I left for Ireland, where I would make Hugh Leonard's *Widow's Peak* in the Wicklow Mountains. I joined an old friend from England, Joan Plowright, and two new ones, Natasha Richardson and her fiancé, Liam Neeson, with whom I'd worked only a year and a half earlier, a lifetime ago it seemed, in *Husbands and Wives.* To focus on something other than the trial came as a relief and a pleasure, and after thirteen years with the same director and crew, it was exhilarating to be at work in an atmosphere so entirely different.

I was returned that summer to long-ago memories of Ireland, of mystical tales told to me by Eileen, my mother, and my grandmother; and of my grandfather's house that moaned in the wind, the black bogs pelted with rain, and the heavy smell of turf fires. Now, in the welcoming of aunts and cousins, after decades of wandering, I was wrapped in a deep sense of belonging. It was as if I had come home.

Far from troubles and scrutiny, Dylan, Satchel, and Tam chased woolly lambs across the hillsides, and in the village they happily blended with the local kids. The previous year, in the midst of all the turbulence, Dylan had chosen another name for herself, a lovely one, and she had asked us not to call her Dylan again. We respected her wishes. Now Satchel, because he had been teased in the school yard as a "book bag," and perhaps inspired by Dylan's name change, chose a fine new name for himself.

Our time in Ireland was only momentarily marred by news that Woody Allen had appealed the custody decision; and then again in midsummer, when he came to Dublin, shattering our newfound peace and privacy with more headlines and loud accusations. In the newspapers we read that he had brought Soon-Yi with him. No one in the family had heard from her since 1992.

As sure as death, Soon-Yi was gone from our lives. Long months ago, her brothers and sisters had begun the painful process of hardening their hearts toward her. Soon-Yi Farrow Previn, schoolgirl, sister, daughter, had metamorphosed into something none of us could comprehend or think about. Knowing my sorrow, a friend urged me to think of her not as a daughter but as a child who had lived among us, without ever understanding what a family is, or what a mother is; she was unable to love us, and felt no commitment to us. She was not a daughter the way Lark, Daisy, Tam, and Dylan are; I tried to think this, to make the betrayal less terrible, the loss more bearable. But in the end, whatever her feelings, or lack of them, I can only love her as my child, and there is nothing to be done about that. I no longer want to see her, but for the rest of my life I will miss her.

We returned to New York in the fall of 1993, still not knowing whether Woody Allen would face criminal prose-

cution for his conduct with Dylan; the police investigation
had gone on for a year. My own position in this matter had
never shifted: my responsibility was to secure the necessary
protection for Dylan. I had always hoped this could be
achieved without putting her through a trial. Now, with the
supreme court decision, I felt confident that, at least for the
immediate future, she would be safe.

On September 24, 1993, Connecticut state's attorney
Frank Maco announced his decision. "I have reviewed an
arrest warrant application submitted by the state police," he
said. "As to the allegations . . . I find that probable cause
exists." Despite this finding, he would not initiate prosecution because of "the risk of exposing the child complainant
to the rigors, uncertainties, and possible traumatization of
such actions . . . I cannot identify a compelling community interest or expectation that justifies my risking the well-
being of the child-victim by exposure to the criminal
process . . . I have conferred with the child and her
mother and they concur with my decision."

In order to undo Woody's adoptions of Dylan and Moses,
we needed to prove that, unbeknownst to the court, a relationship between Woody and Soon-Yi had already existed
prior to the adoptions, a fact both had freely admitted at
first, but that they now denied under oath. Long before the
proceedings began, a housekeeper Woody and I shared told
me she had seen Soon-Yi in his apartment and changed the
sheets and emptied the wastebaskets after her visits.

To the same Judge Roth who had approved the adoptions, we brought proof of fraud including hundreds of
calls between Woody and Soon-Yi, as well as witnesses who
saw Soon-Yi entering and leaving his apartment alone and
other witnesses who saw them in Woody's apartment
throughout 1990 and 1991. There was even the photographer who had taken a widely published photograph of

Woody and Soon-Yi holding hands at a Knicks game in 1990.

After hearing all that, Judge Rene Roth sidestepped the issue of fraud and requested an additional hearing on the "best interest of the children." But I had already spent a half million dollars on the fraud hearing. Faced with a choice between higher education for my children and continuing this litigation, I let it go, at least for the time being. Moses, almost of age, was no longer an issue, and Dylan was protected by the state supreme court.

Woody lost his appeals, the photographers receded, and we found ourselves surrounded by good friends. But as we went about the city, walking, or waiting for buses or cabs, it was hard to ignore the possibility that Woody or Soon-Yi or the limo with the tinted windows might cross our paths. When the older kids settled in to watch a Knicks game on television and the camera suddenly cut to Woody and Soon-Yi, Moses got up and silently left the room. Minutes later the others switched off the set. Even the view I had loved from our apartment windows for thirty years had become painful. I had to break a twelve-year habit of glancing to see which lights were on in the penthouse across the park.

Over the Christmas holidays Fletcher got a job in the packing room at a chic Manhattan clothing store. One day his supervisor, not realizing he was Soon-Yi's brother, asked him to carry packages out to the waiting limo of Woody Allen's girlfriend. Fletcher declined.

That winter the rent-control laws were changed, and our rent was about to be quadrupled. So we let go of the apartment that had been my family's since I was a teenager, to live full-time at Frog Hollow, where, after all, we were happiest. The older kids were in college, graduate school, or law school, and they came home only on weekends or the holidays. Moses, at sixteen, still had two years of high school ahead, so for him it would be more difficult, but he was willing to make the transition to a Connecticut school. As a family we were certain that life in the country would be easier, healthier, and more fun for the younger kids. Although Woody took us to court to prevent us from moving, the judge said we could go. I have lost count of how many times Woody has brought me back into court to challenge the custody decision or to dispute its visitation restrictions. But as of this writing we are still safe, and the children are happier than they have ever been.

So while carpenters fixed up Frog Hollow, during the winter of 1994 we went to Florida, where we rode dolphins, and I made *Miami Rhapsody* with Sarah Jessica Parker and Antonio Banderas.

I wrote to my childhood friend Maria Roach: "This is a time for healing; time to acknowledge the strengths that have seen us through and to be grateful for our blessings. So much has been lost; people I loved dearly and my belief in them, daily life as we knew it and our privacy and peace. We reached a point where we no longer knew what was probable. We did not bring these troubles upon ourselves, but through them I determined to define myself to myself, to others, and to God. This was the goal I set, and so each laceration became a test, a trial I needed to be worthy of. Each scalding survived was a purification. Each plunge into darkness left me struggling for light. Every separate fear and personal humiliation endured served to strip away what was nonessential in me and made me understand: it is by that which cannot be taken away that we can measure ourselves.

"During these last months, my entire orientation has shifted: emotional pain, suffering of the soul, and all the falling away seem to have led me into a deeper consciousness, an awareness, toward a state of (if I may use this word) transcendence, through which we experience our own

existence as a part of the greater whole; as both a non-self
and as a far-greater self, not defined by transitory land-
marks or finite boundaries, but existing purely in relation to
an infinite whole. Through this awareness, and the falling of
the walls, and the evolution of self comes meaningful direction, strength, and serenity. It is also the ultimate weapon
against nothingness.

"I am bonding myself to these thoughts, drawing courage from them, and, carrying only what is essential, I will
travel lightly into an unknown future, trusting we will all be
safe and that a meaningful new life will create itself."

In February the phone in our New York apartment rang: an
agency was telling me about a little girl for whom they had
been unable to find a home, and whom they thought would
be right for us. The kids and I talked it over, and in March
we welcomed an exquisite one-month-old baby girl into the
family. Already smiling and cooing, Kaeli-Shea was a
"Gerber's baby," except that, for reasons no one could explain, she was unable to move her arms.

In May, Woody lost his first appeal of the state supreme
court decision. The court recognized Woody's "tendency to
place inappropriate emphasis on his own wants and needs
and to minimize and even ignore those of his children."
While the five judges stated that the allegations of sexual
abuse of Dylan were inconclusive, they also stated that the
testimony at the trial suggested that abuse did occur.

In June we packed up thirty years' worth of Farrow family stuff, and we left the apartment on Central Park West.
When we arrived at Frog Hollow everyone cheered, and we
moved our things into the newly renovated eight-bedroom
house.

Now, Kaeli-Shea slept in the bassinet beside my bed. She
received physical therapy, and I worked in my garden and
learned my lines, along with some sign language, for a

movie to be shot that winter in Connecticut. *Reckless*, written by Craig Lucas, offered me one of the best roles of my career. Its director, Norman René, my new friend, made a remarkable film and then died not long after it was finished.

Even before we left New York, soon after Kaeli-Shea's arrival, another adoptive parent called to tell me about a boy in an Indian orphanage. He had been abandoned some years earlier in a Calcutta train station. His age was put at five, six, or seven. He was paraplegic as a result of polio. This very frail child was in urgent need of a home, but in all the years that he had been in the orphanage, no one had come forward for him. I told the children about the little boy in India, and there evolved an extraordinary discussion in which the children suggested ways they could each be of help. Everyone wanted this little brother. They urged me to call the agency and hurry the paperwork along, and could we please have a picture. Then, together, we went out and bought a little red wheelchair.

During that first winter at Frog Hollow, Isaiah started to talk, and little by little, Kaeli-Shea began to use her arms. Tam, while receiving braille lessons and "cane mobility" instruction, was fully integrated at the local school. That winter she read *The Diary of Anne Frank* in braille. All the kids made friends quickly, and after the restrictions of apartment living, it was wonderful for them to be able to run outside and play, and invite other children over whenever they wanted.

I was just finishing *Reckless* when Thaddeus arrived from India; they gave me the afternoon off so that the kids and I could meet the plane at JFK. My seventh son was so weak from malnutrition that he spent much of those first months lying down. His legs were like chicken bones and the whites of his large eyes were a dull yellow. His knees, the tops of his feet, and his backside are still scarred from years of dragging himself along the ground.

But we attached ramps to Frog Hollow, and before long Thaddeus, with a dazzling smile, was scooting up and down in his bright red wheelchair. Doctors in the United States don't see much polio these days, so at first they weren't sure how to proceed. Neither leg could support his weight, and one was rigidly bent at the knee, almost at a right angle. There was talk about surgery, and encasing him in a complete body and neck brace because the severe curvature of his spine was causing his ribs to collapse on his organs. But he was just beginning to get used to us and everything else here. He couldn't speak or understand a word of English. We decided to try physical therapy first— maybe we could straighten his leg without surgery. Then he would be able to wear leg braces, and with them he might one day walk with crutches, and there was a chance that his abdominal and back muscles would grow strong enough to support his spine.

Thaddeus won real respect as he endured months of often painful therapy three times a day with plucky good humor and stubborn optimism. It was easy for me to learn how to do the exercises he needed from the therapist who came to our house several times a week, because they were similar to the exercises that had been used for Moses's leg, which he still has to do. We stretched the tendons behind Thaddeus's knee, trying to unlock it; I held his legs while he did his best to walk on his hands wheelbarrow-style. This wasn't easy because he was so weak, and because his left arm has only half strength.

One year after his arrival, braced from his waist through his shoes, Thaddeus pulled himself upright while clinging to a walker, his dark eyes sparkling in triumph. Today, two years later, with the braces and crutches, he can tear around the garden at a good clip, over rocks and through bushes. Although the wheelchair will always be his primary means of getting about, his upper-body muscles are strong, and his spine has straightened. He speaks English now, with a lovely Indian lilt, and he has lots of friends in the second grade at our village school. In the evening I often find him sharing his new reading skills with his little brother Isaiah. Since Thaddeus's arrival his weight has tripled, and he has enough energy to light up the state of Connecticut.

During the time we were waiting for Thaddeus, another agency called to tell me about Minh, a blind girl about three years old, who had spent all her life in a Vietnamese orphanage. No, I kept saying, "We're waiting for a child from India, and that will be it for us. I hope you find another family for Minh." But once you are aware of a specific child, it's difficult to ignore his or her destiny. Photos arrived in the mail showing a tiny pixie of a girl standing against a wall with her fist in her eye.

More than a year had gone by, during which Thaddeus had arrived and become a joy to all of us, when the agency called to say they still had not located a family for Minh. We said yes. The kids were thrilled: Dylan even begged me to ask the agency for a second little girl who would be exactly her age. But I told her that Minh would be the last of the brothers and sisters.

The journey to an orphanage to claim a daughter or son is every bit as extraordinary an experience as giving birth. A year later, in late 1995, when the papers were finally completed, Dylan and I set out with our knapsacks full of presents from the children to their new sister, plus extra treats for the other kids at the orphanage—candy, crayons, baseball hats, and so forth. We flew to Vietnam, stopping in Los Angeles, Seoul, and Bangkok, where we spent the night at an airport hotel before continuing on to Ho Chi Minh City, formerly Saigon.

That evening, as I picked at my dinner, Dylan raced around the rooftop restaurant with two children of a family friend who lives in Vietnam. In bustling downtown Ho Chi Minh City, under a warm, star-filled sky, I thought of the rest of my children just waking in their beds on the other side of this earth, and I thought of little Minh, who by this time tomorrow would be with Dylan and me.

The next day we were taken to the orphanage, a car trip of roughly three hours. As Ho Chi Minh City's crowded suburbs fell away and we sped past the rice fields, I held one momentous thought: I was about to meet a child who is my daughter, and whom I will stand by for the rest of my life. Today she will not understand a word I say, nor will I know scarcely a word of hers, but I will take her in this car away from the orphanage, the only place she has ever known, and I will bring her to the other side of the earth, where her sisters and brothers are waiting in a Connecticut farmhouse. Minh is coming home, home to her family.

There is a brand-new doll and a brown Steiff teddy bear waiting on the spare bed that will be Minh's, in the large corner bedroom where Dylan and Tam sleep. From her windows Minh won't see the views of the lake, the field, and the woods beyond. But Tam has filled a shelf with books for blind children, Dylan has written a beautiful poem, and Satchel and Thaddeus have gone through their things and chosen the toys they feel their sister will like best. Isaiah has wrapped his favorite steam shovel in toilet paper and placed it under Minh's pillow. Lark and I have hung small dresses in the closet and the drawers are filled with size-five clothes—we don't know how big she is, but we guess she is very small. Tam has reminded me to stock up on Asian rice and *nuk-mam*, the Vietnamese fish sauce. Isaiah says, Better get hot dogs. Trang, an invaluable translator and friend during Tam's first months with us, is standing by. Lark, Daisy, Matthew, Sascha, and Carrie will be waiting at the house when we return, and of course Moses. Fletcher is at school in Germany. At the village school, the kindergarten teacher has already rearranged the furniture so that Minh won't bump into anything, and her new classmates are eager to meet her. Like Tam and Thaddeus, she will have an aide during school hours.

What I had been searching for, since the very beginning, since my childhood ended with polio, through my years in convent school and my time with Frank Sinatra and in India, and really every single day, was a life that would be meaningful. Now, in a car outside Ho Chi Minh City, I held Dylan's hand and silently prayed to be better than I am—to be the person Minh and each of my children needs and deserves—and to be worthy of the life I had chosen and the responsibilities that lay ahead.

At the orphanage I hugged my new daughter, and with her mouth overflowing with M&M's, tiny Minh announced that she would sleep next to me on the floor, and she hoped I would give her plenty of candy, a knapsack like my own, and an electric fan.

I named her Frankie-Minh, after Frank Sinatra. He had once told me he had met a little girl who was blind. Hair was blowing across her face, and when he bent over to move it out of her eyes, the child asked, "Mr. Sinatra, what color is the wind?"

And Frank said his own eyes filled so he couldn't see. "Sweetheart," he answered, "the wind moves so fast that none of us have ever seen it."

Frankie-Minh has now been with our family for more than a year. She is six years old, and a single sunbeam, a pure delight to everyone who meets her. In no time she became fluent in English, and already she is learning to read in braille. Tam is able to help her in so many ways, but really all of the kids help one another.

In 1996, after Matthew graduated cum laude from law

school, we returned, as we have every year, to Ireland—this time so I could make *Angela Mooney Dies Again* in Connemara, directed by Tommy McCartle and beautifully written by John McCartle. Matthew joined us in the west of Ireland, in the place where he had been conceived one blissful summer more than a quarter of a century before. To the delight of all the kids large and small, I have bought a thatched cottage in the Wicklow Mountains where the river bends.

As 1997 approaches, Matthew is a lawyer, clerking for a federal court judge, and Sascha is a computer analyst, happily wedded to Carrie, whom I love as my daughter. Lark and Daisy married brothers, and they too are happy; thanks to them, I have three glorious grandchildren. Fletcher and Moses are in college and doing great, while Kaeli-Shea must be the most talkative three-year-old at the Benjamin Bunny Nursery School. Every weekend one or another of the older kids comes to Frog Hollow for a visit.

Tam has made up for her lost school years—today she wins top marks in the eighth grade. She's a whiz at math, and along with Satchel, she is a passionate gardener: by touch, Tam can identify any plant or weed. She and Dylan are close sisters who share a bedroom and confidences. Dylan, at eleven, is a quiet little girl who loves to read, write, and draw. She sings with the school chorus and performs in the town's drama group. Satchel, at nine, is the family philosopher, a voracious reader, and impressively agile in the world of ideas. He is passionate about animals and is a member of the 4-H club.

Outside my window at this moment Thaddeus is sitting with his cat in the red wagon, steering, while Frankie pushes him at top speed. Isaiah and Satchel, totally absorbed, are following the flights of various insects and butterflies. Kaeli-Shea is heading out with a bucket of potato chips. Dylan and her best friend are over on the jungle gym.

I grew up in a family of seven children, I have raised

seven children, now grown up, and again today there are seven children living at home. It feels absolutely right. We have chickens and roosters, two cows, five cats, a dog, rabbits, hamsters, birds, lizards, and tropical fish. We are looking for the right pony.

APPENDIX

I have reproduced the state supreme court decision in its entirety, which perhaps is an unusual document in a memoir. My purpose, however, in doing so is to reassure the reader that extracts from it have not distorted what was decided by the Court. This decision was upheld in appeals to the Appellate Division, First Department, and the New York Court of Appeals. Furthermore, incidents reported prior to the custody trial were included in the testimony at that trial.

SUPREME COURT: NEW YORK COUNTY
INDIVIDUAL ASSIGNMENT PART 6

SU24A

- - - - - - - - - - - - - - - - - - - -x
WOODY ALLEN,

Petitioner,

Index No.
68738/92

- against -

MARIA VILLIERS FARROW, also known as
MIA FARROW,

Respondent.

- - - - - - - - - - - - - - - - - - - -x
ELLIOTT WILK, J.*:

INTRODUCTION

On August 13, 1992, seven days after he learned that his seven-year-old daughter Dylan had accused him of sexual abuse, Woody Allen began this action against Mia Farrow to obtain custody of Dylan, their five-year-old son Satchel, and their fifteen-year-old son Moses.

As mandated by law, Dr. V. Kavirajan, the Connecticut pediatrician to whom Dylan repeated her accusation, reported the charge to the Connecticut State Police. In furtherance of their investigation to determine if a criminal prosecution should be pursued against Mr. Allen, the Connecticut State Police referred Dylan to the Child Sexual Abuse Clinic of Yale-New Haven Hospital. According to Yale-New Haven, the two major questions posed to them were: "Is Dylan telling the truth, and did we think that she was sexually abused?" On March 17, 1993, Yale-New Haven issued a report which concluded that Mr. Allen had not sexually abused Dylan.

This trial began on March 19, 1993. Among the witnesses called by petitioner were Mr. Allen; Ms. Farrow; Dr. Susan Coates, a clinical psychologist who treated Satchel; Dr. Nancy Schultz, a clinical psychologist who treated Dylan; and Dr. David Brodzinsky, a clinical psychologist who spoke with Dylan and Moses pursuant to his assignment in a related Surrogate's Court proceeding. Dr. John Leventhal, a pediatrician who was part of the three-member Yale-New Haven team, testified by deposition. Ms. Farrow called Dr. Stephen Herman, a clinical psychiatrist, who commented on the Yale-New Haven report.

What follows are my findings of fact. Where statements or observations are attributed to witnesses, they are adopted by me as findings of fact.

---

* I acknowledge the assistance of Analisa Torres in the preparation of this opinion.

FINDINGS OF FACT

Mr. Allen is a fifty-seven year old film maker. He has been divorced twice. Both marriages were childless. Ms. Farrow is forty-eight years old. She is an actress who has performed in many of Mr. Allen's movies. Her first marriage, at age twenty-one, ended in divorce two years later. Shortly thereafter, she married André Previn, with whom she had six children, three biological and three adopted.

Matthew and Sascha Previn, twenty-three years old, were born on February 26, 1970. The birth year of Soon-Yi Previn is believed to be 1970 or 1972. She was born in Korea and was adopted in 1977. Lark Previn, twenty years old, was born on February 15, 1973. Fletcher Previn, nineteen years old, was born on March 14, 1974. Daisy Previn, eighteen years old, was born on October 6, 1974.

After eight years of marriage, Ms. Farrow and Mr. Previn were divorced. Ms. Farrow retained custody of the children.

Mr. Allen and Ms. Farrow met in 1980, a few months after Ms. Farrow had adopted Moses Farrow, who was born on January 27, 1978. Mr. Allen preferred that Ms. Farrow's children not be a part of their lives together. Until 1985, Mr. Allen had "virtually a single person's relationship" with Ms. Farrow and viewed her children as an encumbrance. He had no involvement with them and no interest in them. Throughout their relationship, Mr. Allen has maintained his residence on the east side of Manhattan and Ms. Farrow has lived with her children on the west side of Manhattan.

In 1984, Ms. Farrow expressed a desire to have a child with Mr. Allen. He resisted, fearing that a young child would reduce the time that they had available for each other. Only after Ms. Farrow promised that the child would live with her and that Mr. Allen need not be involved with the child's care or upbringing, did he agree.

After six months of unsuccessful attempts to become pregnant, and with Mr. Allen's lukewarm support, Ms. Farrow decided to adopt a child. Mr. Allen chose not to participate in the adoption and Ms. Farrow was the sole adoptive parent. On July 11, 1985, the newborn Dylan joined the Farrow household.

Mr. Allen's attitude toward Dylan changed a few months after the adoption. He began to spend some mornings and evenings at Ms. Farrow's apartment in order to be with Dylan. He visited at Ms. Farrow's country home in Connecticut and accompanied the Farrow-Previn family on extended vacations to Europe in 1987, 1988 and 1989. He remained aloof from Ms. Farrow's other children except for Moses, to whom he was cordial.

In 1986, Ms. Farrow suggested the adoption of another child. Mr. Allen, buoyed by his developing affection for Dylan, was enthusiastic. Before another adoption could be arranged, Ms. Farrow became pregnant with Satchel.

During Ms. Farrow's pregnancy, Mr. Allen did not touch her stomach, listen to the fetus, or try to feel it kick. Because Mr. Allen had shown no interest in her pregnancy and because Ms. Farrow believed him to be squeamish about the delivery process, her friend Casey Pascal acted as her Lamaze coach.

A few months into the pregnancy, Ms. Farrow began to withdraw from Mr. Allen. After Satchel's birth, which occurred on December 19, 1987, she grew more distant from Mr. Allen. Ms. Farrow's attention to Satchel also reduced the time she had available for Dylan. Mr. Allen began to spend more time with Dylan and to intensify his relationship with her.

By then, Ms. Farrow had become concerned with Mr. Allen's behavior toward Dylan. During a trip to Paris, when Dylan was between two and three years old, Ms. Farrow told Mr. Allen that "[y]ou look at her [Dylan] in a sexual way. You fondled her. It's not natural. You're all over her. You don't give her any breathing room. You look at her when she's naked."

Her apprehension was fueled by the intensity of the attention Mr. Allen lavished on Dylan, and by his spending play-time in bed with her, by his reading to her in his bed while dressed in his undershorts, and by his permitting her to suck on his thumb.

Ms. Farrow testified that Mr. Allen was overly attentive and demanding of Dylan's time and attention. He was aggressively affectionate, providing her with little space of her own and with no respect for the integrity of her body. Ms. Farrow, Casey Pascal, Sophie Raven (Dylan's French tutor), and Dr. Coates testified that Mr. Allen focused on Dylan to the exclusion of her siblings, even when Satchel and Moses were present.

In June 1990, the parties became concerned with Satchel's behavior and took him to see Dr. Coates, with whom he then began treatment. At Dr. Coates' request, both parents participated in Satchel's treatment. In the fall of 1990, the parties asked Dr. Coates to evaluate Dylan to determine if she needed therapy. During the course of the evaluation, Ms. Farrow expressed her concern to Dr. Coates that Mr. Allen's behavior with Dylan was not appropriate. Dr. Coates observed:

> I understood why she was worried, because it [Mr. Allen's relationship with Dylan] was intense, . . . I did not see it as sexual, but I saw it as inappropriately intense because it excluded everybody else, and it placed a demand on a child for a kind of acknowledgment that I felt should not be placed on a child . . .

She testified that she worked with Mr. Allen to help him to understand that his behavior with Dylan was inappropriate and that it had to be modified. Dr. Coates also recommended that Dylan enter therapy with Dr. Schultz, with whom Dylan began treatment in April 1991.

In 1991, Ms. Farrow expressed a desire to adopt another

child. Mr. Allen, who had begun to believe that Ms. Farrow was growing more remote from him and that she might discontinue his access to Dylan, said that he would not take "a lousy attitude towards it" if, in return, Ms. Farrow would sponsor his adoption of Dylan and Moses. She said that she agreed after Mr. Allen assured her that "he would not take Dylan for sleep-overs . . . unless I was there. And that if, God forbid, anything should happen to our relationship, that he would never seek custody." The adoptions were concluded in December 1991.

Until 1990, although he had had little contact with any of the Previn children, Mr. Allen had the least to do with Soon-Yi. "She was someone who didn't like me. I had no interest in her, none whatsoever. She was a quiet person who did her work. I never spoke to her." In 1990, Mr. Allen, who had four season tickets to the New York Knicks basketball games, was asked by Soon-Yi if she could go to a game. Mr. Allen agreed.

During the following weeks, when Mr. Allen visited Ms. Farrow's home, he would say hello to Soon-Yi, "which is something I never did in the years prior, but no conversations with her or anything."

Soon-Yi attended more basketball games with Mr. Allen. He testified that "gradually, after the basketball association, we became more friendly. She opened up to me more." By 1991 they were discussing her interests in modeling, art, and psychology. She spoke of her hopes and other aspects of her life.

In September 1991, Soon-Yi entered Drew College in New Jersey. She was naive, socially inexperienced and vulnerable. Mr. Allen testified that she was lonely and unhappy at school, and that she began to speak daily with him by telephone. She spent most weekends at home with Ms. Farrow. There is no evidence that Soon-Yi told Ms. Farrow either that she was lonely or that she had been in daily communication with Mr. Allen.

On January 13, 1992, while in Mr. Allen's apartment, Ms. Farrow discovered six nude photographs of Soon-Yi which had been left on a mantelpiece. She is posed reclining on a couch with her legs spread apart. Ms. Farrow telephoned Mr. Allen to confront him with her discovery of the photographs.

Ms. Farrow returned home, showed the photographs to Soon-Yi and said, "What have you done?" She left the room before Soon-Yi answered. During the following weekend, Ms. Farrow hugged Soon-Yi and said that she loved her and did not blame her. Shortly thereafter, Ms. Farrow asked Soon-Yi how long she had been seeing Mr. Allen. When Soon-Yi referred to her sexual relationship with Mr. Allen, Ms. Farrow hit her on the side of the face and on the shoulders.[1] Ms. Farrow also told her older children what she had learned.

After receiving Ms. Farrow's telephone call, Mr. Allen went to her apartment where, he said, he found her to be "ragingly angry." She begged him to leave. She testified that:

> [w]hen he finally left, he came back less than an hour later, and I was sitting at the table. By then, all of the children were there . . . and it was a rather silent meal. The little ones were chatting and he walked right in and he sat right down at the table as if nothing had happened and starts chatting with . . . the two little ones, said hi to everybody. And one by one the children [Lark, Daisy, Fletcher, Moses and Sascha] took their plates and left. And I'd, I didn't know what to do. And then I went out.

Within the month, both parties retained counsel and attempted to negotiate a settlement of their differences. In an effort to pacify Ms. Farrow, Mr. Allen told her that he was no

---

[1] Ms. Farrow has commenced an action in the Surrogate's Court to vacate Mr. Allen's adoption of Dylan and Moses. In that proceeding, she contends that Mr. Allen began a secret affair with Soon-Yi prior to the date of the adoption. This issue has been reserved for consideration by the Surrogate and has not been addressed by me.

longer seeing Soon-Yi. This was untrue. A temporary arrangement enabled Mr. Allen to visit regularly with Dylan and
Satchel but they were not permitted to visit at his residence. In
addition, Ms. Farrow asked for his assurance that he would
not seek custody of Moses, Dylan or Satchel.

On February 3, 1992, both parties signed documents in
which it was agreed that Mr. Allen would waive custodial
rights to Moses, Dylan and Satchel if Ms. Farrow predeceased
him. On the same day, Mr. Allen signed a second document,
which he did not reveal to Ms. Farrow, in which he disavowed
the waiver, claiming that it was a product of duress and coer-
cion and stating that "I have no intention of abiding by it and
have been advised that it will not hold up legally and that at
worst I can revoke it unilaterally at will."

In February 1992, Ms. Farrow gave Mr. Allen a family
picture Valentine with skewers through the hearts of the children and a knife through the heart of Ms. Farrow. She also
defaced and destroyed several photographs of Mr. Allen and
of Soon-Yi.

In July 1992, Ms. Farrow had a birthday party for Dylan
at her Connecticut home. Mr. Allen came and monopolized
Dylan's time and attention. After Mr. Allen retired to the
guest room for the night, Ms. Farrow affixed to his bathroom
door, a note which called Mr. Allen a child molester. The
reference was to his affair with Soon-Yi.

In the summer of 1992, Soon-Yi was employed as a camp
counselor. During the third week of July, she telephoned Ms.
Farrow to tell her that she had quit her job. She refused to tell
Ms. Farrow where she was staying. A few days later, Ms. Farrow received a letter from the camp advising her that:

> [it] is with sadness and regret that we had to ask
> Soon-Yi to leave camp midway through the first
> camp session. . . . Throughout the entire orienta-
> tion period and continuing during camp, Soon-Yi
> was constantly involved with telephone calls. Phone

calls from a gentleman whose name is Mr. Simon seemed to be her primary focus and this definitely detracted from her concentration on being a counselor.

Mr. Simon was Woody Allen.

On August 4, 1992, Mr. Allen travelled to Ms. Farrow's Connecticut vacation home to spend time with his children. Earlier in the day, Casey Pascal had come for a visit with her three young children and their babysitter, Alison Stickland. Ms. Farrow and Ms. Pascal were shopping when Mr. Allen arrived. Those present were Ms. Pascal's three children; Ms. Stickland; Kristie Groteke, a babysitter employed by Ms. Farrow; Sophie Berge, a French tutor for the children; Dylan; and Satchel.

Ms. Farrow had previously instructed Ms. Groteke that Mr. Allen was not to be left alone with Dylan. For a period of fifteen or twenty minutes during the afternoon, Ms. Groteke was unable to locate Mr. Allen or Dylan. After looking for them in the house, she assumed that they were outside with the others. But neither Ms. Berge nor Ms. Stickland was with Mr. Allen or Dylan. Ms. Groteke made no mention of this to Ms. Farrow on August 4.

During a different portion of the day, Ms. Stickland went to the television room in search of one of Ms. Pascal's children. She observed Mr. Allen kneeling in front of Dylan with his head on her lap, facing her body. Dylan was sitting on the couch staring vacantly in the direction of a television set.

After Ms. Farrow returned home, Ms. Berge noticed that Dylan was not wearing anything under her sundress. She told Ms. Farrow, who asked Ms. Groteke to put underpants on Dylan.

Ms. Stickland testified that during the evening of August 4, she told Ms. Pascal, "I had seen something at Mia's that day that was bothering me." She revealed what she had seen in the television room. On August 5, Ms. Pascal telephoned Ms.

Farrow to tell her what Ms. Stickland had observed. Ms. Farrow testified that after she hung up the telephone, she asked Dylan, who was sitting next to her, "whether it was true that daddy had his face in her lap yesterday." Ms. Farrow testified:

> Dylan said yes. And then she said that she didn't like it one bit, no, he was breathing into her, into her legs, she said. And that he was holding her around the waist and I said, why didn't you get up and she said she tried to but that he put his hands underneath her and touched her. And she showed me where . . . Her behind.

Because she was already uncomfortable with Mr. Allen's inappropriate behavior toward Dylan and because she believed that her concerns were not being taken seriously enough by Dr. Schultz and Dr. Coates, Ms. Farrow videotaped Dylan's statements. Over the next twenty-four hours, Dylan told Ms. Farrow that she had been with Mr. Allen in the attic and that he had touched her privates with his finger.

After Dylan's first comments, Ms. Farrow telephoned her attorney for guidance. She was advised to bring Dylan to her pediatrician, which she did immediately. Dylan did not repeat the accusation of sexual abuse during this visit and Ms. Farrow was advised to return with Dylan on the following day. On the trip home, she explained to her mother that she did not like talking about her privates. On August 6, when Ms. Farrow went back to Dr. Kavirajan's office, Dylan repeated what she had told her mother on August 5. A medical examination conducted on August 9 showed no physical evidence of sexual abuse.

Although Dr. Schultz was vacationing in Europe, Ms. Farrow telephoned her daily for advice. Ms. Farrow also notified Dr. Coates, who was still treating Satchel. She said to Dr. Coates, "it sounds very convincing to me, doesn't it to you. It is so specific. Let's hope it is her fantasy." Dr. Coates immediately notified Mr. Allen of the child's accusation and then contacted the New York City Child Welfare Administration. Seven days later, during a meeting of the lawyers at which settlement discussions were taking place, Mr. Allen began this action for custody.

Dr. Schultz returned from vacation on August 16. She was transported to Connecticut in Mr. Allen's chauffered limousine on August 17, 18 and 21 for therapy sessions with Dylan. Dylan, who had become increasingly resistant to Dr. Schultz, did not want to see her. During the third session, Dylan and Satchel put glue in Dr. Schultz's hair, cut her dress and told her to go away.

On August 24 and 27, Ms. Farrow expressed to Dr. Schultz her anxiety about Dr. Schultz continuing to see Mr. Allen, who had already brought suit for custody of Dylan. She asked if Dr. Schultz would

> . . . please not come for a while until all of this is settled down because . . . I couldn't trust anybody. And she said she understood completely . . . And soon after that . . . I learned that Dr. Schultz had told [New York] child welfare that Dylan had not reported anything to her. And then a week later, either her lawyer or Dr. Schultz called [New York] child welfare and said she just remembered that Dylan had told her that Mr. Allen had put a finger in her vagina. When I heard that I certainly didn't trust Dr. Schultz.

Dr. Schultz testified that on August 19, Paul Williams of the New York Child Welfare Administration asked about her experience with Dylan. She replied that on August 17, Dylan started to tell her what had happened with Mr. Allen but she needed more time to explore this with Dylan. On August 27, she spoke more fully to Mr. Williams about her August 17 session with Dylan and speculated about the significance of what Dylan reported. Mr. Williams testified that on August 19, Dr. Schultz told him that Dylan had not made any statements to her about sexual abuse.

Ms. Farrow did not immediately resume Dylan's therapy because the Connecticut State Police had requested that she not be in therapy during the investigation. Also, it was not clear if the negotiated settlement that the parties were continuing to pursue would include Mr. Allen's participation in the selection of Dylan's new therapist.

Dr. Coates continued to treat Satchel through the fall of 1992. Ms. Farrow expressed to Dr. Coates her unease with the doctor seeing Mr. Allen in conjunction with Satchel's therapy. On October 29, 1992, Ms. Farrow requested that Dr. Coates treat Satchel without the participation of Mr. Allen. Dr. Coates declined, explaining that she did not believe that she could treat Satchel effectively without the full participation of both parents. Satchel's therapy with Dr. Coates was discontinued on November 28, 1992. At Ms. Farrow's request, Dr. Coates recommended a therapist to continue Satchel's therapy. Because of a conflict, the therapist recommended by Dr. Coates was unable to treat Satchel. He did, however, provide the name of another therapist with whom Satchel is currently in treatment.

On December 30, 1992, Dylan was interviewed by a representative of the Connecticut State Police. She told them—at a time Ms. Farrow calculates to be the fall of 1991—that while at Mr. Allen's apartment, she saw him and Soon-Yi having sex. Her reporting was childlike but graphic. She also told the police that Mr. Allen had pushed her face into a plate of hot spaghetti and had threatened to do it again.

Ten days before Yale-New Haven concluded its investigation, Dylan told Ms. Farrow, for the first time, that in Connecticut, while she was climbing up the ladder to a bunk bed, Mr. Allen put his hands under her shorts and touched her. Ms. Farrow testified that as Dylan said this, "she was illustrating graphically where in the genital area."

CONCLUSIONS

A) Woody Allen

Mr. Allen has demonstrated no parenting skills that would qualify him as an adequate custodian for Moses, Dylan or Satchel. His financial contributions to the children's support, his willingness to read to them, to tell them stories, to buy them presents, and to oversee their breakfasts, do not compensate for his absence as a meaningful source of guidance and caring in their lives. These contributions do not excuse his evident lack of familiarity with the most basic details of their day-to-day existences.

He did not bathe his children. He did not dress them, except from time to time, and then only to help them put on their socks and jackets. He knows little of Moses' history, except that he has cerebral palsy; he does not know if he has a doctor. He does not know the name of Dylan and Satchel's pediatrician. He does not know the names of Moses' teachers or about his academic performance. He does not know the name of the children's dentist. He does not know the names of his children's friends. He does not know the names of any of their many pets. He does not know which children shared bedrooms. He attended parent-teacher conferences only when asked to do so by Ms. Farrow.

Mr. Allen has even less knowledge about his children's siblings, with whom he seldom communicated. He apparently did not pay enough attention to his own children to learn from them about their brothers and sisters.

Mr. Allen characterized Ms. Farrow's home as a foster care compound and drew distinctions between her biological and adopted children. When asked how he felt about sleeping with his children's sister, he responded that "she [Soon-Yi] was an adopted child and Dylan was an adopted child." He showed no understanding that the bonds developed between adoptive brothers and sisters are no less worthy of respect and protection than those between biological siblings.

Mr. Allen's reliance on the affidavit which praises his parenting skills, submitted by Ms. Farrow in connection with his petition to adopt Moses and Dylan, is misplaced. Its ultimate probative value will be determined in the pending Surrogate's Court proceeding. In the context of the facts and circumstances of this action, I accord it little weight.

None of the witnesses who testified on Mr. Allen's behalf provided credible evidence that he is an appropriate custodial parent. Indeed, none would venture an opinion that he should be granted custody. When asked, even Mr. Allen could not provide an acceptable reason for a change in custody.

His counsel's last question of him on direct examination was, "Can you tell the Court why you are seeking custody of your children?" Mr. Allen's response was a rambling *non sequitur* which consumed eleven pages of transcript. He said that he did not want to take the children away from Ms. Farrow; that Ms. Farrow maintained a non-traditional household with biological children and adopted children from all over the world; that Soon-Yi was fifteen years older than Dylan and seventeen years older than Satchel; that Ms. Farrow was too angry with Mr. Allen to resolve the problem; and that with him, the children "will be responsibly educated" and "their day-to-day behavior will be done in consultation with their therapist." The most relevant portions of the response—that he is a good father and that Ms. Farrow intentionally turned the children against him—I do not credit. Even if he were correct, under the circumstances of this case, it would be insufficient to warrant a change of custody.

Mr. Allen's deficiencies as a custodial parent are magnified by his affair with Soon-Yi. As Ms. Farrow's companion, he was a frequent visitor at Soon-Yi's home. He accompanied the Farrow-Previns on extended family vacations and he is the father of Soon-Yi's siblings, Moses, Dylan and Satchel. The fact that Mr. Allen ignored Soon-Yi for ten years cannot change the nature of the family constellation and does not create a distance sufficient to convert their affair into a benign relationship between two consenting adults.

Mr. Allen admits that he never considered the consequences of his behavior with Soon-Yi. Dr. Coates and Dr. Brodzinsky testified that Mr. Allen still fails to understand that what he did was wrong. Having isolated Soon-Yi from her family, he left her with no visible support system. He had no consideration for the consequences to her, to Ms. Farrow, to the Previn children for whom he cared little, or to his own children for whom he professes love.

Mr. Allen's response to Dylan's claim of sexual abuse was an attack upon Ms. Farrow, whose parenting ability and emotional stability he impugned without the support of any significant credible evidence. His trial strategy has been to separate his children from their brothers and sisters; to turn the children against their mother; to divide adopted children from biological children; to incite the family against their household help; and to set household employees against each other. His self-absorption, his lack of judgment and his commitment to the continuation of his divisive assault, thereby impeding the healing of the injuries that he has already caused, warrant a careful monitoring of his future contact with the children.

B) Mia Farrow

Few relationships and fewer families can easily bear the microscopic examination to which Ms. Farrow and her children have been subjected. It is evident that she loves children and has devoted a significant portion of her emotional and material wealth to their upbringing. When she is not working she attends to her children. Her weekends and summers are spent in Connecticut with her children. She does not take extended vacations unaccompanied by her children. She is sensitive to the needs of her children, respectful of their opinions, honest with them and quick to address their problems.

Mr. Allen elicited trial testimony that Ms. Farrow favored her biological children over her adopted children; that she manipulated Dylan's sexual abuse complaint, in part through the use of leading questions and the videotape; that she discouraged Dylan and Satchel from maintaining a relationship with Mr. Allen; that she overreacted to Mr. Allen's affair with Soon-Yi; and that she inappropriately exposed Dylan and Satchel to the turmoil created by the discovery of the affair.

The evidence at trial established that Ms. Farrow is a caring and loving mother who has provided a home for both her biological and her adopted children. There is no credible evidence that she unfairly distinguished among her children or that she favored some at the expense of others.

I do not view the Valentine's Day card, the note affixed to the bathroom door in Connecticut, or the destruction of photographs as anything more than expressions of Ms. Farrow's understandable anger and her ability to communicate her distress by word and symbol rather than by action.

There is no credible evidence to support Mr. Allen's contention that Ms. Farrow coached Dylan or that Ms. Farrow acted upon a desire for revenge against him for seducing Soon-Yi. Mr. Allen's resort to the stereotypical "woman scorned" defense is an injudicious attempt to divert attention from his failure to act as a responsible parent and adult.

Ms. Farrow's statement to Dr. Coates that she hoped that Dylan's statements were a fantasy is inconsistent with the notion of brainwashing. In this regard, I also credit the testimony of Ms. Groteke, who was charged with supervising Mr. Allen's August 4 visit with Dylan. She testified that she did not tell Ms. Farrow, until after Dylan's statement of August 5, that Dylan and Mr. Allen were unaccounted for during fifteen or twenty minutes on August 4. It is highly unlikely that Ms. Farrow would have encouraged Dylan to accuse her father of having sexually molested her during a period in which Ms.

Farrow believed they were in the presence of a babysitter. Moreover, I do not believe that Ms. Farrow would have exposed her daughter and her other children to the consequences of the Connecticut investigation and this litigation if she did not believe the possible truth of Dylan's accusation.

In a society where children are too often betrayed by adults who ignore or disbelieve their complaints of abuse, Ms. Farrow's determination to protect Dylan is commendable. Her decision to videotape Dylan's statements, although inadvertently compromising the sexual abuse investigation, was understandable.

Ms. Farrow is not faultless as a parent. It seems probable, although there is no credible testimony to this effect, that prior to the affair with Mr. Allen, Soon-Yi was experiencing problems for which Ms. Farrow was unable to provide adequate support. There is also evidence that there were problems with her relationships with Dylan and Satchel. We do not, however, demand perfection as a qualification for parenting. Ironically, Ms. Farrow's principal shortcoming with respect to responsible parenting appears to have been her continued relationship with Mr. Allen.

Ms. Farrow reacted to Mr. Allen's behavior with her children with a balance of appropriate caution and flexibility. She brought her early concern with Mr. Allen's relationship with Dylan to Dr. Coates and was comforted by the doctor's assurance that Mr. Allen was working to correct his behavior with the child. Even after January 13, 1992, Ms. Farrow continued to provide Mr. Allen with access to her home and to their children, as long as the visits were supervised by a responsible adult. She did her best, although with limited success, to shield her younger children from the turmoil generated by Mr. Allen's affair with Soon-Yi.

Ms. Farrow's refusal to permit Mr. Allen to visit with Dylan after August 4, 1992 was prudent. Her willingness to allow Satchel to have regular supervised visitation with Mr. Allen reflects her understanding of the propriety of balancing

Satchel's need for contact with his father against the danger of Mr. Allen's lack of parental judgment.

Ms. Farrow also recognizes that Mr. Allen and not Soon-Yi is the person responsible for their affair and its impact upon her family. She has communicated to Soon-Yi that she continues to be a welcome member of the Farrow-Previn home.

C) Dylan Farrow

Mr. Allen's relationship with Dylan remains unresolved. The evidence suggests that it is unlikely that he could be successfully prosecuted for sexual abuse. I am less certain, however, than is the Yale-New Haven team, that the evidence proves conclusively that there was no sexual abuse.

Both Dr. Coates and Dr. Schultz expressed their opinions that Mr. Allen did not sexually abuse Dylan. Neither Dr. Coates nor Dr. Schultz has expertise in the field of child sexual abuse. I believe that the opinions of Dr. Coates and Dr. Schultz may have been colored by their loyalty to Mr. Allen. I also believe that therapists would have a natural reluctance to accept the possibility that an act of sexual abuse occurred on their watch. I have considered their opinions, but do not find their testimony to be persuasive with respect to sexual abuse or visitation.

I have also considered the report of the Yale-New Haven team and the deposition testimony of Dr. John M. Leventhal. The Yale-New Haven investigation was conducted over a six-month period by Dr. Leventhal, a pediatrician; Dr. Julia Hamilton, who has a Ph.D. in social work; and Ms. Jennifer Sawyer, who has a master's degree in social work. Responsibility for different aspects of the investigation was divided among the team. The notes of the team members were destroyed prior to the issuance of the report, which, presumably, is an amalgamation of their independent impressions and observations. The unavailability of the notes, together with their unwillingness to testify at this trial except through the deposition of Dr. Leventhal, compromised my ability to scrutinize their findings and resulted in a report which was sanitized and, therefore, less credible.

Dr. Stephen Herman, a clinical psychiatrist who has extensive familiarity with child abuse cases, was called as a witness by Ms. Farrow to comment on the Yale-New Haven report. I share his reservations about the reliability of the report.

Dr. Herman faulted the Yale-New Haven team (1) for making visitation recommendations without seeing the parent interact with the child; (2) for failing to support adequately their conclusion that Dylan has a thought disorder; (3) for drawing any conclusions about Satchel, whom they never saw; (4) for finding that there was no abuse when the supporting data was inconclusive; and (5) for recommending that Ms. Farrow enter into therapy. In addition, I do not think that it was appropriate for Yale-New Haven, without notice to the parties or their counsel, to exceed its mandate and make observations and recommendations which might have an impact on existing litigation in another jurisdiction.

Unlike Yale-New Haven, I am not persuaded that the videotape of Dylan is the product of leading questions or of the child's fantasy.

Richard Marcus, a retired New York City police officer, called by Mr. Allen, testified that he worked with the police sex crimes unit for six years. He claimed to have an intuitive ability to know if a person is truthful or not. He concluded, "based on my experience," that Dylan lacked credibility. I did not find his testimony to be insightful.

I agree with Dr. Herman and Dr. Brodzinsky that we will probably never know what occurred on August 4, 1992. The credible testimony of Ms. Farrow, Dr. Coates, Dr. Leventhal and Mr. Allen does, however, prove that Mr. Allen's behavior toward Dylan was grossly inappropriate and that measures must be taken to protect her.

D) Satchel Farrow

Mr. Allen had a strained and difficult relationship with Satchel during the earliest years of the child's life. Dr. Coates testified, "Satchel would push him away, would not acknowledge him. . . . If he would try to help Satchel getting out of bed or going into bed, he would kick him, at times had scratched his face. They were in trouble." Dr. Coates also testified that as an infant, Satchel would cry when held by Mr. Allen and stop when given to Ms. Farrow. Mr. Allen attributes this to Ms. Farrow's conscious effort to keep him apart from the child.

Although Ms. Farrow consumed much of Satchel's attention, and did not foster a relationship with his father, there is no credible evidence to suggest that she desired to exclude Mr. Allen. Mr. Allen's attention to Dylan left him with less time and patience for Satchel. Dr. Coates attempted to teach Mr. Allen how to interact with Satchel. She encouraged him to be more understanding of his son when Satchel ignored him or acted bored with his gifts. Apparently, success in this area was limited.

In 1991, in the presence of Ms. Farrow and Dylan, Mr. Allen stood next to Satchel's bed, as he did every morning. Satchel screamed at him to go away. When Mr. Allen refused to leave, Satchel kicked him. Mr. Allen grabbed Satchel's leg, started to twist it. Ms. Farrow testified that Mr. Allen said "I'm going to break your fucking leg." Ms. Farrow intervened and separated Mr. Allen from Satchel. Dylan told the Connecticut State Police about this incident.

That Mr. Allen now wants to spend more time with Satchel is commendable. If sincere, he should be encouraged to do so, but only under conditions that promote Satchel's well being.

E) *Moses Farrow*

Mr. Allen's interactions with Moses appear to have been superficial and more a response to Moses' desire for a father—in a family where Mr. Previn was the father of the other six children—than an authentic effort to develop a relationship with the child. When Moses asked, in 1984, if Mr. Allen would be his father, he said "sure" but for years did nothing to make that a reality.

They spent time playing baseball, chess and fishing. Mr. Allen encouraged Moses to play the clarinet. There is no evidence, however, that Mr. Allen used any of their shared areas of interest as a foundation upon which to develop a deeper relationship with his son. What little he offered—a baseball catch, some games of chess, adoption papers—was enough to encourage Moses to dream of more, but insufficient to justify a claim for custody.

After learning of his father's affair with his sister, Moses handed to Mr. Allen a letter that he had written. It states:

> . . . you can't force me to live with you. . . . You have done a horrible, unforgivable, needy, ugly, stupid thing . . . about seeing me for lunch, you can just forget about that . . . we didn't do anything wrong . . . All you did is spoil the little ones, Dylan and Satchel. . . . Every one knows not to have an affair with your son's sister . . . I don't consider you my father anymore. It was a great feeling having a father, but you smashed that feeling and dream with a single act. *I HOPE YOU ARE PROUD TO CRUSH YOUR SON'S DREAM.*

Mr. Allen responded to this letter by attempting to wrest custody of Moses from his mother. His rationale is that the letter was generated by Ms. Farrow. Moses told Dr. Brodzinsky that he wrote the letter and that he did not intend for it to be seen by his mother.

CUSTODY

Section 240(1) of the Domestic Relations Law states that in a custody dispute, the court must "give such direction . . . as . . . justice requires, having regard to the circumstances of the case and of the respective parties and to the best interests of the child."

The case law of this state has made clear that the governing consideration is the best interests of the child. *Eschbach v. Eschbach*, 56 NY2d 167 (1982); *Friederwitzer v. Friederwitzer*, 55 NY2d 89 (1982).

The initial custodial arrangement is critically important. "Priority, not as an absolute but as a weighty factor, should, in the absence of extraordinary circumstances, be accorded to the first custody awarded in litigation or by voluntary agreement." *Nehra v. Uhlar*, 43 NY2d 242, 251 (1977).

"[W]hen children have been living with one parent for a long period of time and the parties have previously agreed that custody shall remain in that parent, their agreement should prevail and custody should be continued unless it is demonstrated that the custodial parent is unfit or perhaps less fit (citations omitted)." *Martin v. Martin*, 74 AD2d 419, 426 (4th Dept 1980).

After considering Ms. Farrow's position as the sole caretaker of the children, the satisfactory fashion in which she has fulfilled that function, the parties' pre-litigation acceptance that she continue in that capacity, and Mr. Allen's serious parental inadequacies, it is clear that the best interests of the children will be served by their continued custody with Ms. Farrow.

VISITATION

Visitation, like custody, is governed by a consideration of the best interests of the child. *Miriam R. v. Arthur D.R.*, 85 AD2d 624 (2d Dept 1981). Absent proof to the contrary, the law presumes that visitation is in the child's best interests. *Wise v. Del Toro*, 122 AD2d 714 (1st Dept 1986). The denial of visitation to a noncustodial parent must be accompanied by compelling reasons and substantial evidence that visitation is detrimental to the child's welfare. *Matter of Farrugia Children*, 106 AD2d 293 (1st Dept 1984); *Gowan v. Menqa*, 178 AD2d 1021 (4th Dept 1991). If the noncustodial parent is a fit person and there are no extraordinary circumstances, there should be reasonable visitation. *Hotze v. Hotze*, 57 AD2d 85 (4th Dept 1977), *appeal denied* 42 NY2d 805.

The overriding consideration is the child's welfare rather than any supposed right of the parent. *Weiss v. Weiss*, 52 NY2d 170, 174-5 (1981); *Hotze v. Hotze, supra* at 87. Visitation should be denied where it may be inimical to the child's welfare by producing serious emotional strain or disturbance. *Hotze v. Hotze, supra* at 88; see also *Miriam R. v. Arthur D.R., supra; cf., State ex rel. H.K. v. M.S.*, 187 AD2d 50 (1st Dept 1993).

This trial included the observations and opinions of more mental health workers than is common to most custody litigation. The parties apparently agreed with Dr. Herman's conclusion that another battery of forensic psychological evaluations would not have been in the children's best interests and would have added little to the available information. Accordingly, none was ordered.

The common theme of the testimony by the mental health witnesses is that Mr. Allen has inflicted serious damage on the children and that healing is necessary. Because, as Dr. Brodzinsky and Dr. Herman observed, this family is in an uncharted therapeutic area, where the course is uncertain and the benefits unknown, the visitation structure that will best promote the healing process and safeguard the children is elusive. What is clear is that Mr. Allen's lack of judgment, insight and impulse control make normal noncustodial visitation with Dylan and Satchel too risky to the children's well-being to be permitted at this time.

A) Dylan

Mr. Allen's request for immediate visitation with Dylan is denied. It is unclear whether Mr. Allen will ever develop the insight and judgment necessary for him to relate to Dylan appropriately. According to Dr. Brodzinsky, even if Dylan was not sexually abused, she feels victimized by her father's relationship with her sister. Dylan has recently begun treatment with a new therapist. Now that this trial is concluded, she is entitled to the time and space necessary to create a protective environment that will promote the therapeutic process. A significant goal of that therapy is to encourage her to fulfill her individual potential, including the resilience to deal with Mr. Allen in a manner which is not injurious to her.

The therapist witnesses agree that Mr. Allen may be able to serve a positive role in Dylan's therapy. Dr. Brodzinsky emphasized that because Dylan is quite fragile and more negatively affected by stress than the average child, she should visit with Mr. Allen only within a therapeutic context. This function, he said, should be undertaken by someone other than Dylan's treating therapist. Unless it interferes with Dylan's individual treatment or is inconsistent with her welfare, this process is to be initiated within six months. A further review of visitation will be considered only after we are able to evaluate the progress of Dylan's therapy.

B) Satchel

Mr. Allen's request for extended and unsupervised visitation with Satchel is denied. He has been visiting regularly with Satchel, under supervised conditions, with the consent of Ms. Farrow. I do not believe that Ms. Farrow has discouraged Satchel's visitation with Mr. Allen or that she has, except for restricting visitation, interfered with Satchel's relationship with his father.

Although, absent exceptional circumstances, a non-custodial parent should not be denied meaningful access to a child, "supervised visitation is not a deprivation to meaningful access." *Lightbourne v. Lighhtbourne,* 179 AD2d 562 (1st Dept 1992).

I do not condition visitation out of concern for Satchel's physical safety. My caution is the product of Mr. Allen's demonstrated inability to understand the impact that his words and deeds have upon the emotional well being of his children.

I believe that Mr. Allen will use Satchel in an attempt to gain information about Dylan and to insinuate himself into her good graces. I believe that Mr. Allen will, if unsupervised, attempt to turn Satchel against the other members of his family. I believe Mr. Allen to be desirous of introducing Soon-Yi into the visitation arrangement without concern for the effect on Satchel, Soon-Yi or the other members of the Farrow family. In short, I believe Mr. Allen to be so self-absorbed, untrustworthy and insensitive, that he should not be permitted to see Satchel without appropriate professional supervision until Mr. Allen demonstrates that supervision is no longer necessary. The supervisor should be someone who is acceptable to both parents, who will be familiarized with the history of this family and who is willing to remain in that capacity for a reasonable period of time. Visitation shall be of two hours' duration, three times weekly, and modifiable by agreement of the parties.

C) Moses

Under the circumstances of this case, giving respect and credence to Ms. Farrow's appreciation of her son's sensitivity and intelligence, as confirmed by Dr. Brodzinsky, I will not require this fifteen-year-old child to visit with his father if he does not wish to do so.

If Moses can be helped by seeing Mr. Allen under conditions in which Moses will not be overwhelmed, then I believe that Ms. Farrow should and will promote such interaction. I hope that Moses will come to understand that the fear of demons often cannot be dispelled without first confronting them.

COUNSEL FEES

Ms. Farrow's application for counsel fees is granted. Mr. Allen compounded the pain that he inflicted upon the Farrow family by bringing this frivolous petition for custody of Dylan, Satchel and Moses.

Domestic Relations Law §237(b) provides that upon an application for custody or visitation, the court may direct a parent to pay the counsel fees of the other parent "as, in the court's discretion, justice requires, having regard to the circumstances of the case and of the respective parties."

Ms. Farrow admits to a substantial net worth, although she is not nearly as wealthy as Mr. Allen. Clearly, she is able to absorb the cost of this litigation, although it has been extraordinarily expensive. However, "[i]ndigency is not a prerequisite to an award of counsel fees (citation omitted). Rather, in exercising its discretionary power to award counsel fees, a court should review the financial circumstances of both parties together with all the other circumstances of the case, which may include the relative merit of the parties' positions." *DeCabrera v.*

Cabrera-Rosete, 70 NY2d R79 881 (1987). Because Mr. Allen's position had no merit, he will bear the entire financial burden of this litigation. If the parties are unable to agree on Ms. Farrow's reasonable counsel fees, a hearing will be conducted for that purpose.

Settle judgment.

DATED: June 7, 1993.

J. S. C.